Constructing Reality in Comparative Theology

Constructing Reality in Comparative Theology

Paul S. Chung

James Clarke & Co.

James Clarke & Co

P.O. Box 60
Cambridge
CB1 2NT
United Kingdom

www.jamesclarke.co
publishing@jamesclarke.co

Hardback ISBN: 978 0 227 17771 6
Paperback ISBN: 978 0 227 17769 3
PDF ISBN: 978 0 227 17772 3
ePub ISBN: 978 0 227 17770 9

British Library Cataloguing in Publication Data
A record is available from the British Library

First published by James Clarke and Co., 2022

Copyright © Paul S. Chung, 2022

All rights reserved. No part of this edition may be reproduced, stored electronically or in any retrieval system, or transmitted in any form or by any means, electronic, mechanical, photocopying, recording, or otherwise, without prior written permission from the Publisher (permissions@jamesclarke.co).

To a Catholic sister, Young Maccarone (1952–)

Contents

Foreword by Ulrich Duchrow		ix
Acknowledgements		xiii
Introduction		1
Chapter 1.	Ernst Troeltsch: Comparative Theology and Historical Research of Religion	5
Chapter 2.	Comparative Theology, Sociological Enquiry, and Power Relations	47
Chapter 3.	Comparative Theology of Grace: Martin Luther and Shinran Shonin	68
Chapter 4.	Karl Barth, Religion and Comparative Theology	98
Chapter 5.	Islam: Religious Discourse, Power and Modernity	121
Chapter 6.	Comparative Theology: Culture and Religion	156
Chapter 7.	Comparative Theology and Interreligious Dialogue	185
Epilogue		210
Bibliography		215
Index		227

Foreword

In *Constructing Reality in Comparative Theology* Paul S. Chung develops comparative theology in terms of the social scientific study of religion. This book therefore leads on from Chung's recent work, *The Social Scientific Study of Religion*, in which he conceptualized a method for constructive theology in the comparative study of religion, in the context of an enquiry into the axial state of world religions. This laid a foundation for a methodology of comparative religion and social scientific experimentation in challenging capitalist modernity, social stratification and civilization. Here, in examining Christian interaction with other religions, Chung constructs his theology of comparative religion in a creative and fresh manner. Through his innovative approach we see the extent to which religious idea or discourse is worked out in social reality for a life-creating and life-respecting culture. Religion may become a source of solidarity and emancipation to cut through the limitations and crisis of today's civilization beset by the pathology of late capitalism.

What is of remarkable significance in Chung's comparative theology is in his interdisciplinary approach to public religion. He reinterprets an ontology of life-world for an effective history of those on the margins (in distinction to Habermas). He then incorporates it into a social system of episteme, and the scientific method of elective affinity becomes critical in dealing with a religious construction of public reality, which is stratified according to bio-political governance, economic injustice, sexual division of labour and racial inequality. To counter this reality of impersonal forces, Chung features comparative theology as built on *theologia crucis* and the gospel of reconciliation in a critical, emancipatory manner.

The existential threat facing humanity, and the planet on which we live, is shown by Chung to be a product of our capitalist society.

His reappraisal of our religious relationships is therefore aimed at a bigger prize, dealing with capitalist modernity and its neocolonial face. In Chung's study of the religious construction of social reality, his comparative theology is concerned with a religious contribution to prophetic ethics, an immanent critique of religious status quo (or disgrace effect and emancipation toward a new model of alternative modernity in transcending dead ends), and of late capitalism and its pathology of clash of civilization.

Chung's deft analysis of the origin of the major world religions and philosophies at a pre-Capitalist state of our existence offers hope, and a prophetic model based on their heritage. We are offered the opportunity to learn from their critique of nascent forms of injustice, greed and corruption. Moreover, Chung shows how, against the majority of believers assimilating to the dominant imperialist capitalism, minorities are at work within these traditions today. They are challenging their faith communities to wake up and follow their original faith documents for the sake of the survival of humanity. In the Abrahamic religions – Judaism, Christianity, and Islam – these minorities are called liberation theologians; in Buddhism they are the International Network of Socially Engaged Buddhists.

In Paul Chung's previous book he outlined his support for these liberation movements in the different religious communities. The present volume continues this trend. Chung's approach to Buddhism is built on social scientific epistemology and reinforces the significance of comparative theology in a critical, emancipatory manner. His method of immanent critique can be obviously seen in his genealogical-hermeneutical articulation in undertaking a critical exegesis of the core Buddhist text for great compassion, while problematizing the same text as it was misused to support ideological power and colonialism in Japanese imperial context.

Furthermore, Chung shows how it is important to cut across Eurocentric scholarship in discussing Islam, and features cultural Renaissance in cosmopolitan Baghdad in the eighth century and philosophical enlightenment in Islamic Spain as the source of the religious construction of cultural reality and its alternative modernity, which should take a different course based on politics of recognition, peace, and symbiosis of civilization. For this task Chung's comparative study of the Calvinist position of election and the Islamic understanding of election differ from Weber's unilateral and unqualified study of Christian theology. Chung is convinced that religious source occupies its emancipatory mandate in challenging the polluted development of religious ideas and capitalist practices over time, which is missing from Weber's sociology of comparative religions. In so doing, Chung relocates Islam as an Abrahamic religion, legitimately within the prophetic tradition of axial religions.

As the danger for humanity is global, only all religions working together have a chance to influence politics to shift the rules for the economy. Chung's approach of critical comparative theology in the context of world religions offers not only a methodology, but also concrete examples of mutually enriching interreligious understanding as a basis for the necessary cooperation. He shows convincingly that it is not abstract interreligious dialogue we need, but a self-critical interaction that redresses oppressive systems of class, caste, gender and more– very congenial with the basic approach of the Axial Age religions.

Ulrich Duchrow
Professor in Theology,
University of Heidelberg

Acknowledgements

Confucius considers morality, education and friendship to be the most important values in human life and society. A moral being is a social being, which is imbued with the Principle (Heavenly Tao); social life cannot be properly apprehended without morality, upon which justice can be built. Morality and rectifying justice come to terms with one another.

Writing this book on comparative theology and the religious construction of reality, I sense that this Confucian disposition and value still remains an undercurrent in my scholarship and cultural taste. The Principle appears as meaning in the mode of givenness, without being exhausted by it. It is *totaliter aliter* which houses human life as justice and integrity, awakening and renewing moral meaning of life in dynamic and progressive ways. It sharpens language to go alongside justice and moral integrity. Religious source and tradition become life-world in guiding one's practical style of life, cultural taste and solidarity, while one's critical consciousness engages in the questionable domain of the religious field and power structure. It is this that has led me to reconsider a philosophy of phenomenology (Edmund Husserl) by looking at Max Weber's comparative sociology of world religions through the materialist, symbolic lens. This philosophical, sociological methodology facilitates the endeavour of elaborating a constructive theology of comparative religions, dealing with culture, society and religion, while appreciating the contribution of comparative theology in an exegetical framework.

I must acknowledge a Catholic sister, Young Maccarone, whose generous funds made this writing project possible. I value a lively dialogue with her in matters pertaining to the beauty of the religious other, as we are both on the way to religious truth. I extend thanks to Prof. Ulrich Duchrow at Heidelberg, who honours me with his forewords to both

The Social Scientific Study of Religion and this work. His pioneering book *Transcending Greedy Money and Interreligious Solidarity for Just Relations* remains a driving force in my materialist, symbolic enquiry into religion, language, culture and capitalist modernity.

Gratitude must also go to Peter Watters for his careful proofreading and valuable comments in sharpening and clarifying arguments, analysis and synthesis. Finally, I extend thanks to all the team at The Lutterworth Press for helping bring these two books to light.

Paul S. Chung
Pentecost, Berkeley, CA 2021

Introduction

In *The Social Scientific Study of Religion* I sought to elaborate a sociological (or archaeological in a specific sense) hermeneutical method in dealing with the elective affinity between religious ideas and material interests, seeking its fitting relation through the lens of reflexive sociology. Archaeological analysis of religious discourse and power relations are explicated in diverse fields or spaces in analyzing the reality of social stratification embedded with inequality and hierarchy.

Here, the social theory of division of labour, rational organization of society, its system of authority, and domination are seen and examined in connection with discourse analysis, material interests (grounded in the practical, ethical way of life), and power relations (prestige, monopoly and privilege distributed among status groups). These avenues are explored in order to expand the definition and methodology of comparative theology which has previously been restricted to textual comparison alone. In so doing, I also develop further themes that I began to explore in some of my previous publications, particularly *Comparative Theology among Multiple Modernities*. This development can be seen especially in the chapters on Troeltsch, on Luther and Buddhism, and on Barth. In the five years since that volume's publication, I have uncovered more parallels and and crossovers between these thinkers and traditions, which I am pleased to be able to share now.

Weber's theological character and Protestant ethic can be revised, and his thesis revised in terms of an elective affinity between religious belief, political power and social stratification. This expanded understanding, as one hermeneutical basis for comparative theology, is used here for a comparative study of Buddhism and Islam. By focusing on the social economic structure throughout the history of religion and society, this comparative study runs in a different course from Francis Clooney's commentarial comparative theology, which is based only on textual comparison.

In connection with *The Social Scientific Study of Religion*, the present volume examines the Christian interaction with other religions in the interreligious context, and advances a constructive theology of comparative religions. For this purpose it undertakes a hermeneutical reappraisal of Western classic theologians in order to develop a religious construction of reality. Selecting several important theologians (Martin Luther, John Calvin, Ernst Troeltsch, Karl Barth and Paul Tillich) in the interreligious context, it discusses the significance of comparative theology in dealing with political power, social stratification and social economic structure. This understanding refers to a theology of culture, while including race, sexuality and gender to position comparative theology as a constructive theology of comparative religions.

Chapter 1 discusses Ernst Troeltsch as a classic example of comparative theology in reference to Weber, examining his contribution to historical, critical enquiry of comparative religions within the universal history of religion. His historical method and the universal history of religions can be appreciated in reference to the philosophy of religion and sociological hermeneutics. Troeltsch is indebted to Dilthey's historical hermeneutics, but their historicism tends to be vulnerable to relativism and psychological understanding. In order to critically improve on the limitations and conceptual insufficiencies, Troeltsch's historical program and philosophy of religion for comparative theology are viewed in a framework of phenomenological, materialist clarification and revision.

Chapter 2 investigates the extent to which a sociological enquiry of comparative religions would be mutually beneficial in a Buddhist-Christian com-reading. There is a focus on the Buddhist text of *Bodhicaryāvatāra* (*The Way of the Bodhisattva*) in connection with the Buddhist principle of dependent origination. A theory of problematization takes on the complex relation between emptiness and compassion, while taking issue with its questionable identity between Zen, militarist killing, and body politics in the Japanese colonial context.

Chapter 3 constructs a comparative theology of grace in reading Martin Luther together with Shin Buddhism and evaluating Pure Land Buddhism's contribution to a different, alternative form of modernity in Japan. Comparative theology in this regard draws attention to each religious tradition in its own terms and uniqueness between Reformation theology and Pure Land Buddhism in Japan. Finally, Robert Bellah's evaluation of Pure Land Buddhism, and its path to modernity in Japan, are included.

Chapter 4 is a study of Karl Barth, explicating his theological insight into comparative theology and world religions. A hermeneutical retrieval can be made to present a new face of Barth in dealing with his notion of *Aufhebung* (sublimation) concerning the relationship between revelation and religions. It is interesting to consider the extent to which the revelation (the source of the gospel) can be dialectically and analogically related to the religions (especially in his evaluation of Hindu *bhakti* religion and Pure Land Buddhism in Japan); this enquiry continues to investigate the revelation in light of God's reconciliation with the world. Barth's revelational particularism then leads to an inclusive openness toward religious others.

Chapter 5 lays out the history of Islam, viewing contributions and limitations from a historical, sociological perspective. A comparative study of Islam unfolds in terms of a religious construction of reality. The chapter scrutinizes the discourse of Eurocentrism, and then draws attention to the source of Islam, religious discourse, and the historical development of political power. The study distinguishes the Mecca model from the Medina model in order to cut through the debate between political Islam and secularism. Through a critical mode of enquiry, the Meccan model is presented as the source of immanent critique in finding elective affinity between the Islamic source and the historical course of development toward 'Protestant' Islam. The Islamic idea of predestination and Weber's definition of Calvinist Predestination are considered in terms of Calvin's own position. Comparative theology helps in enriching the position of the self for semantic retrieval through reading the other. Thus, a constructive study of Islam reinterprets the potential of an Islamic source for religious humanism, critical reasoning, democracy and civil society.

Chapter 6 takes on the political, cultural significance of comparative theology, considering culture and religion in an interdisciplinary manner. A theology of culture gains prominence in cultural diversity and religious pluralism, and thus a multicultural reality requires an interdisciplinary approach to religion and culture in reinforcing the significance of a social scientific enquiry for comparative theology. It can be seen that a social theory of cultural stratification helps comparative theology to engage in cultural religious issues (race, gender, ethnicity, sexuality and social status) in terms of a social theory of discourse, symbolic domination, and power relations. A theory of social stratification can be framed in terms of life-world enquiry, in which a task of theology of culture is used as a significant part of comparative theology.

Chapter 7 is a study of comparative theology, in league with Tillich and Barth, to make it more amenable to social scientific study of religion and culture. Appreciating their respective insights into interreligious dialogue, the social scientific approach to religion is advanced in terms of a theory of life-world, which incorporates a cultural-narrative model in a hermeneutical frame of reference. This social phenomenology can be brought into a proleptic theological configuration of reconciliation and *theologia crucis*.

The Epilogue outlines the way comparative theology can be featured and advanced in a new direction, as engaged in a religious construction of social reality in a sociological hermeneutical framework, which underwrites a materialist, symbolic approach. The comparative project of reading together (*Homo lector*) in a commentarial sense can be renewed and enriched through *Homo socius* by way of *Homo ethicus* in religious studies.

Chapter 1

Ernst Troeltsch: Comparative Theology and Historical Research of Religion

Ernst Troeltsch (1865–1923) remains a classic example of theocentric theology involved in featuring its constructive dimension in terms of God, humanity, history and religion. His major concern was with clarifying the nature of the historical development of religion, its sociological problems, and philosophy of value.[1]

In this chapter, Troeltsch's historical, sociological enquiry is compared with Weber. Their sociological enquiry is revised and critically updated through the lens of reflexive sociology (Bourdieu). Troeltsch's historical-critical method can be revived in taking on the comparative study of religion. His insight is decisive in a constructive theology of comparative religions, religious ethics, historical research, and philosophy of religion. On the other hand, he also has limitations concerning the problem of historical relativism and religious a priori. Life-worldly enquiry helps to cut through Troeltsch's philosophy of religion embedded within irrational and mystic leaning.

With critical modification in mind, Troeltsch is appraised as an influential figure in facilitating constructing theology in the comparative study of religions. His theocentric theology is considered in terms of a biblical symbol of reconciliation, which reinforces his eschatological orientation in the recognition of and solidarity with the dominated in history and society. An Excursus deals with a critical note on Troeltsch's

---

1. Troeltsch, 'My Books (1922),' in *Religion in History*, pp. 374–5.

personalistic type of religion in reference to Hindu *bhakti* religion and Amida Buddhism.

1. Weber and Troeltsch in Comparison

Troeltsch began an academic friendship with Max Weber in 1897/8, when Weber took up the chair of national economy at Heidelberg. Weber was involved in the 'Association for Social Policy' and the 'Evangelical Social Congress.'[2] In 1904 Troeltsch joined 'The Evangelical Social Congress,' in which he sought to deal with the relation between Protestant theology and social political problems at his time. Troeltsch formed a close relationship with Weber, and they shared a house in Heidelberg and travelled together to the United States in 1904.

As a historical theologian Troeltsch was trained in the school of the history of religions, especially in reference to Friedrich Schleiermacher (1768–1834) and his biographer and editor of the former's works, Wilhelm Dilthey (1833–1911). When Troeltsch joined the philosophical faculty at the University of Berlin as a philosopher, in 1915, he sought to develop his philosophy of religion in the historical, sociological frame of reference. He clarified the epistemological problem in focusing on the relation between the religious a priori and the non-theoretical, psychological component; he sought to substantiate his philosophy of religion in dialogue with the neo-Kantian school of Heinrich Rickert and Wilhelm Windelband.[3]

Weber remains one of the most important figures in the development of Troeltsch's philosophy of religion, his theology, and his social ethical teaching of Christianity. Troeltsch's book *The Social Teaching of the Christian Churches* (originally published in 1911) is regarded to be the standard in dealing with the history of Christian social ethics. He influenced H. Richard Niebuhr, who writes of his book *Christ and Culture*. Niebuhr writes: 'In one sense [it] undertakes to do no more than to supplement and in part to correct [Troeltsch's] work on *The Social Teaching*.'[4]

It is useful to consider Weber in dealing with Troeltsch's contribution. Weber distinguishes three problems in his study of religions. First, major religious ideas affect the secular ethic and economic behaviours of the average believer. Second, the group formation of status has an

---

2. Drescher, *Ernst Troeltsch*, p. 102.
3. Troeltsch, 'My Books (1922),' in *Religion in History*, p. 374.
4. Niebuhr, *Christ and Culture*, p. xii.

effect on religious ideas in historical development. Third, comparison between the West and other civilizations is made in considering the causes and consequences of religious beliefs, as they relate to economic development and rationalization. In the sociological study of religious ideas and economic behaviour, status group is involved in developing its style of practical life, social prestige and the status situation.

Reflexive Sociology and Revisionist Model

However, Weber's interpretative sociology can be modified in terms of several central categories of reflexive sociology, which can be viewed in a phenomenological frame of reference. In developing a critical theory of social stratification and power relations, one's resources (capital) in multiple and differentiated spheres produce a character structure (habitus) that generates a particular style of behaviour. Social position (status or class) influences individual disposition or habitus, while the latter indicates and internalizes the former.

Habitus becomes a generative framework for cultural tastes in an individual and collective sense in the social fields, characterizing an aesthetic dimension of the practical style of life. It includes categories of perception and appreciation by which to acknowledge particular objects as legitimate and meaningful.[5] Habitus or cultural ethos for practical lifestyles or for political opinion is not merely rooted in the social status position, but it can be clarified in explicating the extent to which religious ideas would come to terms with material interests. This social scientific experiment is decisive in a religious construction of reality in which constructive theology is bound to the study of comparative religions.

The practical style of life, social prestige and status situation can be reinforced in the context of social struggle, competition and domination underlying rationalization and social division. This infrastructure is reproduced, specialized and differentiated, because the social process is linked to capital, habitus and social fields together with power relations and legitimation in authority and domination. In the process of reproduction the distribution of resources and its inequality are justified through symbolic power and its system of violence. This sophistication incorporates social reproduction, social change, and the role of agent into an account of stratification.[6]

---

5. Bourdieu, *Distinction*, p. 101.
6. Riley, 'Bourdieu's Class Theory,' *Catalyst*. vol. 1. Nr. 2. (Summer 2017), pp. 110–12.

Religious Discourse and Social Stratification

The connection between habitus and capital helps to revise Weber's theory of status and class by sharpening the relation between status and class in the intersectional fields. For Weber, the economic determination underlies the class situation or market situation, but it does not condition the group formation. In contrast to class situation, status situation refers to every typical component of the life, which is determined by a specific, social estimation of status honour, whether positive or negative. This status perspective becomes crucial in Weber's theory of social stratification constituting an institutional approach to the relation between political power, religious discourse (motivational variant) and economic formation.

However, Weber's major concern falls in analyzing religious discourse in its ideal typical type in influencing a practical way of life among agents, especially through their economic ethics. Thus he undermines the significance of the class position for status position. If the social position of the agent, according to his/her volumes and structures of capital, provides his/her specific value, cultural taste and effect, the relation between agent and capital of symbolic goods makes Weber's differentiation of class from status redundant. Space of lifestyles entails an affinity between taste, status and class, so class differences are seen in habitus as an embodied form of capital, which becomes an indicator of class or status by internalizing social position and space.[7]

This perspective helps to modify and sharpen Weber's theory of relation between ideas and interests in the practical style of life in terms of religious-ethical disposition and its cultural taste and prestige. Ideas become a reflection or a driving force in reinforcing material interests within status stratification. The material and ideal interests are dialectically combined, and society becomes influenced by idea formation; political power also suffocates the economic situation or co-determines social institutions with it.

Here, a possibility is implied for analyzing the extent to which the material interests would misuse or disgrace the source of religious ideas by serving the purpose of the status group. But such critical enquiry into disgrace effect of material interest upon religious ideas remains restrained in Weber. In Weber's account, religious rationalization would be advanced by commercial developments in connection with the emergence of priestly education. A priesthood supported toward

---

7. Ibid., pp. 128–9.

autonomy and religious rationalism in the urban commerce, that is bourgeois strata. An analysis is made of the material conditions and status situation in different social groups, in which particular styles of life are expressed by some religious ideas.[8] The concept of the ideal type facilitates Weber in treating the elective affinity between religious idea (Puritan Calvinism) and the spirit of capitalism in the course of history.

Having said this, Troeltsch finds a considerable significance in Weber's sociological method and elaborates his comparative study of social ethics within the entire history of Christian religion. For him Weber's sociology of ideal type reinforces a critical enquiry into seeing religious factors as the background of social, ethical forces in historical contexts.[9]

Troeltsch: The Political and the Social

Troeltsch contends that Weber's standpoint is based on economic history and social history. Weber's study of the Protestant ethic and the spirit of capitalism demonstrates the best example of the standpoint of religious idea and economic history on the question: 'What influences did the religious community on its side receive from the politico-social formation?'[10]

Weber's use of the term 'ideal type' is found between the content of a religious idea and cultural economic interests. By an elective process of elements, it avoids subjectivist, psychological extrapolation, as it comes to a point of consonance between religious discourse and cultural, material formation and interest. In a similar vein, Troeltsch defines the 'social' as a section of the general sociological phenomena, rather than as being exhausted by the economic or the political condition. Sociological relations are not regulated by the political dominion of the state, nor by economic interest. The social problem consists in the political community, and the sociological phenomena, though the latter is essentially un-political, has a great influence on the life of the state.[11]

The social sphere or field can be seen as civil society in distinction from political society (state), and civil society is considered in terms of social resource or capital within the organization of stratification. Social resource is largely based on social connection and its phenomena like status organization and institution (social capital), in which it is

---

8. Bendix, *Max Weber*, pp. 95–6.
9. Troeltsch, 'My Books (1922),' in *Religion in History*, p. 372.
10. Troeltsch, *The Social Teaching of the Christian Churches*, I, p. 34.
11. Ibid., p. 28.

distinguished from cultural capital (education and credentials) and economic capital (occupation and income resource). An agent has multiple dimensions in each sphere or field in social division of labour, stratified and diffused in a hierarchical spectrum. An agent's special space or position is considerably flexible, in accordance to accumulation of each source in terms of struggle, competition and domination. Religion or the religious field has relative autonomy and it is involved in multidimensional sources to justify its discourse, teaching and authority through compromise and negotiation. Sociological formation is related to the state and also the economic order of society to which the religious structure of society seeks to assimilate. Troeltsch's concern is to formulate the ethical, historical, or cultural-philosophical interest, when he investigates the actual influence of the sociological religious theory upon other social groups.[12]

Given this, the Church is an institution endowed with grace and salvation (the Christ of Church as the Redeemer); the sect is a voluntary society characterized by the experience of the new birth (The Christ of the sect as the Lord); mysticism is a purely personal and inward experience (the Christ of mysticism as an inward spiritual principle like the divine seed or spark).[13] However, Troeltsch goes beyond Weber by formulating religious and social problem in terms of his historical, critical method, and the ethical, theological, or cultural-philosophical enquiry. Christianity as a pre-eminently historical force can be explored by the Christian ethos, and a history of Christian ethic should be seen in its connection with the universal history of religions and civilization.[14]

A method of ideal type intersects with historical, critical method (critique, analogy and correlation), in which historical study retains a sociological implication; it treats Christian social ethics in a different historical context, as well as religious ethics in the universal history of world religions. His position is characterized by the slogan: 'everything is tottering,' because modern historical study showed that Christianity was influenced and transformed in historical development in its interaction with Hellenistic culture and philosophy.[15] The sociology of the ideal type can be renewed and enhanced in a historical, critical frame of reference, in which the social typology or model can retain more historical clarity and significance than Weber.

---

12. Ibid., pp. 34, 37 endnote 9.
13. Troeltsch, *The Social Teaching*, II, pp. 993–4.
14. Troeltsch, *The Social Teaching*, I, pp. 25, 37. Footnote 9.
15. Troeltsch, *The Christian Faith*, p. xvii.

Comparative Ethics, Sociological Research, and Religious Source

Troeltsch was alerted by Weber to the challenge of the Marxist theory of substructure and superstructures, and he sought to critically respond to the Marxist assumption. He investigated the history of religion, especially Christianity, by its social, political environment. 'Thus the Christian ethic of the present day and the future will also only be an adjustment to the world-situation'[16] through compromise and involvement.

In the face of European culture dissolving, it is useful to construct a new, contemporary cultural synthesis. A Eurocentric vision would no longer be tenable; it is 'in the midst of the storm of building a new world, where every ancient world must be tested for practical workability or unworkability. ... The earth quakes under our feet, and the various possibilities for the future dance circles around us, especially where the World War has meant a complete revolution, in Germany and in Russia.'[17] Nevertheless, this does not mean that the search for truth and justice falls back merely into skepticism. He undertook to construct a new cultural synthesis in interaction with other cultures, while participating in the foundation of the German Democratic Party in opposition to the Kaiser.[18]

Given this, he appears to be a constructive theologian in interpreting the Christian belief system to be more relevant to pressing social challenges than ever. His concern of social ethics is prominent in the political context. For him even Christian ethos in its divine love entails a socialism in light of the kingdom of God. His critical thinking is based on the eschatology. As he writes: 'The life beyond this world is, in very deed, the inspiration of the life that now is.'[19] As the apex of theology, ethics has the task of analyzing theological norms, belief systems and arguments from a moral, individual and social-ethical standpoint; it has to evaluate whether these are appropriate in a socially responsible manner to life in society, culture and institutions. Based on sociological developments, he applies the sociological question to the entire history of Christianity.

Taken all together, his research focuses upon the extent to which sociological effects would be taken on by the historical development of

---

16. Troeltsch, *The Social Teaching* II, p. 1013.
17. Cited in Troeltsch, *The Christian Faith*, p. xxi.
18. Troeltsch, *The Christian Faith*, Introduction by Garrett E. Paul, p. xxii.
19. Troeltsch, *The Social Teaching* II, p. 1006.

Christianity in terms of the 'social'; the latter does not deduce from the absolute character of Christianity and its social doctrine. The 'social' is related to sociological formations of status group, which the religious structure has to assimilate through compromise or interaction. This refers to the significance of social stratification. The whole Christian world depends upon the fundamental sociological condition, and so the sociological effect on Christian thought and dogma becomes crucial. A study of religion is advanced in terms of exploring the relation between religion and social stratification in its dialectical influence.

This responds to the Marxist assumption in which the economic basis gives an account of the phenomenon of religion; here, religious discourse is generally in the service of the political power and the sociological formation. However, Troeltsch's ideal type of Christian ethics in historical formation is not concerned with analysis of class, social capital, and social conflict in competition and struggle. This perspective redefines Troeltsch's sociology of religion through social stratification by strengthening his historical approach to the universal history of religion. This synthesized method and enquiry facilitates an endeavour in developing a constructive theology of comparative religions, and each religious and sociological formation is undertaken in its own historical location and interactions within differentiated fields; it takes into consideration religious ideas and ethics through critical involvement with society and history.

Moreover, such a perspective sharpens Troeltsch's basic question which reads in the twofold sense: 'What was the actual influence of the sociological religious fundamental theory upon other social groups?' 'On the other hand, what influences did the religious community on its side receive from the politic-social formations?'[20]

Troeltsch's research focuses upon the extent to which philosophical, sociological effects would be taken on by the historical development of Christianity in terms of the 'Social,' which cannot be deduced from the social doctrine of Christianity. Religious formation as faith community is bound to the political, social institution and power structure. As he writes, 'This sociological section is composed of the various questions which arise out of economic life, the sociological tension between various groups with different customs and aims, division of labour, class organization, and some other interests, which cannot be directly characterized as political, but which actually have a great influence on the collective life of the State; ... The "social problem", therefore, really

---

20. Troeltsch, *The Social Teaching* I, p. 34.

consists in the relation between the political community and these sociological phenomena'[21]

This finds a parallel with Weber's theory of social stratification, which is mainly concerned with three interconnected areas: economic status (wealth/class situation – economic society), political status (power/parties – political society), and social-cultural status (status situation in honor or prestige – civil society). A multiple form of power in economic, political, and social-cultural spheres is to be secured in terms of the legal order as an additional factor, though the latter does not become the primary source of power.[22]

Weber's theory of social stratification takes on the issue of religion and status group in driving social differentiation and rationalization. A specific complex of social relations is engendered and specialized, and the value of social networks is involved in producing and reproducing a social form of cultural capital or cultural knowledge. Stated in terms of reflexive sociology, multiple forms of capital can be classified in terms of usable resources and powers; cultural capital then becomes efficacious as a power or a resource in social institutions and bureaucratic authority, along with economic capital.[23]

Along with a theory of social stratification, Troeltsch's basic question is formulated in dealing with the influence of religious discource upon social group, while considering political social influence upon the religious community.[24] From his basic questions, Troeltsch conceptualizes elective affinity through the reciprocity between sociological religious theory and the political, social, economic formation. Christian religious influence is relevant in the political and economic sphere, while the latter also determines the religious interest and its historical development.[25] Troeltsch safeguards himself from the Marxist method by which 'to represent the whole of Christianity as an ideological reflection of economic development.'[26] But he articulates the influence of social stimulus and economic influences upon religious thought, though the religious idea plays a major role in interaction with social condition.

---

21. Ibid., p. 28.
22. *From Marx Weber*, p. 180.
23. Bourdieu and Wacquant, *An Invitation to Reflexive Sociology*, pp. 117–20.
24. Troeltsch, *The Social Teaching* I, p. 34.
25. Ibid., p. 37. Footnote 9.
26. Troeltsch, *The Social Teaching* II, p. 1002.

More than Weber, Troeltsch develops his enquiry in terms of social condition and history of religion 'within the general current of historical evolution.'[27] Thus the concept of the casual connection or elective affinity is considerably widened and altered in taking on the cooperating relationship between religious thought, political conditions and social, economic forces.[28] It entails an enquiry into the degree to which the institutional arrangement would be favourable or detrimental to the religious theory and its practical style of life. A sociological analysis of the history of religion is made in terms of a historical, critical method in treating the cultural context, political formation and institution.

In the interaction of all phenomena in the history of civilization, there is no point reaching 'beyond correlative involvement and mutual influence.'[29] Historical method of correlation places limitations on all absolute claims of human knowledge under critical scrutiny. This historical method facilitates Troeltsch incorporating sociological enquiry into the historical problem with the religious source and its historical spectrum, in terms of the principle of interconnection within the universal historical framework. His broadened perspective remains decisive in his study of Calvin, Calvinism and capitalism. Troeltsch's historical, sociological study of Calvinism and capitalism widens out the causal relationship, encompassing primitive Calvinism in Geneva and its political tendency to democracy characterized by the principle: 'By the people and for the people.' This political democracy has been explicated in connection with Beza and Monarchomachi and popular sovereignty.[30]

The Christian element in the Calvinist justification of capitalism would be greatly miscomprehended without considering the religious source, in other words, 'the Christian Social elements of Calvinist doctrine;' it is merged into a form of Christian Socialism. The capitalist has the duty to increase the capital and to utilize it for the good of society. The charitable activity of the Church was exercised in support of the local poor. Only productive credit for business purposes is allowed, but not usury credit. The fight against usury and the exploitation of the poor in the Genevan church imprints a mark of

---

27. Ibid., p. 1003.
28. Ibid.
29. Troeltsch, 'Historical and Dogmatic Method in Theology (1898),' in *Religion in History*, p. 14.
30. Troeltsch, *Social Teaching* II, pp. 630, 633.

social humanism.[31] 'The Christian Socialism of the English people at the present day is essentially of Calvinist origin.'[32] This appraisal takes a different course from Weber's thesis of Calvinism and capitalism.

2. Historical Method, Comparative Religions and Absoluteness

From Weber Troeltsch learns 'a new way of seeing things,'[33] but what distinguishes him from Weber is seen in his historical method: historical criticism, the importance of analogy, and correlation. All tradition is placed under scrutiny, which comes from the legacy of the Enlightenment, especially Kant's critical philosophy. There exist only judgments of probability in the realm of history. Because of probability in historical events, the historian has the capacity of discerning analogy between the events of the past and those of the present. Through analogy the unknown of the past is interpreted by the known of the present; this discerns a qualified similarity in the midst of dissimilarities within history.[34] The principle of analogy is related to the correlation underlying all historical happenings as knit together. The historical is identical with the relative within the mutual interrelation of all historical developments.[35]

Troeltsch maintains that historians acknowledge and recognize the interaction and interplay of all events in a historical setting in terms of the principle of correlation. His notion of correlation expresses that every human event is embedded within interconnection, as tightened together within a relationship of correlation.[36] His history-of-religions method starts from the totality of historical reality, subjecting all tradition to critical scrutiny of the interconnection.[37] The religious a priori plays at work within the correlation, because Troeltsch ascribes

---

31. For more details see Chung, "Ernst Troeltsch: Political Ethics and Comparative Religions," in Chung, *Critical Theory and Political Theology*, pp. 283–4.
32. Troeltsch, *Social Teaching* II, p. 649.
33. Introduction by James L. Adams to Ernst Troeltsch, *The Absoluteness of Christianity and the History of Religion*, p. 16.
34. Ibid., p. 9
35. Troeltsch, 'Historical and Dogmatic Method in Theology (1898),' in *Religion in History*, p. 13.
36. Ibid., p. 14.
37. Troeltsch, 'The Dogmatics of the History-of-Religions School (1913),' ibid., p. 88.

the life of the spirit in general to the recognition of the interwovenness of all human events (including the religious and the non-religious or the Christian and the non-Christian).[38]

This perspective contradicts an attempt to elevate Christianity as the absolute religion (Hegel). Hegel fails to elaborate the historical, critical method, making the historical data fit into his Procrustean framework; here, Christianity is isolated from the actual historical stream, or from other religions, and it is conceptualized in the sense of absolute religion.[39]

Troeltsch wonders whether the Christian faith could 'embrace historical thinking without nullifying its many universal values.'[40] Comparison between religions has a shattering effect upon the native outlook of absoluteness, paving a path for a new thinking of searching constant relationships; through comparison, analysis, new synthesis and combination we may come to reach the absoluteness as 'the most comprehensive integrating principles.'[41]

Religious A Priori and Comparative Religions

In his research program, the historical enquiry occupies a central place within the framework of the universal history of religion. His theory is influenced by Wilhelm Dilthey's hermeneutic, while he incorporates a notion of religious a priori into theological and philosophical transcendentalism.[42] This transcendental side is connected with Troeltsch's recognition of the neo-Kantian school in which he gives an account of the relationship between psychology and epistemology. If the epistemology demonstrates a productive capacity of positing valid insights, then it is not psychologically derived.

At this point, Troeltsch introduces a concept of the religious a priori: expression of the autonomy of reason, while the universally necessary is to be psychologically grasped.[43] Troeltsch takes on overcoming both dogmatic supernaturalism and mere psychologism through the concept of the religious a priori. The divine spirit, which is actively present in

---

38. Troeltsch, 'On the Question of the Religious A Priori (1909),' ibid., p. 33.
39. Troeltsch, *The Absoluteness of Christianity and the History of Religions*, pp. 11–2.
40. Ibid., p. 132.
41. Ibid., p. 133.
42. Troeltsch, 'On the Question of the Religious A Priori (1909),' in *Religion in History*, p. 33.
43. Ibid., p. 35.

human spirit, is the real ground of every religious a priori. He does not relinquish the dimension of religious feeling in Schleiermacher, but seeks to secure a yearning for the absolute, in other words, for religion in the general question of life.[44]

The religious a priori can be defined as the longing for the divine reality or the wholly Other, such that the religious a priori occupies a status of religious rationality in its distinct manner, which embraces moral values and a moral worldview; in other words, it becomes an undercurrent in religious construction of reality. This perspective reinforces Troeltsch's notion of religious a priori, by revising it in reference to history, society and culture.

Schleiermacher was an important influence on Troeltsch, as was Dilthey. As Troeltsch writes, 'the unconditioned nature of every *a priori*, and the continuity and logical nature of the historical forms of reason, appear to point to an active presence of the absolute spirit in the realm of the finite, to an activity of the universe, as Schleiermacher says, in individual souls.'[45]

Troeltsch's historicism is critically driven by the enquirer, as well as affirming the aspect of religious a priori (dependent feeing and intuition) in the study of world religions; it underlies the analogical imagination and correlation among all historical events. This perspective entails a neo-Kantian moment in Troeltsch, which transcends aimless or rampant relativism, or ethical relativism. It takes into account 'the rationally necessary and autonomous consideration and evaluation of the real from ethical, religious and teleological-aesthetic points of view.'[46]

He may pave a path toward conceptualizing a constructive theology of comparative religions, within the framework of universal history of religions, in terms of the historical method and sociological investigation. He assumes a post-Eurocentric orientation in recognition of other religious ways, while keeping Christian particularity, especially in light of God's future. His historical, sociological enquiry, which entails a post-Eurocentric character, makes it pertinent to develop Christian social ethics in a dialogical manner with world religions in the non-West. Troeltsch's contemporary synthesis of European culture does not necessarily mean an encapsulation into a Eurocentric vision.[47]

---

44. Ibid., p. 34.
45. Ibid., p. 41.
46. Ibid., pp. 35–6.
47. Troeltsch, *The Christian Faith*, p. xxii.

Typology of Absoluteness and Comparative Theology

Troeltsch's study of comparative religions helps in the endeavour to advance a constructive theology in the interreligious context. He introduces two types of absoluteness with several divisions; (1) native absoluteness, (2) artificial, apologetic absoluteness, (3) supernatural absoluteness, (4) rational absoluteness, and (5) evolutionary absoluteness.

All religions are born with an absolute claim, and the naive absoluteness in the historically evolved religions emphasizes the deep, inner relationship between bearers of revelation and God; the naive claims underlying the supernatural absoluteness are legitimized and measured by the liberating and redeeming power stemming from faith.[48] There arises an artificial, apologetic absoluteness out of the naive absoluteness under the pressure of the circumstances. This apologetic project embellishing the religious doctrine comes into conflict with the historical way of thinking. Only one's own position is taken to be positive, whereas all others are treated in a negative manner. This position leads to 'the controlling idea of supernatural absoluteness' in a decisive and fundamental sense of definition.[49]

However, given the supernatural absoluteness, the Christian position has been challenged by philosophical speculations, systems of philosophy, ethical forces and cultural development. The Christian position is to adopt all of these as belonging to its own truth, because they are assumed to be directed by God. For instance, rational articulation by the Church explained idealist movements of ethical and religious reform as remnants of the primordial revelation given to Christian religion; all truth prior to or outside Christianity is declared to be a remnant of the preparatory work of the Logos incarnated in Christ.[50]

The high point of this artificial rationalization can be seen in the Middle Ages, to the point where Christian apologetics took over the philosophy of Aristotle from Jewish and Islamic theology; it complements natural reason with the supernatural authority of Christian dogma. This artificial rational system results from contrast, comparison and reflection, which can be seen in the Thomist system or the Protestant dogmatic system undergirding the literalist inspiration of the Scripture.[51]

---

48. Troeltsch, *The Absoluteness of Christianity and the History of Religions*, p. 147.
49. Ibid., p. 151.
50. Ibid., p. 152.
51. Ibid., pp. 154–5.

Troeltsch distances himself from Christian apologetics. His scientific procedure moves, instead, from contrast toward synthesis, and it runs beyond previously maintained dogmatic presuppositions toward renewing, expanding and synthesizing their basic principle. In this methodical procession, the common point of reference made in comparison and relationship is freed from what was dogmatically secured as the objective or the centre of the whole. Epistemological enquiries call into question the whole basis upon which previous thinking and philosophical assumptions were built. They challenge the fundamental concepts regarding the object of theological reflection; the modern natural scientific view collides with the old doctrine of the Scripture and church doctrine, posing a threat to the apologetic, supernatural idea of history.

A constructive theology of comparative religions in Troeltsch's fashion investigates the sacred events in accordance with historical scientific enquiries; it also acknowledges a resemblance between the religions of past and present, or between Christian and non-Christian religions. This task requires a scientific study of a universal history of religion, which is embedded with its various types of absoluteness and its different faith communities, dogmas, religious ethics, sacred texts, revelations and theologies. This scientific stance makes it difficult for the artificial absoluteness to be maintained. Troeltsch contends that 'supernatural and rational absoluteness gave rise to *evolutionary absoluteness*.'[52] In this evolutionary, or in a better term, historical culmination of absoluteness, Troeltsch comprehends Christianity as unique and supernaturally revealed truth, in other words, the 'absolute' religion. Although this truth is absolutely certain, it is not yet exhaustive without disregarding other truths. The relativity and similarity, which are found in the claims of the various religions, cannot threaten the validity of Christianity.

In comparison of value orientations among religions, Troeltsch comes to form a criterion of judgment which is related to something common and universally valid within them; this common element 'inheres in the higher religious and ethical forms of thought.'[53] The principle of normativeness and universal validity are common to all religions, while the absolute is still maintained. But the normative and universal goal, which is considered as something perfect and complete, is not exhausted in its human cultural realization; it goes beyond history, belonging to the future.

---

52. Ibid., p. 157.
53. Ibid., p. 98.

Such a principle appears, as seen in a psychological and epistemological perspective, to be the concept of a goal toward which humankind strives; this reality provides the creative force at work in the human conception of a goal; it refers to one's forward-driving restlessness, and a yearning for the Absolute that is moving in resistance to the merely natural world. It requires a shift towards 'retracing all [human] goals and orientations to a transcendent force that actuates our deepest strivings and is connected with the creative core of reality.'[54] In the goal-oriented character of reality, Troeltsch discovers the permanent element in the concept of evolutionary development as directed toward the absolute goal of the human spirit; 'the various eruptions, breakthroughs, and manifestations of the higher spiritual life.'[55]

At this juncture, Troeltsch recognizes 'Christianity as the highest religious truth,' – indeed, 'as the focal point and culmination of all religious developments.'[56] What is decisive in Troeltsch's typology is to see Christianity as 'the pinnacle of all religious development;' it is also 'the basis and presupposition for every distinct and meaningful development in man's religious life in the future.'[57] Christian faith among the great religions refers to 'the strongest and most concentrated revelation of personalistic religious apprehension.'[58] This position is based on personal conviction, which emerges from comparative observation and evaluation. It has little to do with a dogmatic approach in its absolutization of Christianity.

Nonetheless, absolute truth belongs to the future, which appears in the judgment of God. We remain in approximation to God's future, while taking part in the divine living power in our midst.[59] 'The universally valid ... works teleologically within history.' In the relative, Troeltsch holds, there is a token of the absolute, which transcends history,[60] in other words, it implies an eschatological reservation of historical forms of religion.

---

54. Ibid., p. 100.
55. Ibid.
56. Ibid., p. 107.
57. Ibid., p. 131.
58. Ibid., p. 112.
59. Ibid., p. 115.
60. Ibid., p. 106.

Historical Relativity and the Norms of Value

Troeltsch is not concerned with filtering social norms and values out of the history of Christianity and establishing a finished and permanent principle of religion. Rather, he relies upon the guiding hand of God in the Judeo-Christian sense, leading humanity historically within history; God left 'to Jesus the disclosure and consummation of the salvation of the future.'[61]

This said, Troeltsch may appear to stand within the Christian confessional tradition, in which he affirms that Christian faith is grounded in revelation in accordance with the apostolic concept of the economic Trinity. History is conceptualized as proceeding from God; thus 'our faith in the highest revelation binds the eternal and the temporal close together.'[62] His historical thinking does not necessarily seek to deconstruct faith and the dogmatic belief system; rather the latter could be reinterpreted within the history of religions in order to make it more relevant to the modern world. This implies a constructive side of comparative theology, in which one's religious discourse and belief system is to be refined in a fresh and creative relationship with other religions and traditions. The textual study in comparison remains decisive, while the textual study stands under historical critical examination. Comparative theology after comparison, which proceeds with critique, analogy, religious a priori, and correlation, moves in undertaking semantic retrieval, and rendering the compared synthesis to contemporary relevance. Faith refers to itself in a concrete thought-content, and it does not originate only from the individual subject; it is grounded in the archetype, the personality of the founding prophet or revealer. It depends upon the embodiment of revelation and is embedded with 'communal work of great epochs of intellectual history and whole generations.'[63]

Seen in the context of historical criticism, Christianity is regarded as a climax in the historical development of its actualization of the consciousness of God. Troeltsch does not bring relativism into contradiction with absolutism, but combines the two in terms of synthesis and evaluation; historical relativity is therefore connected with norms of value. 'Thus the modern study of history leads to the task of comparing

---

61. Ibid., p. 162.
62. Troeltsch, *The Christian Faith*, p. 107.
63. Troeltsch, 'Faith and History (1910),' in *Religion in History*, p. 134.

the major forms of religious orientation from a single, inclusive perspective, and this places a new and even more extensive restriction on relativism.'[64]

In his 1923 lecture at the University of Oxford ('The Place of Christianity among the World Religions'),[65] Troeltsch takes the superiority of Christianity to be no longer valid. It cannot be accepted as the convergence or culmination point for all other religions, without reservation. 'It is the loftiest and most spiritual revelation we know at all. It has the highest validity.'[66] For Troeltsch 'each of the faiths may experience its contact with the divine life.'[67] It is unfortunate that this statement is called 'nominalistic, unlimited relativism', or a form of henotheism.[68] His concern is rather to elaborate the contact of religious others with the divine life, because this divine life is grounded in the triune God.

Already in 'On the Possibility of a Liberal Christianity (1910),' Troeltsch finds it difficult to deify the person of Jesus as an absolutely central position in the sense of a universal world-redeemer – it is also difficult to regard Jesus as the culmination of humanity and his cosmic significance. At the same time, he does not reject the distinctively Christian idea of God without further ado, because he acknowledges its life-giving embodiment in Jesus as the revelation of God. 'Jesus will always keep on living wherever the Prophetic-Christian belief in God is alive.'[69]

Taken together, he contends in his 1923 lecture that 'the Divine Life is not One, but Many.' 'To apprehend the One in the Many constitutes the special character of love.'[70] This theocentric, historical stance embraces all the relativism as well as subjectivism; this stance is always concerned

---

64. Troeltsch, *The Absoluteness of Christianity and the History of Religions*, p. 92.
65. Troeltsch, 'The Place of Christianity among the World Religions,' in *Christian Thought*, pp. 1–36.
66. Cited in 'Introduction' in Troeltsch, *The Absoluteness of Christianity and the History of Religion*, p. 13.
67. Ibid., p. 17.
68. Ibid.
69. Troeltsch, 'On the Possibility of a Liberal Christianity (1910),' in *Religion in History*, p. 348.
70. Troeltsch, 'The Place of Christianity among the World Religions,' in *Christian Thought*, pp. 32, 35.

with a question of proximate values,[71] because being in history means moving in a way that is relative and open-ended; it is in contrast to absolute knowledge in the Hegelian sense.

Troeltsch's notion of 'polymorphous truth'[72] does not necessarily classify his stance into a religious pluralist one imbued with a double belongingness to the two different religious traditions. To be historical is to be relative, and this principle does not necessitate one's double belonging to the two different religions. It would be naive to argue that the double belongingness to the two different historical religions would bring the different, relative religious truths to completion. In the textual comparison an interstice remains for synthesizing of the semantic articulation to be shared between the two religious traditions, but such synthesis stands under continual correction and critique for future. To be historical is to be problematic at any given time; correlation looks forward, going beyond self-righteous syncretism.

Troeltsch's position on doctrine such as the Trinity affirms his position as a critical historian, who places historical manifestations and developments of all religions under the mystery and future of God. This position characterizes his stance as one which affirms Christian uniqueness, while recognizing that of other religions; the latter is driven through religious a priori toward the mystery of God. Without Prophetic-Christian faith in God, one cannot become a critical historian in recognition of the people of other cultures and religions.

Along with Troeltsch, however, H. Richard Niebuhr repeats the limitations of Troeltsch's historical relativism, dealing with the relation between Christ and culture. Christianity was relative, but it has come to Christians as an absolute claim. Such a claim appeals to Western people, while they still live in the midst of relativity.[73] For instance, according to Niebuhr, conscience is transhistorical, but the morality of cultural values is historical and connected with the maintenance of perishable things in the world. A synthesis is possible only in individual acts of achievement, and finally we are justified only by faith.[74]

However, Niebuhr sidesteps a dogmatic side of Troeltsch, who maintains that 'the dogmatic doctrine of the religious significance of Christ should precede ... the discussion of the specific concepts of the

---

71. Troeltsch, 'On the Possibility of a Liberal Christianity (1910),' in *Religion in History*, p. 357.
72. Knitter, *No Other Name?*, p. 30.
73. Niebuhr, *Christ and Culture*, p. 182.
74. Ibid.

Christian faith as a whole; it is their presupposition and foundation.'[75] More than Schleiermacher, Troeltsch affirms the doctrine of Christ as a divine revelation in accordance with the Pauline-Johannine teaching, such that he relates the specific meaning of Jesus' suffering and death to the Reformation doctrine of justification, which is based on the absolute forgiveness of all sins consisting in a sacrificial death.[76]

His concept of revelation is based on dynamic understanding in which revelation exists not in isolation, but rather in its effects through the doctrine of the Holy Spirit underlying 'a personally convincing revelation.'[77] In the dynamic concept of a productive, progressive revelation, he considers the concept of reproductive revelation in which there is a surging consciousness of the unity between the human and divine spirits (the great religious personalities included). However, Troeltsch does not identify Christian revelation with the non-Christian ones, instead, he argues that the revelation itself can be encountered in its subsequent development and rendering. In a dogmatic exposition of faith, he holds, faith is saturated by revelation, which becomes accessible in the first place.[78]

Troeltsch's position steers between relativism and absolutism and requires a turn toward a transcendental force actuating out deepest strivings and relating our goal and orientations to the creative core of reality.[79] As he writes, 'the kingdom of God, just because it transcends history, cannot limit and shape history. Earthly history remains the foundation and the presupposition of the final personal decision and sanctification; but in itself it goes on its way as a mixture of reason and natural instinct, and it can never be bound in any bonds except in a relative degree and for a temporary space.'[80]

This statement characterizes Troeltsch's eschatological stance, which is expressed: 'the life beyond this world is, in very deed, the inspiration of the life that now is.'[81] The evolutionary goal in the eschatological light is not constructed from a scientifically established law of cause and effect

---

75. Troeltsch, *The Christian Faith*, p. 277.
76. Ibid., p. 278.
77. Ibid., p. 45.
78. Ibid., p. 49.
79. Troeltsch, *The Absoluteness of Christianity and the History of Religion*, p. 100.
80. Cited in Niebuhr, *Christ and Culture*, p. 182.
81. Troeltsch, *The Social Teaching* II, p. 1006.

in the sense of Social Darwinism, or from Hegel's historical dialectics of the spirit. Rather, Troeltsch asserts that God has immediacy to people of every epoch through the religious a priori. This position does not abolish the flux of evolution and becoming. The present is completely filled by the immediate nearness of God, and thus the distinctive character of the non-theoretical (or irrational) validity is moments in the process of becoming. Each moment has an immediate, individual significance of its own in a direct relationship to God.[82]

Thus, the great religions are related to each other in a stage-by-stage causal process, standing in a parallel relationship. Jewish, Christians, Hindu, Chinese, European, and other Oriental people will have a different basic framework for each contribution and construction in the history of evolution of religion.[83] His eschatological thinking in a historical frame of reference sounds closer to Weber's dictum: 'It is not necessary to become Caesar in order to understand Caesar.'[84]

3. Troeltsch, Philosophy of Religion and Life-world

Troeltsch provides both a philosophy of religion and a theology, in dealing with the polarity between mythos (life) and logos (thought) with a strong emphasis on the significance of history. '*Logos* and *Mythos* in Theology and Philosophy of Religion (1913),' he sought to explicate the relationship between theology and philosophy of religion in terms of logos and mythos. He takes a living, historical personality as the central symbol; every age can interpret this as the great religious resource for all humanity creatively from its own historical perspective. He articulates the symbolism of the religious mind and the immediacy of experience over against Kant.[85]

In the early stage of his thought, Troeltsch constructed a general history of the development of the religious spirit in the common life, especially through Schleiermacher and Dilthey's philosophy of history. Later, Troeltsch undertook a transition from Dilthey's psychological understanding to a neo-Kantian un-psychological theory of validity,

---

82. Troeltsch, '*Logos* and *Mythos* in Theology and Philosophy of Religion (1913),' in *Religion in History*, p. 67.
83. Troeltsch, 'Rival Methods for the Study of Religion (1916),' ibid., p. 76.
84. Weber, 'The Nature of Social Action,' in *Weber Selections*, p. 8.
85. Troeltsch, '*Logos* and *Mythos* in Theology and Philosophy of Religion,' in *Religion in History*, pp. 54, 71, Note 1.

which was known during his time as the phenomenological school, represented by Wilhelm Windelband and Heinrich Rickert.[86]

Troeltsch argues that Kant recognized an a priori in ethical, religious, and telelogic-aesthetic reason. Indeed, Kant in his division between understanding and reason includes the power of judgment as an intermediary between understanding and reason; the latter contains 'in itself *a priori* … a proper principle for seeking laws, although merely a subjective one.'[87] The original consciousness in human cognition of understanding and reason is given in feeling, because it refers to consciousness prior to reflection based on understanding and reason. In the third *Critique*, Kant analyzes how an a priori feeling can be accounted for; more precisely his idea of aesthetic judgment based on feeling can have universal validity or subjective universality. Ideas of God, the soul, and the world as a whole are represented in aesthetic ideas to us. Troeltsch's constructive synthesis of Kant and Dilthey for a religious a priori can provide the historical, sociological grounds for a philosophical approach to religion and its pluralist thesis, which is grounded in the Kantian distinction between noumenal reality and its phenomenal appearances.

In effect, this philosophical enquiry of religion is also undertaken in John Hick's synthesis of the Real in and of itself in each of the great religious traditions, while underlying a radical reorientation of human life from self-centredness to reality-centredness.[88]

Religious a priori in a theocentric-personalist framework comes to terms with a neo-Kantian synthesis of reality-centredness, reinforcing the importance of anthropological significance in human religious experience. Each tradition among world religions can be comparatively explored and constituted in terms of critique, analogy and correlation within the universal history of religion, despite differences of truth claims.

Religious A Priori and Neo-Kantian Epistemology

Troeltsch would have a lack of conceptual clarity regarding the relationship between religious experience and a priori validity. His philosophy of religion falls on theocentric-personalist orientation, while including the non-theoretical and irrational component, leading to mysticism

---

86. Troeltsch, 'My Books (1922),' ibid., pp. 370–1.
87. Kant, *Critique of the Power of Judgment*, pp. 5, 177.
88. Hick, *An Interpretation of Religion*, p. 4.

in the case of Meister Eckhart and Neoplatonism; despite discrete entities between God and the subject, the subjects act, feel and think only in God.[89]

In Troeltsch's mystical leaning, however, it would be difficult to affirm the religious a priori as religious rationality, because it is exposed to historical influence, as well as social conditions. It ceases to be a priori in historical effectiveness and social location since it doesn't take on the character of transcendental validity. Already in his conception of religious a priori, Troeltsch feels a difficulty in bringing up the integration between the a priori and the psychological with the aim of constituting an irrational unity of life.[90] Can we generalize a mystical experience of the Absolute in terms of autonomous validity, while allowing a distinction between theoretical and non-theoretical validity?

Edmund Husserl's theory of life-world can help in breaking through Troeltsch's epistemological limitations, and deserves special attention. Husserl discerns the problem of psychological historicism in Dilthey's philosophy of historicism, criticizing it as a cultural formation because of epistemological flaws, which give it a lack of objective validity.[91] The philosophy of life-world holds a central problem regarding how to make sense of the normative character of epistemic claims to knowledge and truth within the value-relevant and descriptive stance. If norms and values are considered to be truly valid, this validity remains an undercurrent in shaping the subjective evaluation of its normative validity. The reference to norm and value (life-world) is a theoretical performance for the historian to establish the historical significance of a phenomenon. This performance, under influence of the life-world, becomes a guiding principle, which interacts with the historian's personal evaluation based on his/her own values and biases regarding the subject matter. All factual material constitutes the data for the epistemological subject, while applying its scientific methods and normative values deriving from its own a priori. The epistemological subject and the logical a priori should be the point of departure for a logic of historical science.[92]

Thus, Troeltsch maintains that we have a completely objective, purely phenomenological teleology in which historical method on an a posteriori basis refers to the 'ideographic method' aiming at the individual and the

---

89. Troeltsch, 'Logos and *Mythos*,' in *Religion in History*, p. 68.
90. Troeltsch, 'On the Question of the Religious A Priori (1909),' ibid., p. 40.
91. Husserl, 'The Critique of Historicism,' in *The Essential Husserl*, p. 25.
92. Troeltsch, 'Modern Philosophy of History (1904),' in *Religion in History*, p. 285.

particular; the scientific-universal method in natural science refers to the nomothetic one. The difference between the methods of natural science and historical science is based on the distinguished types of natural science and human science, and it is deduced epistemologically; what is involved in this problem is deduction and abstraction[93] in terms of natural sciences as nomothetic (aiming at general laws); but historical sciences are of idiographic character, because they by focus their theoretical interest upon the individual and unique. However, to constitute historical fact by a value relation, it is necessary to take into account 'the way historical knowledge is interwoven with historical events.'[94]

This position is closer to Dilthey, who elaborates a critique of historical reason in contrast to Kant's critique of pure reason. Dilthey argues that all experience, all thought, and all knowledge emerge from the interaction between individual and historical context. Only through history do we come to know ourselves, and our knowledge is extended through the interpretation of the external world of life.

Of special significance in Dilthey's project is an overwhelming sense of the relativity of all perspective; human thought is inevitably embedded with historical life. For instance, in the study of the historical movement, we can experience individual role and participation in a historical context and from the individual personality. One's unique and creative breakthrough cannot be adequately comprehended without considering one's life connection with the social, cultural, historical environment. All understanding always remains partial and can never be completed, because the connectedness is a category emerging from life itself.[95]

Life-world and Epistemology

Husserl's theory of life-world can be a mediator for Dilthey's hermeneutics of history, though it simultaensouly challenges its subjectivistic relativism without reference to history as the objective validity. In Husserl's conviction there is a universal a priori science of universal human sciences in contrast to the neo-Kantian formal classification of the sciences; nomothetic is equated with natural scientific method, while historical science is equated with the idiographic method.

Husserl's idea of a universal a priori human science provides the theoretical basis of valid knowledge, that is, objectivity in the human

---

93. Ibid., p. 291.
94. Gadamer, *Truth and Method*, p. 506.
95. Dilthey, 'The Rise of Hermeneutics (1900),' p. 217.

sciences;[96] it should be seen and founded in light of the life-world. In other words, Husserl's phenomenology can be seen as a scientific philosophy of life, which is undertaken in correlation between the intuitive perception (*noesis*) and the ideal meaning of *noema*, which is moved and affected under the life-world. Husserl proposes the notion of life-world for universal, objective validity, and in doing so takes issue with mathematical natural science in its idealizing of nature itself or the world through technization.[97] Even Kant's transcendentalism is not capable of penetrating into the role of life-world at work in human subjective life.[98]

Religious a priori is located with the life-world, and is culturally affected and socially constituted. Since Kant paves a path to the aesthetic dimension in religious studies, then aesthetic judgment anticipates common sense shared by everyone. Pure feeling in an aesthetic judgment claims objective validity, universality and necessity. The subjective and personal character of the judgment of taste is expressed in the maxim *de gustibus non disputandum* (In matters of taste, there can be no disputes).[99]

Unlike for Kant, however, religious feeling or cultural taste emerge out of a relation to wider objective structures of the social world and cultural tradition. The way in which the unconscious of the social (life-world) can be explored objectively and subjectively can be explicated in terms of people's religious longing, habitus and practices. In this way it unveils the 'unthought' under the influence of the social world. It is necessary to consider that the multiple spaces and fields in a society are constituted and stratified by symbolic capital, goods and economic interests.[100]

A genetic phenomenology accounts for the extent to which the social life-world is established and maintained through consciousness and its polythetic acts of constitution; the latter are patterned according to the accumulation of past experience. For Husserl, lived experience itself, and the objective moment constituted in it, can be seen as possession or knowledge in the form of a habitus.[101]

---

96. Jalbert, 'Husserl's Position between Dilthey and the Windelband-Rickert School of Neo-Kantianism,' p. 290.
97. Husserl, 'The Mathematization of Nature,' in *The Essential Husserl*, pp. 338, 352.
98. Ibid., p. 360.
99. Otto, *The Idea of the Holy*, p. 149.
100. Bourdieu, *Distinction*, pp. 485–500.
101. Throop and Murphy, 'Bourdieu and Phenomenology: A Critical Assessment,' *Anthropological Theory* Vol 2 (2), p. 193.

In dealing with the habitus, Husserl is more concerned with the pre-given structures of consciousness in terms of intentionality, and their correlation is adumbrated in the processes of retention, reflection and protention in the semantic circle, which fuses different horizons for a synthesis of deepened and enriched meaning. The structures of the life-world are often unrecognizable to those individuals acting and reacting within it. Phenomenological enquiry avoids an attempt to understand structures of consciousness simply as the product of a dialectical 'internalization' of objective structures (Bourdieu or Berger). If there is a correlation between social structure and religious a priori, there is no pure religious a priori. A religious or aesthetic taste or social disposition is formed in the intersection between historical effect and social location.

Troeltsch and Religious Epistemology

Troeltsch appreciates Rickert's epistemology, and qualifies his religious a priori in terms of historical criticism. He finds Hegel's system unsatisfactory, because Hegel makes the nomothetic universal into the dynamic force and the ultimate goal of the idiographic particular. In doing so, Hegel marginalized 'the particularity and individuality of history,' while changing 'the whole of history into a valueless preliminary stage of the realization of the universal concept.'[102]

Troeltsch puts priority on historical method over against the nomothetic sciences, because the latter simplify the empirical world; their cognitive value 'cannot ultimately be an end itself.'[103] In a nomothetic type of natural scientific knowledge there is no capacity for comprehending the irrational particular. This type of knowledge is not capable of being accessible to the epistemological need for value construction, which requires an idiographic or historical discipline.[104] For Troeltsch, everything historical remains irrational-mystical and individual, despite all references to absolute values. He expresses this reality as our fate and destination.[105] Should everything historical be judged to be irrational, individual, and even mystical, such that we must succumb to it as our fate and destination?

---

102. Troeltsch, 'Modern Philosophy of History (1907),' in *Religion in History*, p. 293.
103. Ibid., p. 296.
104. Ibid., p. 298.
105. Ibid., p. 305.

Religious a priori can then be qualified in an epistemological sense within the horizon of life-world, in which the human religious experience of the Absolute would be dynamically related to the process of understanding. Everything historical as irrational and mystic can be expressed and understood through linguistic competence, which renews its psychological side in the reference to the Absolute. A theory of life-world critically renews Troeltsch's concern about objective reality in recognition of the individual, the unique, and even the irrational-mystic through linguistic-hermeneutical enquiry. For instance, we may discover truths in different cultures and traditions. Their truths are generally verifiable for them, while they are not the same as other forms of the ruth at all. Despite all relativity and difference, the objects of life-world, common to all, are operative as a general structure or framework in all their relative features and conceptions. Language is capable of translating and interpreting the differences or relativities for communication and exchange with one another.

A constructive theology of comparative religions is of a theocentric, linguistic character, because God's infinity is beyond human comprehension or imaginative construction, or even mystical irrationality. It takes up a radical inclusiveness in light of God's reconciliation sustaining human longing for God, as well as by relativizing imaginative construction. God, as seen in the light of being the source of the life-world, is corrective of human understanding through the process of adumbration, critical distance, and a new synthesis, while transforming as the source of life and emancipation human biases, dominion and corruptions. This critical constructive method calls into question what is taken for granted, or what has been done in the theological tradition; this question requires a task of revising, correcting and refining intellectual conviction and judgments, going beyond our present position. 'Faith in God, if God is taken seriously as the ultimate point of reference in terms of which all else is to be understood and relativized.'[106]

Troeltsch Revision: Faith-Epistemology and Religion

Religion can be comprehended in terms of life-world, in which religion is involved in the dialectical dynamic process and structure. It concerns cumulative tradition in historical and cultural development (rituals, art, music, economic ethics, and theologies, among others) and personal

---

106. Kaufman, *In Face of Mystery*, p. 8.

piety or faith.[107] According to Alfred C. Smith, personal faith has a significance in the comparative study of religion, because faith is a divine-human complex whose human component should be the subject matter of religious studies. The personal faith, grounded in a dialectical process involved in the relationship between the mundane and the transcendent, is not to be confined within any intelligible limits. 'Faith' and 'cumulative tradition' are central in the comparative study of religion. Cumulative tradition is the material form of the faith of past generations as well the present. In the first place, faith generates the tradition, while faith is nourished and patterned by the tradition; yet faith precedes and transcends the tradition, and in turn sustains it.[108]

There is an affinity between Alfred C. Smith and Troeltsch in dealing with faith and cumulative tradition. In Troeltsch's account, faith consists of an attitude of belief, which is based on tradition, authority, and community of conviction; but it is not exhausted by this customary usage of belief. Faith is seen in a willing surrender to God and an openness to divine fulfillment, and is identical with religion itself.[109] This faith-knowledge interplay relates to the transcendental, and the latter is wholly inaccessible even to the historical, critical method, because such knowledge in its basic content is specifically religious and symbolic.[110] Faith-knowledge shows itself to be a cognitive principle in its own right, because faith epistemology aims at a relationship to divine reality as mediated by religion. The religions of faith interpret the world mythically in connection to the significance of religious *heroes*, and it crystalizes their mythos around ethical-religious values. This perspective of faith of religions is true of Mosaic and prophetic religion as well as Islam.[111]

If Smith adopts a personalist approach, comprehending faith as constant in human history, comparative study of religion indicates that a form of faith varies and changes from one religious tradition to another, but not in kind. So faith should be the ultimate subject matter of the study of religion. However, Troeltsch's faith-epistemology is elaborated in terms of the combination between logos and mythos in historical-sociological frame of reference. He draws attention to the sociological dimension of religion, going beyond purely individual and personal constructs. The sociological perspective provides a critical, dynamic engagement

---

107. Smith, *The Meaning and End of Religion*, p. 194.
108. Smith, *Faith and Belief*, p. 5.
109. Troeltsch, 'Faith,' in *Religion in History*, p. 121.
110. Ibid., p. 128.
111. Ibid., p. 126.

in seeking through new syntheses to meet present conditions and to adapt it to future exigencies.[112] A social philosophy of religion contends that religion exists only as a historical given, and a religious system is conditioned by the secular world in its historical vicissitudes and modifications.[113]

Despite this difference, Troeltsch's faith-epistemology within a theocentric-personalist framework does not necessarily contrast with Smith's view of religion as dynamic dialectics between cumulative tradition and personal faith. It is then necessary to incorporate a theocentric-personalistic stance in the comparative study of religion into the dynamism of the life-world.

Here, Treotlsch's philosophy of religion and its faith-epistemology can be revised and enhanced in a hermeneutical frame of reference. This sociological hermeneutical enquiry analyzes the cumulative tradition of religion in terms of historical, critical method, and it explicates the extent to which the religious discourse would be embedded with the multiple fields of material interests and symbolic goods in its social formation and stratification. Institutional side and political power come into focus in which religious a priori and one's faith-life is conditioned, influenced, and interacted by other different streams of cumulative tradition.

Troeltsch and Post-Eurocentric Direction

Troeltsch affirms the Prophetic-Christian belief in God, while recognizing an infinite plurality of spiritual worlds. Thus 'there are still other religious life-contexts with their own redeemers and paradigmatic figures.'[114] In so doing, there are still other circles and sources of light set within the great divine life of the world, which originate from the depths of the divine life. 'Every epoch stands immediately before God, and we stand immediately before God precisely as gathered together in the circle of light radiating from Jesus.'[115]

The radiating light of God's revelation in Christ does not necessarily come into conflict or competition with the unique experience among other religions within the universal history of religions. Troeltsch's

---

112. Troeltsch, 'The Dogmatics of the History-of-Religions School (1913),' ibid., p. 103.
113. Troeltsch, 'The Social Philosophy of Christianity (1922),' ibid., p. 218.
114. Troeltsch, 'On the Possibility of a Liberal Christianity (1910),' ibid., p. 349.
115. Ibid., p. 350.

attitude of agreement, involvement and renewal for a new synthesis can be seen in his account: 'in the movement of God's life ... God sits on the Divine throne (*im Regiment*) with God's truth prevailing. ... What we perceive to be the truth binding our conscience cannot be wholly false and must point toward the future. We may devote ourselves, therefore, seriously and faithfully to the task that we comprehend, and leave the rest to God.'[116]

His theocentric stance would come to terms with a sociological concept of multiple modernities, though the sociological concept of the axial civilization and religions does not occupy his thought. His historical method within the universal history of modernity retains a post-Eurocentric orientation and can assert that different histories, different cultures and different circumstances give rise to quite different modern cultures and societies.

According to Troeltsch, a version of social Darwinism is impossible, because 'history manifests no gradual ascent to higher orientations as far as the vast majority of mankind is concerned.' As he continues, 'by no means, however, are the great religions that burst forth in this way related to each other in a stage-by-stage causal process. They stand, rather, in a parallel relationship.' With regard to the world of the East Asian religions, 'our conclusion is that while the modern study of history cannot avoid forming concepts of normative principles, it cannot arrive at such concepts by proofs for the absolute realization of a universal principle.'[117]

Modernity was born in Europe, and it is assumed as a process of worldwide diffusion; however, multiple forms of modernity should be discovered in different traits and characteristics in different societies and civilizations. European and Western modernity are just one of the diverse forms that modernity has taken on over the past two centuries. Troeltsch would support an alternative reality of plurality and hybrid, as seen in the project of multiple modernities engaging in the fusion of diverse patterns and forms. His project of historical sociology is appreciated in his dismantling of the Eurocentric presumption in terms of comparative study of world religions.

Certainly, Troeltsch's study of comparative religions helps me to advance religious social ethics in the interreligious context for the politics of recognition and multiple modernities. In his theocentric, historical stance, Troeltsch is grounded on the Prophetic-Christian

---

116. Ibid., p. 359.
117. Troeltsch, *The Absoluteness of Christianity and the History of Religion*, p. 70.

belief in God, while assuming an infinite plurality of spiritual worlds. For him 'there are still other religious life-contexts with their own redeemers and paradigmatic figures.'[118] There are still other circles and sources of light, within the great divine life of the world coming out of the depths of the divine life. This insight makes it possible to conceptualize his comparative theology of divine lights as the ensemble of semantic texts, which can be intelligibly described in their particular terms and contexts.[119] If the cultural practice and its symbolic structure are taken 'as a means of saying something of something,' the notion of a text as an ensemble of texts extends beyond written materials.[120]

Religious texts, together with cultural meaningful practices, may become the sematic text, if seen in the light of cultural life-world. This perspective facilitates an effort in undertaking an analysis of the many different meanings of rationalization in regard to the cultural, political, economic development in the non-West. In other words, historical critical enquiry within the universal history of religions facilitates an endeavour to analyze multiple forms of modernity in different ways in distinction from a Eurocentric manner. A notion of alternative modernities (Charles Taylor) or multiple modernities (Eisenstadt) refers to an attempt to conceptualize non-Western forms of modernity, which is not exhausted by the Western metanarrative of rationalization or modernity.[121]

4. Comparative Theology and Religions

Troeltsch constructed a general history of the development of the religious spirit or religious a priori in the common life, especially through Dilthey's historical psychology. Schleiermacher, an influential figure on Dilthey, holds good in Troeltsch. Troeltsch takes Schleiermacher as a path for his own development, but he contends that the modern study of history finds it difficult to accept Schleiermacher's position without reservation; in the latter, Christianity is bestowed with a higher power in the rise of the spirit. Troeltsch argues that it is out of the question to attempt 'to construe Christianity … as the absolute, history-transcending realization of the spirit.'[122]

---

118. Geertz, *The Interpretation of Cultures*, p. 14.
119. Ibid., p. 14.
120. Ibid., p. 449.
121. *Alternative Modernities,* ed. Gaonkar.
122. Troeltsch, *The Absoluteness of Christianity and the History of Religion*, p. 41.

Troeltsch's philosophy of religion encompasses religious validity (or religious a priori) as well as the non-theoretical (or irrational and mystical) elements. This mystical component within the framework of personalistic theism provides a background for Troeltsch's understanding of faith. However, he designates piety in a broader concept, paying due respect to the Holy in all of its aspects; it refers to the totality of the subjective religious life, while faith is comprehended as the cognitive element of religion, determining piety.[123] Thus, Troeltsch combines piety with faith through the conception of a personal, ethical God. In this union faith is designated as the cognitive element of piety, because it is a matter of trust and surrender to divine reality which is apprehended by thought. The cognitive element depends upon revelation, and faith is primarily in the fundamental revelation.[124] He breaks through some limitations of Schleiermacher's piety-centredness.

Later, he made a shift from the psychological description to a neo-Kantian theory of validity. Troeltsch acknowledges in Kant's philosophy that an a priori plays a substantial part in ethical, religious, and teleologic-aesthetic reason. Kant makes the division between understanding and reason, while accepting the power of judgment as an intermediary between understanding and reason. Religious-aesthetic reason contains a priori in itself, although it is merely a subjective universality. An a priori feeling in his idea of aesthetic judgment can have universal validity or subjective universality.

In Kant's analysis of the judgment in his third *Critique*, aesthetic judgment is set in opposition to logical judgment. In the distinction between the aesthetic and logical judgment, Kant separates the faculty of judgment based on feeling of the beautiful and the sublime for universal validity from discursive, conceptual concept and inference. The Kantian term 'aesthetic' marks the peculiarity of the former in contrast to logical judgment.

Comparative Theology with a Different Interpretation

Troeltsch's constructive synthesis of Kant and Dilthey for a religious a priori marks a significant contribution to the philosophy of religion, as well as the notion of religious rationality in complementing Weber's value rationality. Religious a priori in the form of religious rationality

---

123. Troeltsch, 'Faith,' in *Religion in History*, p. 122.
124. Ibid., p. 124.

can provide historical, sociological ground in interaction with a philosophical approach to religion.

Troeltsch's epistemology within the religious a priori may come to terms with John Hick's synthesis of reality-centredness, which is based on the Kantian distinction between noumenal reality and its phenomenal appearances. Kant locates the idea of God within the realm of morality, because God is postulated rather than experienced. However, Hick modifies Kant's epistemological model by stating that God is a reality encountered in religious experience. His basic epistemology is based on Thomas Aquinas: 'The thing known is in the knower according to the mode of the knower (*Summa Theologica*, II/II, Q.1, art. 2).'[125] Hick's synthesis of the Real in and of itself in each of the great religious traditions makes a radical reorientation of human life from self-centredness to reality-centredness.[126] Nonetheless, Troeltsch would be suspicious of Hick's pluralism hypothesis; the latter tends to sidestep an analysis of the sociological reality and historical significance in shaping and conditioning religious symbols, the sacred texts, doctrine, and religious ethical influence upon economic development. A domestic form of revelation in a Christian context is, according to Troeltsch, not surpassed by the sheer relativization for the pluralism thesis.

It is Gordon Kaufmann who draws attention to Troeltsch in order to develop his constructive theology in recognition of extra-biblical materials, philosophical ideas and natural scientific achievements, while undercutting limitations of a one-dimensional biblicism as well as a one-dimensional experientialism; here Kaufmann takes issue with Tillich's method of correlation, in which divine revelation provides definitive answers to the fundamental questions as raised by human reason and experience.[127] For Kaufmann, Troeltsch calls into question the universalistic claim of Christianity for possessing the truth which is valid for all humanity. Because of the embeddedness of Christianity in history and culture, 'the essence of Christianity' in the confessional approach is deemed to be 'vague, subjectivistic, undisciplined, and at best pertinent only to the West.'[128]

Troeltsch is concerned with considering the history of *religion* as *history* of religion in which a theory of constructing Christianity as the absolute religion is out of the question on the basis of a historical way

---

125. Hick, *God has Many Names*, p. 49.
126. Hick, *An Interpretation of Religion*, p. 4.
127. Kaufmann, *In face of Mystery*, p. 23.
128. Ibid., p. 24.

of thinking. 'In the correlative interconnection of all historical events' everything historical is identical with the relative.[129] For Troeltsch, the Christian religion is a purely historical phenomenon which is subject to all cultural limitations and social conditions. It requires historical research and method in the universally verified sense, because what is historical means what is relative.

His notion of historical relativism, according to Kaufman, implies the radical historical character of humanity, such that society came to constitute itself in and through history; all customs, practices, institutions, ideas, morality and values of a society remain relative to history and to the society in every respect, going through different histories and societies in advancing their own distinctive customs, institutions, religion and ethical value.[130]

In this regard, it is of special importance for Kaufmann to overcome an ahistorical way of thinking about Christian faith and theology, in which the concept of essence or an unchanging core of truth expresses itself differently in the various forms of historical Christianity. Thus, he makes the essence of God-talk into the controlling principle in his constructive theology. The essence of God-talk has no essentialist claims, because Kaufmann is not convinced that any such essence of God-talk is to be discovered in terms of a close examination of theistic traditions.[131]

The essence of God-talk, framed within four major categories (God/world/humanity/Christ), requires a wider Christology which challenges the traditional Christological deification of the man Jesus. Kaufmann's radical theocentrism maintains that divine creativity itself in God's incarnation is seen as a christic principle or Christ-event in the more complex pattern of personal/social relationships surrounding and including the man Jesus. God is conceptualized as the mysterious serendipitous creativity in terms of the evolutionary-historical process working throughout the world, whose image is the man Jesus.[132] This ecological-processive reality runs counter to the reified mythic picture of Jesus.

However, the essence of God-talk as the mysterious serendipitous creativity does not fit Troeltsch's interest; for Troeltsch a sociological

---

129. Troeltsch, *The Absoluteness of Christianity and the History of Religion*, p. 63.
130. Ibid., p. 117.
131. Kaufmann, *In face of Mystery*, pp. 29–30.
132. Ibid., p. 384.

enquiry of diverse types of Christian social teaching is undertaken in the historical course of time, in which his theocentric theology does not undermine the subject matter of Christian revelation and faith. Religious a priori can be conceptualized in reference to the divine referent as the objective reality. It can be manifested and formulated in religious symbols, faith, mythical narratives and social ethical attitudes among religions.

A pluralistic project of global theology according to Hick focuses on the reality of the Eternal One who belongs to the basic problem in the philosophy of religion. A global theology is philosophically grounded in the basically cognitive character of religious experience, which leads to a distinction between the Eternal One in itself (the infinite reality) and the Eternal One as experienced, thought, and expressed by us. However, Troeltsch's historicism thesis is grounded in a theocentric-historical frame of reference, which is sociologically distinguished from Hick's pluralism hypothesis. In the case of the latter, the Real in itself in a Kantian sense is elevated to be the Eternal One as 'the same infinite divine reality.'[133] The latter encompasses the personalistic personae of theistic religions as well as the nonpersonal awareness of the Absolute in nontheistic religions, in all of which the Eternal One is represented as the sameness in different culturally conditioned perceptions.

Hick's position conflates Christian revelation with Hindu manifestations in *bhakti* religion. The ultimate reality (Brahman) is no less than its personalist manifestations, especially in the case of Ramanuja. Given this, a critical question is raised concerning the extent to which the Eternal One would be generalized or totalized into the God of Judeo-Christianity or vice versa; God has many different names, but in sameness: 'the Allah of Islam, the Krishna and the Shiva of theistic Hinduism, the Brahman of advaitic Hinduism, the Dharmakaya or the Sunyata of Mahayana Buddhism, and the nirvana of Theravada Buddhism.'[134] Hick's pluralism is of an ahistorical character, marginalizing the historical difference and sociological uniqueness in each religious tradition, and subjugating all differences and pluralist expressions to the Eternal One. Would a human individual take a standpoint under the Eternal One, which cannot be known to the human being? How do we know that all is the One? Should the rich differentiation and determination of empirical content and religious experiences in the universal history of religion be plunged into a night in which all cows are black?

---

133. Hick, *God has Many Names*, p. 52.
134. Ibid., p. 24.

Against this 'colonialist' totalization of the sameness, life-worldly enquiry into religious a priori is concerned with analogical expression of the Eternal One in terms of similarity in dissimilarity, in which the Eternal One as *totaliter aliter* is not subsumed into the philosophical logic of the sameness. Rather the eternal One is comprehended in terms of the divine freedom and mystery; in it the different religious ways become the texts of semantics to be deciphered and interpreted in each historical, cultural difference and uniqueness. One should await the absolute religion in close conjunction with the end of all history. 'There must be complete twilight before the owl of Minerva can begin its flight in the land of the realized absolute principle.'[135]

Comparative Theology, Interreligious Ethics, and Reconciliation

For Troeltsch, the concept 'relative' means that all historical phenomena are unique; every independent structure leads to a perspective that embraces broader and still broader horizons, until finally it opens out onto the whole. A comprehensive perspective allows for us to form universal judgments and evaluations. Relativity does not necessarily mean denial of the values appearing in the individual configurations, which have the power to encounter and influence one another; as a result of such interaction the individual is led to discern its inner truth and necessity, choosing among values at every moment of history. These values take part in the peculiarities of the situation to which they belong. The scientific study of history does not exclude norms and values nor undergird a rampant relativism without purpose and meaning. Troeltsch does not make an either/or choice between relativism and absolutism, but seeks to combine them in a synthetic way in light of divine transcendence.

Troeltsch holds that 'individual' and 'unique' or 'everything new and creative' emerges from the transcendent depths of history, and these elements come to actualization in relation to the given. What is unique and individual is a new creation in light of the theocentric principle. The substantive components and principles of life take shape in the depths of the soul, and these are creative regulators of historical life. One's understanding of history must be drawn from history itself, and history must be separated from epistemology or a philosophy of culture and

---

135. Troeltsch, *The Absoluteness of Christianity and the History of Religion*, p. 69.

metaphysics.[136] There is a transcendent depth to history out of which 'individual and unique' emerges. Religious personality becomes the arbiter in dealing with comparison and evaluation, when it comes to the comparative study of world religions. Such a criterion is a matter of personal conviction, thus subjective; 'It is, in short, a personal, ethically oriented, religious conviction acquired by comparison and evaluation.'[137] Certainly, Troeltsch is not averse to the objective basis in the research of the major religious orientations and belief system and its assessment; but 'its ultimate determination remains a matter of personal, subjective, inner conviction.'[138]

Taking a step further, his theocentric principle is the source of the religious a priori, which can be integrated into life-worldly enquiry, and which could strengthen his epistemology. It cuts across his entanglement with neo-Kantian objectivity as well as psychological, mystic leaning. The gospel ethic then becomes noteworthy in Troeltsch. The gospel together with the Scripture, he holds, 'exerts its influence ever anew' and Christian confessional teachings 'concern social life and the whole of civilization.' 'Whether in agreement or opposition, in dependence or in change of meaning, all the modern ecclesiastical social doctrines are determined by this point of view.'[139] Jesus in the Gospel ethic was confronted with the Jewish priestly aristocracy through his solidarity with the oppressed, and the lowest of the low in the human family. The Gospel message of the kingdom of God refers to the vision of an ideal ethical and religious situation that is given to the destitute against the dominant forces of contemporary human society. 'It is … undeniable that the message of Jesus, in its sympathy with poverty and suffering, does apply more particularly to the poor.'[140]

Sociological characteristics determine the background and meaning of the Gospel ethic, which is 'melting down of earthly smallness and worldliness in the Fire of the Divine Love.'[141] Individualism and universalism are closely connected with the religious root of the Gospel ethic, such that 'the sociological thought of the Gospel has been able to react again and again against ecclesiastical tyranny.'[142] In the coming reign of God the poor and the suffering are promised to 'have their tears

---

136. Ibid., p. 88.
137. Ibid., pp. 96–7.
138. Ibid., p. 97.
139. Troeltsch, *The Social Teaching* I, p. 25.
140. Ibid., p. 60.
141. Ibid., p. 56.
142. Ibid., p. 58.

wiped away and all their desires satisfied.'[143] In this direction Troeltsch characterizes the Gospel ethic in terms of 'the religious Communism of Love,' which is differentiated from all other forms of communism.[144]

In a similar vein, Weber seeks to conceptualize a religious ethic of ultimate ends or conviction in reference to ethic of responsibility. In 'Politics as a Vocation' (1919), Weber distinguishes an ethic of responsibility from an ethic of conviction.[145] His conception of political ethic is qualified in three components: passion in the sense of matter-of-factness, a feeling of responsibility, and a sense of proportion.[146] Along with the ethic of responsibility, Weber also introduces the absolute ethic of the Gospel. This ethic is kept in line with the acosmic (world-denying) ethic of love which does not ask for consequence. It refers to 'the religious Communism of Love' in Troeltsch. Weber's argument is that an ethic of ultimate ends (not identical with irresponsibility) is founded in the religious realm, while an ethic of responsibility is not identical with unprincipled opportunism. An ethic of ultimate ends feels responsible for 'the flame of protesting against the injustice of the social order.'[147] The religious ethic of brotherliness and sisterhood remains the fundamental imperative of all ethically rationalized religions: to help widows and orphans in distress, to care for the sick and the poor brother and sister of faith, and to give alms.[148]

As we have seen, Weber was confronted with the reality of the iron cage brought through capitalist rationalization. The reality of the iron cage can be paradoxically seen in the resurgence of polytheism in the value spheres. Now, we are confronted with the different gods of the spheres of various orders and values, which assume the form of impersonal force, standing in irreconcilable conflict and in eternal struggle.[149] The symbol of the iron cage of bureaucratization has caused a polytheism of value spheres imbued with the reality of impersonal forces. Against this reality of impersonal force, however, Weber holds an alternative through responsible ethic, which is imbued with religious prophetic conviction. However, he remains restrained in his minimalist approach

---

143. Ibid., p. 61.
144. Ibid., p. 62.
145. Weber, 'Politics as a Vocation,' in *From Max Weber*, p. 78.
146. Ibid., p. 116.
147. Ibid., p. 121.
148. Weber, 'Religious Directions of the World and Their Directions,' ibid., p. 330.
149. Weber, 'Science as a Vocation,' ibid., p. 139.

to religious moral rationality, because he appears to recommend our fate as the surrender to impersonal forces. His minimalist approach is not capable of demonstrating an aspect of challenging the reality of impersonal forces, in terms of analyzing the extent to which the knowledge and power structure could be established as the legitimate realm of bureaucracy or reification.

Troeltsch's problem can also be seen in his excessive attachment to religious individualism, because he dissociates the prophetic movement and its social change from Christianity; he is content with his excessive emphasis on the 'radical disengagement of God and of souls from the world.'[150] Built on individualist ethics, Troeltsch remains restrained in highlighting the prophetic side of the Gospel ethics transcending the acosmic type of mystic universalism (Spinoza). Rather, it is imperative to relocate the theocentric principle within the symbol of reconciliation, in which *theologia crucis* becomes central in combining the anamnestic reasoning of Jesus' solidarity with those excluded, unfit and deviant – *massa perditionis*. It underpins a prophetic, anamnestic vision that inspires collective responsibility for failure to avert imminent disaster in the past or to improve social conditions beset by inequality, domination and violence.

The divine lights can be positioned within the eschatology, which is related to people of all other cultures and religions. If every epoch stands in immediate relation to God, multiple religious expressions of divine truth are deepened and enlightened within the circle of light radiating from Jesus. God's future underlying the relation between divine life and lights of the world can be seen in light of the gospel of reconciliation, in which God does not abandon humanity, culture and the world.

In a critical revision of Troeltsch, it is important to construct comparative theology in the double sense; first a hermeneutical project of reading together with other religious traditions; then comprehension of the human being as a cultural being in terms of ethical being. Sociological theory of religion comes to terms with understanding the human being as an interpreting animal. Comparative theology becomes a critical, constructive project, which seeks to refine and reinterpret the Christian message, belief system and religious symbols in reading other religious texts and recognition of their religious practices and tradition. One's faith is not undermined; rather it is taken as the basic presupposition underlying comparative theology. One's faith is enriched

---

150. Troeltsch, *The Absoluteness of Christianity and the History of Religions*, p. 110.

and deepened toward the synthetic understanding of one's religious particularity; in recognition of the other's power of transformation, a comparative theology reinforces and widens one's faith in the process of semantic retrieval in engagement with other religions.

A religious a priori or longing for divine transcendence can be seen in all religious symbols, ritual manifestation and moral practices; it can be expressed concerning social organization, economic attitude and political system. These are taken as the semantic fields to be deciphered intellectually or described densely in their own terms. This perspective characterizes comparative theology in elaborating religious discourse and its construction of social reality in a critical, emancipatory manner. It is driven by problematization, immanent critique, synthesis and emancipation in dealing with prejudices and obscurities in historical accumulation and the disgrace effect of religious discourse in connection with the divine reality.

Excursus: A Critical Note on Troeltsch's Personalistic Type of Religion

Troeltsch articulates the significance of historical critical research in the comparative study of the main religious orientations among world religions. In dealing with a criterion of value within each historical situation and its presupposition, he is concerned with comparing the different manifestations and correlating them in order to disclose a higher, transcendent life in God. His comparative interest lies in exploring the faith in God living in every higher religion.[151] This aspect, restricted to relativism, constitutes a faith epistemology in comparing and measuring the major forms of religious orientations. His historical method does not privilege Christian religion, because it is comprehended as a relative phenomenon in the course of history. In the fulcrum of the historical mode of research, the historical is identical with the relative.[152] It does not exclude norms, but it seeks to discern norms and see them as a unified whole toward a common goal; the goal is not yet completely realized, but belongs to the future.[153] A personal conviction does not derive from a dogmatic approach, but 'from comparative observation and absorption in hypothetically adopted value.'[154] In his historical research

---

151. Ibid., p. 95.
152. Ibid., p. 86.
153. Ibid., p. 91.
154. Ibid., p. 107.

of Christianity, Troeltsch confirms that the Christian orientation and its reliability are rooted in the realm of personal religious faith. Prophetic and Christian personalism entails its superiority in the historical course over other religious paths.[155]

In the study of Pure Land Buddhism, however, it is difficult to affirm Troeltsch's characterization of Christianity only as the personalistic religion of redemption, in which its highest value is discernable in the history of religions. According to Troeltsch, all other religious orientations have not yet achieved the breakthrough to personalism.[156] He argues that divinity in the Indian religions is comprehended to be impersonal but eternally existent, while requiring self-renunciation and strenuous spiritual exercises.[157] Although both Brahmanic acosmism and Buddhist quietism are examples of the redemption concept, they did not go through discovering the value of personal life. In the Brahmanic development, Troeltsch observes that the divine turns into the Eternal and Immutable, whereas the world is finite and transitory; all pain and joy are mere illusion. Knowledge of the divine means emancipation from the world as a way of blending God and the soul into one; in other words, it implies 'absolutely indistinguishable unity' between Brahman and the soul. The only way to the divine is a way of self-redemption through contemplation (gnosis included) and asceticism.[158]

Troeltsch, however, does not acknowledge that Ramanuja's type of *bhakti* religion entails the dimension of the personalism with its universal reorientation to all. In the Buddhist development Troeltsch observes that the divine is totally transmuted into the void of bliss lying behind the world (emptiness). It makes self-redemption possible through the Four Noble Truths in subduing the will and attaining right knowledge, which crowns the endeavour of participation in the emptiness. The higher world in both cases is to be pursued by the enlightened in terms of self-exertion and the natural power of the soul. Troeltsch's evaluation is related only to the Vedanta within Hinduism and Theravada Buddhism. He is not capable of acknowledging the *bhakti* tradition as well as the faith tradition in the Mahayana tradition.

According to Troeltsch, the higher religious life is alleged to have four sets of ideas: God, the world, the soul, and the world of the transcendent.[159]

---

155. Ibid., pp. 124, 159.
156. Ibid., p. 129.
157. Ibid., p. 110.
158. Ibid., p. 111.
159. Ibid., p. 113.

What makes Christian religion into the strongest revelation of personalistic religion is its understanding of God and faith. He makes a choice between meditation (on Transcendent Being or non-Being) and redemption through faith in participation in the personality character of God. The higher goal and the greater profundity of life, Troeltsch holds, are found in the personalistic religion in historical development. Despite his personal conviction of Christian personalism, Troeltsch does not establish the history of Christianity as 'a finished and permanent principle of religion.'[160] Relativity and similarity can be found in the claims of the various religions which cannot pose a threat to Christianity.[161]

Nonetheless, Pure Land Buddhism is an example of Buddhist breakthrough to personalism in juxtaposition with Christian personalism, which does not culminate in the most perfect form and manifestation. A comparative study of the Reformation teaching of grace with Buddhist teaching of grace is an indispensable regime. This comparative theology is explored in Chapter 3.

---

160. Ibid., p. 162.
161. Ibid., p. 159.

Chapter 2

Comparative Theology, Sociological Enquiry, and Power Relations

This chapter deals with the extent to which a comparative theology and sociological enquiry would be mutually beneficial through clarification and elucidation in a Buddhist-Christian context. I have explored this in more detail in my book *Comparative Theology among Multiple Modernities*, but will summarise those arguments here in order to set up the more exercises in comparative theology that I propose to undertake in the following chapters.

First, I will briefly demonstrate how the sort of comparative theology explored here deals with a sociological enquiry of religious discourse and comparative reading in a hermeneutical manner, including power relations, problematization and immanent critique. Francis Clooney's comparative theology is instrumental here; it is based on the concept of *Homo lector* (the reading person) in the commentarial exegesis of textual juxtaposition, but it is also possible to elaborate a sociological hermeneutic and its reading strategy with respect to the social and ethical dimensions of human life. This social scientific experiment aims at examining the degree to which religious ideas or discourses would be bound with power structures and material interests in the course of time and the social context.

Second, for this task it is necessary to analyze the Buddhist text of *Bodhicaryāvatāra* (*The Way of the Bodhisattva*) in connection with the Buddhist principle of dependent origination. A historical survey of the meaning of *bodhicitta* can be undertaken, and the wisdom of emptiness can be explicated in diverse Buddhist contexts through exegetical work.

Then, it is possible to critically examine Christian commentary of this religious text.

Third, the relevance of the *bodhicitta* idea with the *Heart Sutra*, is discussed, while taking issue with a questionable regime of emptiness and karma in the Japanese colonial context, as well as in the modern Japanese interpretation. Comparative theology and sociological enquiry can be advanced in taking issue with the Japanese Buddhist approach, while interpreting the Buddhist text of *Bodhicaryāvatāra* and *Heart Sutra* in a different manner. Its negative effect of disgrace is analyzed, in a bio-political manner, as a way of problematizing the complex relation of political power over the colonized body (comfort women) and the religious discourse of violence (militaristic killing).

Finally, an axial enquiry can be made into Buddhist religion (theoretical attitude imbued with narrative thinking) as an immanent critique in unveiling ideological distortion of religious ideas.

1. Social Scientific Experiment and Comparative Theology

A comparative theology can be articulated in sociological enquiry, which is informed by a hermeneutical frame of reference. It aims at exploring the degree to which religious discourse would be enmeshed with the material interests and power relations in history and society. For this, it is vital to do meticulous exegetical work in taking on religious discourse, its social formation and its ethical significance.

A theory of problematization is incorporated into an exegetical work of the sacred texts, while explicating how and why a particular body of knowledge (Buddhist discourse of emptiness and karma) is entitled to be set up as a hegemonic discourse in subjugation of its other aspect (compassion) in a (post-) colonial regime. It requires an archaeological analysis of discursive formation and performance in connection with the social background (institutional support, political decision, techniques of public assistance, and cultural validity). Power-knowledge relations can be contained and conjoined in religious discourse, which reinforces the effects of the power;[1] this implies underwriting a social aspect of the religious construction of reality.

This perspective reinforces a critical theory of religion, which attempts to investigate the way religious discourse and status group find consonance with political power, economic motivation and cultural value. Such enquiry is concerned with the bio-political strategy, which

---

1. Foucault, *Discipline and Punish*, p. 27.

is connected with symbolic power, authority and domination. It features a critical side of comparative theology in its constructive thrust to the point of solidarity and emancipation; a critical comparative theology focuses on the way exegetical language in sacred texts would cut across the mode of representation espoused with social conditions and power structures. If religious discourse of confession becomes a basis for a steady proliferation of discourses concerned with sexuality, then the multiplication of discourses concerning sex are embedded within a network of formation, rationalization, and specialization through power exercises. At this level of articulation, there is a hermeneutical function inscribed into discursive formation and practices.[2]

A hermeneutical strategy in religious study involves a horizon of intelligibility from the sacred literatures, as well as examining the social performance of religious discourse. There is no religion without a sacred text or texts; even a radical Zen Buddhist understands the direct realization of the Buddha-mind within the textual tradition. He or she cannot be located at the level of exteriority purged of any religious or anthropological background. Textually formed rationality and its religious discourse have far-reaching consequences in its dissemination and influence upon society, political motivation, economic attitude, education, and cultural value.

A comparative theology puts into brackets or problematizes what is taken for granted in religious episteme, by refraining from the domain of the problem; it renders the problematic regime as an object of critical analysis in unveiling adulteration of an idea with material interest and dominion. Comparative theology retains a critical function in focusing on the disgrace effect of religious discourse, which is produced by its negative effect; it is seen in alliance with the interests of the dominant group and their hegemony. In effect, religious discourse is made into ideology in justifying the status quo. It points to a regime of problems which are embedded in accommodation, hegemony and privilege. Immanent critique focuses on contradictions or the disgrace effect that exists between religious ideas and their social practices, seeking a potential for emancipatory change.

Homo Lector *and Self-Effacement*

For his comparative theology, Clooney does not utilize the studied traditions as fitting and suitable in order to serve the home tradition of comparative theologians. Rather, he values their legitimacy and universal

---

2. Foucault, *History of Sexuality* 1, p. 61.

validity without downplaying other traditions.³ It is important for Clooney to develop comparative theology in terms of *collectio* (reading together) in which he 'intends a rethinking of every theological issue and a rereading of every theological text' by involving sacred texts of other traditions.⁴ He is interested in rewriting Christian theological tradition from the newly composed engagement. His position is of a rigorous commentarial significance, while he makes an intelligent commitment to the sacred texts. He insists that a *Homo lector* must favour self-effacement before the text, by emphasizing a humble attitude instead of a value-neutral position. A humble practice 'discloses productive ways of thinking and changes the reader, as she or he is drawn into the world of the text,' in face of 'the implications of [their] truths.'⁵

However, the position of self-effacement tends to lose a critical attitude toward the problem of religious texts and their patriarchal, authoritative tradition. This vulnerability of submission to religious authorities, power structures and institutionalization is therefore an obstacle to Clooney's descriptive position in which a constructive side is undermined in his comparative reading of a text, such as the *Summa Theologiae* and Advaita. He safeguards comparative theology against a constructive side of undertaking any changes in any particular doctrines or abandoning them. Only the rereading of a tradition's doctrines is recommended in a meticulous and painstaking manner in terms of the other tradition and its text compared. As he writes, 'Comparative Theological reading does not require the abandonment of any particular doctrines, nor a revisionist interpretation of the meaning of any particular doctrine; indeed, comparative theological reading depends on the perdurance of what is said, read, taught, written in a tradition; those who expect from comparative theology sensational new teachings should inevitably by disappointed.'⁶ His model of comparative theology is consonant with George Lindbeck's postliberal theology concerned with the nature of doctrine in the intratextual manner. If religious discourse is inscribed into material interests and justifies the social system of the caste in Indian society, to what extent would comparative theology reinterpret the religious text and its discourse, problematizing the regime in question and upholding the immanent critique?

---

3. Clooney, *Theology after Vedanta*, pp. 5–6.
4. Ibid.
5. Clooney, *The Truth, the Way, the Life*, pp. 9, 10.
6. Clooney, *Theology after Vedanta*, 189. pp. 116–7.

Given this, a sociological-hermeneutical enquiry is a way of undertaking a semantic notion of synthesis of meaning compared in the two traditions through fusion of horizons. It further frames such semantic experimentation in a symbolic materialist analysis of power relations within social stratification or in the context of colonialism. A bio-political strategy is concerned with explicating the degree to which religious discourse would be embedded with a political system of domination and institutional support in misusing religious texts. Such strategy is analyzed and advanced in terms of the problematization or critical distance in suspending what is taken for granted. This enquiry remains crucial within the framework of the religious construction of reality, and it requires commentarial, exegetical work on religious texts in terms of immanent critique, solidarity and emancipation.[7]

Sociological Interpretation and Homo Socius

Along with the concern of Clooney's comparative theology, however, it is important to articulate a sociological enquiry within a hermeneutical framework. This will deal with the sacred literatures as historically transmitted, socially conditioned, interest-bound, and embedded with power relations. This post-metaphysical stance incorporates an archaeological art in deciphering discursive formation, and analyzing the epistemic system in formation, transformation and rupture[8] into the semantic articulation between religious discourse and its special manifestation in history and society. A new meaning occurs in the procedure of the encounter and interpretation, which approaches the truth in an open-ended way; it implies an art of fusion of horizons.[9]

This sociological hermeneutic allows for self-effacement in the initial stage of appreciation in authentic listening and learning; it then proceeds to find elective affinity between religious ideas and material interests along power relations, in order to undertake a careful and deliberate reading praxis. It is concerned with prophetic insight, which is underlined in the religious texts for immanent critique and emancipation. This critical, semantic enquiry considers plurality and ambiguity, in which religions entail exercises in resistance to self-idolatry

---

7. For more detail, see Chung, *Comparative Theology among Multiple Modernities*, pp. 230–32.
8. Foucault, *The Archeology of Knowledge*, p. 131.
9. Gadamer, *Truth and Method*, pp. 306–7.

or the absolutization of religious doctrine and their power systems in the nexus of institutionalization and the dominant form of knowledge.

It can be argued that American evangelicals form strong symbolic boundaries when challenged by 'outsiders,' but they also acknowledge that this is not the full story and is perhaps a necessary simplification.[10] Against this trend, it is an indispensable task of the comparative theologian as a reading agent to allow for that boundary to be challenged and changed. A genuine conversation with the text appreciates the meaning and truth of the religious classics, while testing their applicability or non-applicability to the public sphere in the strategy of resistance, difference and irregularity.[11]

Indeed, religious language can be expressed as social discourse, which is enmeshed within political motivation and the status quo of the power structure; we see such an example in Buddhist idea of emptiness, which tends to justify imperial militarism; it is also applied to the Christian distortion of symbol of the cross turned into crucifix and crusade.

The life-world of *Homo lector* is kept alive instead of being bracketed. It helps to have an attitude of appreciation in dealing with other sacred texts, through the angle of self-effacement and suspension of the reader's values; it correlates with a critical method of problematizing religious ideas in serving material interests and the privilege of the dominant, scrutinizing social elements such as the background of institutions, political legitimacy, economic motivation and social process.

Thus, *Homo lector* becomes *Homo socius* and *ethicus* without a mere submission to the hierarchical and oppressive elements of the religious texts and tradition. The social scientific experiment facilitates projecting a critical comparative theology in dealing with the extent to which religious discourse intersects with reality in history and society stratified and organized in inequality, injustice and symbolic domination. Thus, exegetical work on religious texts becomes the fulcrum in constituting critical comparative theology in its constructive and emancipatory frame.

2. *Bodhicaryāvatāra*: Text Reading and Interpretation

If faith is in search of understanding, 'faith and understanding,' a faith-epistemology, is not separated but articulated in a semantic circle, which is undertaken through dialogue with the Other. Here the term 'semantic

---

10. Smith, *American Evangelicalism*, pp. 124–44.
11. Tracy, *Plurality and Ambiguity*, pp. 93, 102.

Comparative Theology, Sociological Enquiry, and Power Relations 53

circle' is used in connection with Husserl's responsible critique and emancipation, referring to the textual world along with the non-textual background (politics, economics and culture); it is used to differentiate itself from a term 'hermeneutical circle' which is concerned mainly with the totality of textual literature in terms of the part-whole pair.

In a Buddhist context, faith (devotion in taking in the Three Jewels—the Buddha, Dharma, and sangha monastery) is so closely connected with intellect, that this connection is a crucial factor in Nāgārjuna; he was the second-century Indian representative of Mahayana Buddhism.[12] Buddhist integration of faith and reason does not necessarily contradict Christian position of faith and underdtanding, rather such respective epistemology can be enhanced and deepend in compataive reading of different sacred texts. Indeed. God is the mystery of the world more than faith.

For mutual learning and elucidation, it is important to view the language of faith in the commentarial, exegetical framework, in dealing with the Buddhist sacred text of *Bodhicaryāvatāra*. The *Bodhicaryāvatāra* is versed as *The Way of the Bodhisattva*, which is assumed to have been compiled in Sanskrit by a Buddhist philosopher, Śāntideva, who lived in India in the eighth century (approximately between 685 and 763 CE).[13] *The Way of the Bodhisattva* is respected as the most important source with reference to Nāgārjuna's *Precious Garland*[14] and Asaṅga's *Bodhisattva* Levels. In the Cittamātra (mind-only) school, however, *bodhicitta* refers to the *tathāgatagarbha* (Buddha-womb) or *ālayavijñāna* (substratum-consciousness); it is identified with the Buddha nature or Buddha essence, or even the cosmic body of the Buddha (dharmakāya). The term 'bodhicitta' is the root of enlightenment, as rendered in modern translation as the 'thought of enlightenment' or 'desire of enlightenment' (or sometimes 'awakening'). 'Bodhi' means the state of being Buddha, the awakened, or it is enlightenment or awakening. 'Citta' has its common meaning as mind, thought, attention, or desire. What is central in the path to full enlightenment is the three essentials such as bodhicitta, great compassion (the altruistic mind of awakening), and the wisdom of emptiness.

Given diverse meanings and applications, Francis Brassard concerns the soteriological significance, involving the religious idea of *bodhicitta*

---

12. The Dalai Lama, *Practicing Wisdom*, p. 3.
13. Brassard, *The Concept of Bodhicitta in Śāntideva's Bodhicaryāvatāra*, N, p. 16. Williams identified the perdiof of Śāntideva's life (c. 695–743); see Williams, *Mahayana Buddhism*, p. 58.
14. Dunne and McClinton, ed. and trans., *The Precious Garland*.

is articulated. It is important to develop the Buddhist soteriology in terms of sociological enquiry, in which the notion of *bodhicitta* can be explored in the historical context by finding elective affinity between the *Bodhisattva* ideal and the social way of life.

Bodhicitta *and Two Levels of Truth*

Bodhicitta has a dual character: the conventional *bodhicitta* and the ultimate *bodhicitta*. The cultivation of the former is the means to elaborate compassion for all sentient beings. Cultivation of the latter qualifies the mind to realize the phenomenal world in terms of suffering, impermanence and emptiness, which is not expressed by concept or speech.[15]

A distinction is made between the conventional *bodhicitta* and the ultimate *bodhicitta*, and it remains crucial in the Mādhyamika tradition. The Middle Way epistemology serves as an antidote to one's mental perception and emotional attachment to the phenomenal world, while religious language and discourse are 'relatively' utilized to explain the deeper reality of the religious experience of emptiness, more than reduced to a skillful means.[16]

Nāgārjuna (first to second century CE), the founder of the Middle Way, distinguished the two truths in terms of ultimate truth and relative truth. In his keen appreciation of the dynamics of reality he equates emptiness with interdependent origination; the emptiness can be defined as relativity. 'Interdependent origination – that is what we call emptiness. That is a conventional designation. It is also the Middle Way.'[17] Nāgārjuna maintains that 'Buddhas resort to two truths: worldly conventional truth and ultimate truth.'[18] For him, relative and absolute are declared to be the two truths. However, the absolute is not within the reach of our intellectual capacity, because the intellect resides in the relative.[19] There is the basic discrepancy between the two dfferent entities, which refer to one single reality of the ultimate absolute reality as well as the phenomenal reality.[20]

---

15. Williams, *Mahayana Buddhism*, p. 203.
16. Brassard, *Concept of Bodhicitta*, p. 34.
17. Strong, *The Experience of Buddhism*, p. 160.
18. Ibid., p. 159.
19. Cited in The Dalai Lama, *Practicing Wisdom*, p. 17.
20. Ibid., p. 19.

Bodhicitta *in Comparative Reading*

Paul Williams was a former practising Buddhist, but now as Roman Catholic,[21] he argues that the 'Bodhicaryāvatāra is the Bodhisattva's path to Buddhahood.' It is linked to the Madhyamakāvatāra, while it is 'distinguished by a poetic sensitivity and fervour which makes it one of the gems of Buddhist and world spirituality literature.'[22] In Bodhicaryāvatāra (3:8-10), the aspiration of a Bodhisattva is portrayed as generating bodhicitta compassion:

> *May I be the doctor and the medicine*
> *And may I be the nurse*
> *For all sick beings in the world*
> *Until everyone is healed.*[23]

In this poetic expression *bodhicitta* embraces the nature of emptiness and compassion in terms of the ultimate type of *bodhicitta*. The ultimate *bodhicitta*, when truly generated, retains deep compassion for the suffering of all those in suffering. However, Śāntideva sidesteps the Buddhist coherent ethics of the Eightfold Path, under the influence of Madhymaka philosophy.[24]

On the contrary, Perry Schmidt-Leukel seeks to discern a certain form of knowledge of personal God in the Buddhist text. He argues: '*Everybody has a dim or implicit knowledge of Nirvāṇa by longing for happiness.*'[25] He introduces the *Bodhicaryāvatāra* (8:129): 'All those who are suffering in the world are so out of longing for their own happiness. All those who are happy in the world are so out of longing for the happiness of another.'[26] It is important to make the Mahayanist distinction between a dynamic nirvana (ethical practice of a *Bodhisattva*) and a static nirvana (emptiness).[27] The dynamic nirvana relates to

---

21. Williams, *The Unexpected Way*.
22. Williams, *Mahayana Buddhism*, p. 58.
23. Ibid., p. 203.
24. Williams, *Unexpected Way*, p. 203.
25. Schmidt-Leukel, 'Finding God in the *Bodhicaryāvatāra*,' *Journal of Comparative Scripture*, no. 6 (July, 2015), p. 23; emphasis in original.
26. Ibid.
27. Nagao, *Madhiyamika and Yogācāra*, pp. 23-34; Makransky, *Buddhahood Embodied*, pp. 85-7.

Śāntideva's nirvana-emptiness (3:11): '*Nirvāṇa* is the leaving behind of everything. ... If I have to give up everything, it is better to give it to all beings.'[28] The *Bodhicaryāvatāra* teaches the way of generating and cultivating *bodhicitta* and wisdom (*prajñā*), thus, it is the perfect realization of emptiness – the perfection of *bodhicitta*. The relationship between *bodhicitta* and wisdom in the *Bodhicaryāvatāra* is combined, so altruism and wisdom characterize the true spirit of *bodhicitta*.

Ultimate *bodhicitta*, equal to the *dharmakāya*, transcends this world and cannot be expressed in terms of concepts or language. This reality 'devoid of any self-sufficient, independent nature,' or intrinsic reality, has nothing to do with 'some ontological category' or inconceivable entity, which is 'separate from the things and events.'[29] Against this argument, however, it can be maintained that the ultimate *bodhicitta* is seen as the mind stream of a *Bodhisattva* or Buddha, as endowed with great compassion and directly cognizes emptiness.[30] For Śāntideva, 'The absolute truth is not within the reach of intellect, / For intellect is grounded in the relative.'[31] In sum, the two truths are imbued with the twofold nature of one single reality, such that there is a basic discrepancy between the conceptual perception of reality and reality as it is. But in understanding the world of conventional truth, it is possible to examine the ultimate truth, while and fully recognizing the discrepancy existing between our conceptual perception and reality.[32]

For Schmidt-Leukel, '*Concepts are adequate if they serve as suitable means for developing bodhicitta.*'[33] Great compassion can be identified with the selfless love and true happiness. So, God can be known in genuine love and in spiritual longing for happiness. The terms 'God' and '*Nirvāṇa*' are 'expressive of different, yet equally authentic patterns or ways of experiencing the same reality.'[34]

It is important to underatsnd that Śāntideva's critique of God (*īśvara*) does not necessarily mean a harsh rejection of any kind of theism. Seen in light of dependent origination, God as the creator must be logically dependent upon the creation of the world.[35] In this comparative reading,

---

28. Schmidt-Leukel, 'Finding God,' p. 24.
29. The Dalai Lama, *Practicing Wisdom*, pp. 90–1.
30. Williams, *Mahayana Buddhism*, p. 203.
31. The Dalai Lama, *Practicing Wisdom*, p. 17.
32. Ibid., p. 19.
33. Schmidt-Leukel, 'Finding God,' p. 27; emphasis in original.
34. Ibid., p. 28.
35. Ibid., p. 30.

a Christian bias of God is inscribed into Buddhist terrain, but it undermines the Buddhist struggle against the Vedanta's attachment to the Brahman comprehended in the dialectical relation between the qualities and non-qualities. This comparative theology is questionable, because the Buddhist notion of dependent origination should be first explored in the Buddhist struggle with Vedanta theology, and its notion of reincarnation and karma underwriting the social system of the caste. Then it is necessary to explore the history of interpretation of such religious discourse in competition, conflict, and even rupture. Going through the historical study of religious discourse, its formation and practice, a comparative theologian may arrive at a semantic retrieval of the religious idea, such as dependent origination, in a creative and fresh manner in problematizing what is taken for granted in the epistemic tradition through responsible critique and emancipation. A semantic circle is necessary in unveiling the layered meaning of the religious discourse.

Critical Exegesis

A Christian commentarial analysis goes that far by enquiring whether the whole idea of God is inconceivable, because Śāntideva called God inconceivable. Even in Mādhyamikas, the Buddha is designated as 'the Inconceivable' in the third Hymn to the Inconceivable among the famous Four Hymns, as ascribed to Nāgārjuna.

Nāgārjuna conceptualizes two aspects of a single reality of emptiness, but does not credit metaphysical, ontological inconceivability to the Buddha. By way of the conventional truth, it is possible to grasp the ultimate truth of emptiness as grounded in dependent origination.

We read in the opening statement of *Fundamentals of the Middle Way* (1:1-2):

> *He who taught dependent origination—*
> *... To you, who is supreme speaker*
> *among all fully enlightened buddhas, I pay homage.*[36]

Indeed, Nāgārjuna pays homage to this Buddha and teaches a doctrine of dependently origination as free from intrinsic existence, but he rejects the theory of inherent self-existence in which the world should be unchanging and timeless, which is central in Vedanta theology. This

---

36. Nagarjuna's *Fundamentals of the Middle Way*, cited in Tenzin Gyatso, *Essence of the Heart Sutra*, p. 122.

position problematizies a Christian commentarial work and notices incommensurability, or the unbridgeable gulf between Buddhist dependent origination and Christian theism for God the Inconceivable. A Christian inverted scheme of interpretation adulterates its theism into Buddhist non-theistic terrain. However, Schmidt-Leukel argues that Buddhist acceptance of the Christian God would be seen as 'a further suitable means of developing *bodhicitta*.'[37]

His reading of the Middle Way school might be relevant in an interpretive key concept from the Mind-only school, in which dynamic nirvana, or the conventional truth, is defined as the manifestation of the inconceivable or emptiness. If the conventional truth can be seen as the manifestation of the unmanifest, the moral practice of *bodhicitta* is more valued for the soteriological path than for sacramental worship; from Śāntideva we read, 'Merely desiring the benefit [of all beings] is more meritorious than worshipping the Buddhas; still more so is striving for the perfect happiness of all beings (1:27).'[38] However, it is difficult to bring a Christian radical concept of God into the Buddhist way of *bodhicitta* and wisdom of emptiness. He interprets the relationship between conventional truth and ultimate truth as basically one of possible means to an ultimate end, in which 'conventional truth can … be seen as the manifestation of the unmanifest.'[39]

A question could occur whether Śāntideva might buttress the wisdom of emptiness in terms of the absolute or independent nature of God over creation. In other words, God is dependent upon the world, as conversely the world is dependent upon God – perhaps a theocentric imagination would be undertaken in encounter with Buddhist insight. God the Mystery is not discarded in St. Paul (Romans 11:33-34). God may be all in all (1 Corinthian 15:28)

3. Problematization of Absolute Nothingness

The *Bodhisattva* practice of compassion becomes crucial in a Mahayana Buddhist's quest. It is also imbued with the meaning of the *Heart Sutra* (*The Heart of the Prajñāpāramitā Sutra*).[40] Historically, the *Heart of Wisdom* is part of the *Perfection of Wisdom Sutras* assumed

---

37. Schmidt-Leukel, 'Finding God,' p. 32.
38. Ibid., p. 33.
39. Ibid., pp. 26, n., 28.
40. Simmer-Brown, 'Preface,' in Conze, trans., *Buddhist Wisdom*, p. xxiii.

to be composed approximately in the period between 100 BCE and 600 CE. The *Heart Sutra* in the Chinese version begins the teaching on emptiness, while in the Tibetan version the Buddha first gave this teaching on emptiness.[41]

A profound unity between compassion and wisdom is the central theme of the *Perfection of Wisdom Sutras* in which empty refers to 'empty' of any inherent self-existence, or something like an essence self-identity as permanent and inalienable. As we read in the text of the *Heart Sutra*, 'even the five aggregates are empty of intrinsic existence. Form is emptiness, emptiness is form; emptiness is not other than form, form too is not other than emptiness.'[42]

Nāgārjuna's social perspective is grounded in the wisdom of emptiness, while sharpening the *Bodhisattva* practice of compassion through social justice. As he argues, 'Just as unworthy sons are punished out of a wish to make them worthy, so punishment should be enforced with compassion and not from hatred or concern with wealth. Once you have examined the fierce murderers and judged them correctly, you should banish them without killing or torturing them.'[43]

In his *Counsels*, we further read: 'Cause the blind, the sick, the humble, the unprotected, the destitute, and the crippled, all equally to attain food and drink without omission.'[44] In a recent Buddhist breakthrough to social justice, Thich Nhat Hanh conceptualizes his socially engaged Buddhism in the principle of dependent origination as expounded in the *Heart Sutra*.[45]

This vantage point runs counter to Japanese Imperial Buddhism, which butressed emptiness as the principle to justify a militaristic practice of Zen; it can be seen in the genocide of innocent victims. D.T. Suzuki (1870–1966) attempted to analyze the process of enlightenment in a practical way, considerably affecting Buddhist ideas and material interests in historical development as well as in the social, political network of power relations.[46] In Suzuki's *Zen and Japanese Culture*, we read his militaristic interpretation of emptiness:

---

41. Gyatso, *Essence of the Heart Sutra*, p. 65.
42. Ibid., p. 60.
43. Thurman, 'Guidelines for Buddhist Social Activism Based on Nagarjuna's Jewel Garland of Counsels,' cited in Ken Jones, *The New Social Face of Buddhism*, p. 47
44. Cited in Jones, *New Social Face of Buddhism*, p. 48.
45. Thich Nhat Hanh, *The Heart of Understanding*.
46. Suzuki, *Essays in Zen Buddhism*, p. 168.

> The art of swordsmanship distinguishes between the sword that kills and the sword that gives life. ... He had no desire to harm anybody, but the enemy appears and makes himself a victim. ... The swordsman turns into an artist of the first grade, engaged in producing a work of genuine originality.[47]

A Second Lieutenant Tanaka in the Imperial Japanese army was inspired by this miliaristic teaching during the sack of Nanjing, the Chinese holocaust (December 1937–January 1938), which saw mass killing of capitiulaed soldiers, ravaging of Chinese citizens and rapes of women. This has been covered in more detail elsewhere,[48] but in short, a particular interpretation of the Buddhist doctrine of the 'Buddha-heart', based in turn on the Mādhyamika-school theory of Śūnyatā, creates a metaphysics of nothingness without ethics.[49] This can be found to be at fault for the ruthless violence committed by Japanese imperial soldiers.

In the militaristic context of killing, 'killing' of the others is undergirded by the stage of 'no mind,' which is central in the Buddhist metaphysics of emptiness as absolute nothingness. It is used as the pretext to relativize or even nullify the responsibility of the perpetrator. The political technology of the body and murder is sanctioned through religious discourse. The emptiness and *bodhicitta* in the Nāgārjuna-Śāntideva tradition contradicts the modern Japanese version of emptiness as absolute nothingness.

Critique and Textual Com-reading

Masao Abe, one of the important Japanese Buddhist philosophers in the Kyoto school, affirms nirvana or Enlightenment as the Subjective realization, in which 'everything and everyone are respectively realized as they are.' 'Nirvana is nothing but a person's realization of the existential true Self as the ultimate ground.'[50] Everything in samsara (a suffering reality of world) and everyone is fulfilled.

Abe affirms the Buddhist cardinal principle of dependent origination, in which true nirvana (Sunyata) as absolute nothingness, is the real source of both non-attached wisdom and great compassion. However, Abe seems self-contradictory, when he argues that Sunyata is absolute nothingness,

---

47. Cited in Jones, *New Social Face of Buddhism*, p. 116.
48. See Chung, *Comparative Theology among Multiple Modernities*, pp. 244f.
49. Ives, ed., *Divine Emptiness and Historical Fullness*, pp. 51–2.
50. Abe, *Zen and Western Thought*, p. 176.

the total dynamic movement of emptying. That is without attachment to the self and others. In fact, he undermines the significance of the great Compassion in its social critical dimension, while overemphasizing the non-discriminating mind beyond good and evil in the Nietzschean sense of nihilism. In Abe's interpretation of the famous passage in the *Heart Sutra*, 'Form is emptiness and the very emptiness is form,'[51] the very emptiness as form is versed as the absolute nothingness.

At this point, his interpretation is problematic, because the very emptiness as form refers to the great Compassion, especially for those sick, the impoverished, and the disadvantaged. This frame of interpretation is in league with the most distinguished Mahayana philosopher, Nagarjuna (c.150–c.250 CE). In his ideal of the compassionate welfare state, Nagarjuna inspires a Buddhist type of socialism in the tradition of the Middle Way School. His religious discourse remains a chief source for engaged Buddhism today. In Nagarjuna's advice to King Udayi, we read: 'Always care compassionately for the sick, the unprotected, those stricken; with suffering, the lowly and the poor.'[52] The great Compassion in the tradition of Nagarjuna (c.150–c. 250 CE), the Middle Way School remains a source of immanent critique pertaining to the Japanese Zen Buddhist distortion of the Sunyata to champion military genocide during the Japanese colonial time (Nanjing massacre, December 1937).

In fact, Abe comprehends true nirvana as a way of accepting everything without discrimination, even social and historical evils. But he does not formulate an ethical dimension of great Compassion with social critical significance for those stricken and on the margins. Furthermore, in the Buddhist-Christian-Jewish context, Abe attempts to comprehend the Holocaust in terms of a doctrine of karma. It implies volition or action through body, speech and mind in an individual and collective sense. This is united in the unfathomable depth of ignorance (avida). However, Abe's statement becomes questionable: 'Without the religious dimension as the ground, the sociohistorical dimension is groundless and rootless.'[53] In league with D.T. Suzuki, Abe argues that the history of humankind 'is nothing but a grand drama visualizing the Buddhist doctrine of karmic immortality.'[54] The chain of karmic causation, like an immense ocean, is applied to accounting for the problem of evil in Buddhism.

---

51. Ives, ed. *Divine Emptiness and Historical Fullness*, p. 51.
52. Harvey, *An Introduction to Buddhist Ethics*, p. 199.
53. Ibid., p. 179.
54. Ibid., p. 64.

Can the reality of the Holocaust be explained merely by the Buddhist doctrine of the collective karma innate in human existence? If the universal or collective karma innate in human existence is the basis in which the Holocaust is ultimately rooted, where is the place of the religious dimension of anti-Semitism and the sole responsibility of the perpetrator in Abe's version of the collective karma?

Abe is associated specifically with the radical Zen tradition in China; but the Buddhist teaching of karma in the historical and textual context puts emphasis on ethically right action in reference to the Brahmanical teaching in the *Upanishads*. In the *Svetasvatara Upanishad* (400–200 BCE) we read that the performer of action bears fruit and he/she wanders in the circle of transmigration according to his/her karma. Karmas are likened to seeds, whose results are known as fruits. Karmic fruitfulness is implicated as generous donation, which is central in the Mahayana doctrine of six paramitas (perfections).

In contrast to a degenerate form of fatalism (*niyati*), the historical Buddha emphasizes the importance of human action and its effects in terms of the idea of karma. This teaching is based on the freedom of choice, reacting against the karmic results of previous action in the Brahmanic teaching. For the Buddha, not everything that happens to a person is rooted in karma. 'Thus the Buddha criticized theories which saw all experiences and associated actions as due either to past karma, the diktat of a God, or pure chance.'[55] This textual position breaks through Abe's Zen interpretation of the karma only through absolute nothingness. The exegetical-hermeneutical stance is of special significance in interreligious exchange. In fact, Buddhist life-world embraces the emptiness experience as great compassion for those suffering in the world (dukka), while promoting social justice in compassionate solidarity with those wretched and victimized.

In the process of 'reading together,' it is significant to construct an interreligious epistemology. There is valid suspicion regarding what is taken for granted in the religious world through problematization. A critical reflection of meaning in religious texts is explicated in an endeavour to highlight the source of the immanent critique. Religious discourse is analyzed in examining the extent to which it would be bound to material interests and power relations. This comparative practice of com-reading marks a new regime of social scientific approach to religion and culture.

---

55. Ibid., p. 24.

Bio-political Strategy and Semantic Enquiry

What is crucial in comparative theology and sociological enquiry is to analyze the extent to which religious ideas would be used and deployed via material interests and political motivation under bio-political directives in the colonial time. The body is directly involved in a political field in the colonial context, in which religious ideas sanction the government's bio-political strategy in mobilizing and enlisting the human body to colonial militarism. The sovereign's power is literally and publicly inscribed on the people's body in a manner controlled, governed and well-administered for its governmentality. Bio-political governmentality in the Japanese colonial time can be further seen in its subjugation of the body of the colonized self with respect to military mobilization, and comfort women for sexual needs of the imperial troops. In the political investment of the colonized body, religious discourse is involved in diffusing it, gaining the support of the apparatuses and institution in the colonial context. In the technology of colonial power over the subjugated body, the latter's soul is born out of methods of punishment, supervision and subjection. 'The soul is the effect and instrument of a political anatomy; the soul is the prison of the body.'[56]

A bio-political enquiry sees that the issue of the military comfort station was primarily institutionalized in a bio-political arrangement through Japanese military involvement and its personnel. The coercion is inherent in the system of the comfort station, assuming many diverse forms in the context of gender, ethnic inequality and colonial rule.[57] Such a perspective reinforces an anthropological study, facilitating a cultural analysis of the bodies of comfort women in terms of 'a gendered structural violence.' It focuses on explicating the correlation between Japanese colonial economy, its sexual culture, and the Korean culture of patriarchy.[58]

As well as the cultural side of hierarchy, the textual reading is important as well. Japanese reading is grounded in a radical tradition of Zen by tainting it with the Buddhist doctrine of karmic immortality. This seems to be closer to the Brahmanic position of karmic causation in the justification of the caste system. Without analyzing the social condition of textual reading, a commentarial comparative theology would

---

56. Foucault, *Discipline and Punish*, p. 30.
57. Yoshiaki, *Comfort Woman*, p. 8.
58. Soh, *The Comfort Woman*, p. xii.

be vulnerable to symbolic power and violence perpetrated in religious discourse and its accommodation to the status quo. It loses a critical side of dependent origination, mediation and moral integrity only for an absolute nothingness adulterated by political motivation and its colonialist position.

Against this commentarial representation, it is important to articulate an effective strategy of social scientific experiment by examining the art of comparison as a creative procedure. Textual juxtaposition may produce new meaning with the arbitrary choice of texts on the part of comparative agent.[59] In the juxtaposition for a comparative reading, one articulates the coordination as rules for using texts together in one's own religious commentarial tradition (as applied to the other religious texts). Superimposition (*adhyasa*) of one text on another for enhancing meditation on the latter (applied to other religious texts); the comparative conversation in an analogical procedure; in this intentional, creative act of juxtaposition the transmutive process (through eiphor or diaphor) is described as semantic motion (phora) implicit in the term 'metaphor,' or the metaphoric process. The eiphor implies a strategy in outreaching and extending meaning through comparison, while diaphor seeks to create new meaning in terms of juxtaposition and synthesis.[60]

Finally, the semantic notion appeals to the practice of collage in selection and combination to engender new meaning through deconstruction and the subsequent constructive reading. The use of collage runs counter to the notion of intentionality, and it favours a writing which is productive outside of the ideology of communication. Such skill of collage is concerned with different readings of the texts by unsettling the two different traditions of religions through decontextualization and reconceptualization.[61]

Given this, Clooney's comparative theology is of a constructive character in its minimalist approach by way of juxtaposition, collage and synthesis, but in his semantic motion, the comparativist's *noesis* (the subjective activity producing meaning) undermines a critical enquiry of the religious discourse in social location in reference to political systems and institutional ratifications. The skill of collage exists in exteriority, that is, outside of the ideology of communication; religious discourse juxtaposed in comparison becomes a general referent of intelligibility, but such a collage is exposed to be blind to the social condition of

---

59. Clooney, *Theology after Vedanta*, p. 154.
60. Ibid., p. 172.
61. Ibid., p. 174.

misusing and distorting religious discourse (emptiness, karma, and Enlightenment) for the sake of material interests and symbolic violence.

To what extent would a theory of juxtaposition deal with the Buddhist tradition of interpretation in competition, conflict and rupture concerning the cardinal principle of emptiness or dependent origination? In the superimposition of the one text upon another, a Buddhist principle of emptiness correlates with ethical compassion, but the other tradition transcends it for absolute nothingness. A skill of superimposition is no longer tenable in the epistemological rupture within the Buddhist tradition.

If the traditional interpretations are put into brackets, how would the procedure of collage become effective and productive concerning the religious discourse of emptiness through decontextualization and recontextualization? Is it feasible for comparative theology to exist in exteriority outside of the ideology of communication? When written discourse is adulterated by a political system of domination, should textual reading, its anamnestic rationality, and speech activity in solidarity with the innocent victims be required in deconstruction of the disgrace effect? Certainly, a synthesis of meaning requires a creative act of juxtaposition, but it should be undertaken by problematizing the elective affinity between religious discourse and material interests embedded within power structure and social location.

A critical comparative theology embraces the social scientific approach in scrutinizing the social material function of religious discourse for responsible critique and emancipation; such a project is grounded in anamnestic reasoning of those victims; it seeks to unveil the extent to which the fabrication of religious discourse would emerge from power, desire and political governmentality in domesticating and controlling the dominated through its instinctive violence and domination. It requires the perpetual critique of the existing structure of the grand unifying form of religious discourse and power structue, which seeks to legitimize social stratification and sanction its gendered inscribed inequality and injustice.

Buddhist Axiality and Critique

The Buddha's own teaching can serve as the immanent critique, as it deals with colonialist militarization of the Buddhist teaching of karma and emptiness. The Buddha shakes the Brahmanic tradition to the core, disregarding the distinction of birth and the caste order, and he completed the axial transition in terms of ethicizing the world. He rejected the Upanishadic equation of atman with Brahman, arguing that these entities have no essential reality. A conception of the emptiness, which is grounded in *anatta* (non-self) is to be understood in Buddhist critique of the essential reality seen in the Upanishadic equation between atman and Brahman underlying the social reality of the caste. This refers to the new Buddhist model of reality as the critique of, as well as alternative to, the prevailing model of the Brahmanic religion.

What the Buddha shared with Brahmanism, however, can be seen in the threefold belief system: samsara (the round of rebirth), karma (retribution of action), moksa (liberation). In the Four Noble Truths there is an emphasis on the noble Eightfold Path with ethical significance toward nirvana. The Buddha rejected the hereditary status of the Brahmin and the caste system, and he articulated the significance of an ethical way of life and universalized ahimsa, which can be still found in Vedic texts. This ethical orientation contradicts the Japanese interpretation of emptiness and killing, which would be more relevant in the story of killing as the karma duty in the *Bhagavad Gita*.

Robert Bellah characterizes Buddhism as an axial religion because it entails the aspect of the theory as well as the logical aspect intertwined with symbols and narratives. What is remarkable in Buddhism as an axial religion is seen in its systematic thought-accompanying narrative and symbolic thought. The combination between theoretic thinking and narrative thinking is important to the understanding of the Axial Age:

> Narrative, in short, is more than literature, it is the way we understand our lives. ... Great literature speaks to the deepest level of our humanity; it helps us better understand who we are. Narrative is not only the way we understand our personal and collective identities, it is the source of our ethics, our politics, and our religion. ... Mythic (narrative) culture ... is older than theoretic culture and remains to this day an indispensable way of relating to the world.[62]

The Buddhist breakthrough is expressed in the integration of theoretical reflexivity and narrativity in which it becomes an alternative to the prevailing model of the Brahmanic tradition. It entails a strong ethical component with non-violence and no-killing. In the Four Noble Truths there is the path from suffering (*dukkha*) to nirvana (enlightenment), which is formulated in systematic and narrative thought, emphasizing

---

62. Bellah, *Religion in Human Evolution*, p. 280.

the equality of all human beings in their capacity to follow the path to liberation.[63]

Buddhist axiality is characterized by critique, equality and ethical precepts, taking issue with injustice and violence embedded with the Hindu teaching of samsara and karma; emptiness is seen in terms of dependent origination and contradicts a nihilism underlying militarization of religious ideas. This axial enquiry does not concur with justifying the unjustifiable; in other words, past horrors must not be excused as a necessary precondition for a better future. It is unbearable to think of countless victims in history and society as stepping stones underlying and sanctioning the path of inevitable development. The axial enquiry can be further elaborated in terms of anamnestic reflection in reparation for the innocent victim from the results of what has been done in history and society.

Comparative Theology and Ethical Significance

In the project of critical comparative theology, it is also important to acknowledge that the Christian symbol of the cross has undergone similar ramifications. On the one hand, an ethical vision for solidarity with the poor is reinforced in connection with its ideal content of God's sacrificial love. On the other hand, it is also blasphemed, even accommodated to serve the power of the colonialist, turning into a crucifix of dominion, genocide and racism.

In the reading of Sermon on the Mount, the Dalai Lama finds an inspiration—'the sun makes no discrimination where it shines.' A Christian advocacy (Matthew 5:38-42)—'Love your enemies and pray for your persecutors'—values *bodhisattva* ideals as expounded in the *Compendium of Practices*—'If you do not practice compassion toward your enemy then toward whom can you practice it?'[64] A Buddhist reading of the Gospel must be appreciated and valued, while in the Christian reading of non-Christian sacred texts the subject matter of the gospel (living voice of God) comes to terms with compassion and enlightenment; each tradition in mutual learning and respect has little to do with becoming a form of hegemony in domestication of the Other.

---

63. Ibid., p. 542.
64. The Dalai Lama, *The Good Heart*, p. 49.

Chapter 3

Comparative Theology of Grace: Martin Luther and Shinran Shonin

I have explored the relation betweem Matin Luther's theology and Buddhism in more detail in my book *Martin Luther and Buddhism*.[1] But I seek to elaborate the more exercises and arguments in comparative theology that I propose to undertake in the following chapter.

In dealing with the history of effect in the different religious worlds brought by Luther and Shinran, a comparative study of grace is important, even imperative in the interreligious context. A sociological study of religion takes into account religious discourse in the historical background and social aspect of the religious construction of reality; such an experiment facilitates constructing comparative theology in terms of textual reading, religious ideas, and their impact on political motivation, social stratification and cultural value.

For this constructive orientation, the religious discourse of grace and compassion can be thematized in the textual world between Luther and Shinran. (1) The comparative experiment requires *historical* study in dealing with Shinran's teaching of salvation in comparison with his teacher, Honen (1133–1212). It seeks to comprehend Shinran's epistemological difference and uniqueness in its historical, social background, clarifying his own model in reference to the traditional Buddhist discourse. (2) The comparative enquiry requires a critical exegesis of Luther's teaching of justification, while examining medieval Catholic

---

1. Chung, *Martin Luther and Buddhism*, 381–398.

teaching. A tripartite model is to be patterned to characterize Luther's position.

(3) Based on this historical research, a comparative reading is performed concerning Luther and Shinran; focusing on Christ and the Buddhist notion of Amida; it is useful to take up together the Buddhist notion of faith (*shinjin*) and Luther's notion of faith (*fiducia*) in terms of *analogical* procedure. Based on *semantic retrieval of meaning*, it is necessary to analyze an idea of the recognition of the Other layered in Luther; a synthesis of new meaning for Buddhist theology is constructed for prayerful exchange. (4) A constructive interpretation is made in synthesizing justification with justice underlying the religious construction of reality. Weber's sociological reading of religious ideas (calling) and economic traditionalism in Luther is critiqued. Luther is considered as the source of the immanent critique over and against the Protestant grand narrative of capitalist modernity. Similarly, there is a critical reflection of Shin Buddhism and economic rationalization in Japan, which facilitates constructing social reality and rationality in the religious, cultural framework.

1. Japan and Pure Land Teaching

The Pure Land faith is based on the narrative of the bodhisattva named Dharmakara; he was regarded as a king who heard Buddha's teaching and awakened the aspiration for enlightenment. In fact, he gave up the throne and became a monk with the name Dharmakara. His basic vision was bound to the benefiting of others. He attained Buddhahood and is now dwelling in the Land of bliss west of this world.[2]

Pure Land teaching came to Japan, in the run up to the Kamakura age (1185–1333). Japan was conditioned and plagued by civil warfare, economic collapse and social cultural problems. This reality gave a strong impetus to the eschatological expection of the Last Days (*mappo*). As George Sansom writes, there was 'a striking account of material conditions in the capital in the years from 1177 to 1182. It is a dreadful tale of storms, earthquakes, conflagrations, plagues, starvation, and cold, when infants could be seen clinging to the breasts of their dead mothers and shivering men stole images of the Buddha for firewood and corpses remained unburied.'[3]

---

2. Ueda and Hirota, *Shinran*, p. 108.
3. Sansom, *History of Japan to 1334*, p. 286.

The specific concept of *mappo* evolved within the Japanese Pure Land and culminated in the thought of Shinran, but its general idea that we are living in a degenerate age has ancient roots in the Chinese Buddhist tradition where Pure Land Buddhism arose.[4] However, Shinran's uniqueness in the Buddhist tradition lies in his appealing to the universal grace of Amida and in challenging other Buddhist practices of self-awakening, while transcending its narrow-minded position. He was involved in the various strands of Pure Land teaching proposed by Genku Honen (1133–1212), his teacher, and finally Shinran expounded his teaching as the true teaching of the Pure Land (Jodo Shinshu).

To clearly articulate Shinran's own development, it is first necessary to briefly examine his teacher Honen's instruction. Honen took up the three disciplines of precepts, concentration and wisdom as the most important teachings. In his formative practice, the Chinese monk Shan-tao's (613–81) commentary on the *Meditation Sutra* became an inspiration for Honen to put an end to struggle in the year of 1175. According to Shan-tao it is of utmost importance to recite the practice of the name of Amida Buddha, which is in accordance with the Original Vow of that Buddha.[5]

Honen based himself on the exclusive practice of *nenbutsu* (meditating on and invoking the name of Buddha), which belittles other Buddhist teachings. The easy practice is grounded in an act of a deep faith in Amida's Vow. Honen made a strong impact on Shinran, who adopted Honen's position as the starting point and made his own breakthrough by differentiating himself from his teacher Honen.[6]

Shinran's Breakthrough and Development

Shinran received his training as a *doso* (a minor priest) at the headquarters of the Tendai Order. However, he was not capble of attaining enlightenment, despite the Tendai teaching and other practices of Zen meditation.[7] After spending twenty years of life as a Tendai monk, in the year of 1201 he decided to become a student at the feet of Honen. Shinran's study under Honen constituted the second phase of his formation and development. He committed humself to Honen's teaching, in contrast

---

4. For detailed analysis of *mappo* see Kirkland, 'The Chinese Background of the Concept of MAPPÔ.'
5. Coates and Ishizuka, *Honen*, p. 187.
6. Chung, *Comparative Theology Among Multiple Modernities*, pp. 44–45.
7. *The Essential Shinran,* comp. and ed. Bloom, pp. 2, 6.

to the traditional path of self-power. In the year of 1205 Shinran was arranged to marry under the permission of Honen.

In 1207, however, two women who had converted to the Honen teaching were charged in court with improper relationships with Honen's disciples. The court made the decision to abolish the community, forcing the leading members to be exiled, Shinran included. These members were sentenced to death or dispossessed of their priesthood.[8] In his exile in the Echigo region, Shinran lived together with common peasantry and and experienced their plight. These common people – socially marginalized, economically poor, and intellectually uneducated – were crucial for Shinran to radicalize the unconditional boundless compassion and grace of Amida.

His teacher Honen was eventually pardoned, but Shinran remained a defrocked priest (a married layman). Spending the years of exile (1207–12), the court lifted his banishment, and thereafter significant transformation occurred in Shinran's religious life in 1213. He stopped the practice of recitation through a radical understanding of Shan-tao's (613–81) teaching; he became convinced that no recitation is needed, but rather faith alone is the true way to receive the Buddha's compassion. Shinran, with his family, moved to the village of Inada in Kashima. Here, from 1212 to 1235, his teaching became popular among the peasants and townspeople.[9]

For Shinran, 'With our evil natures hard to subdue, our minds are like asps and scorpions. As the practice of virtue is mixed poison, we call it false, vain practice.'[10] An epistemological rupture occurred in Shinran's thought which was embedded with the lift of his exile and the plight of the peasant. A religious idea is bound up in social life, breaking through the prevailing religious episteme; as its religious discourse grasps the heart of mass religiosity, its practice is disseminated and constructs the social reality in a religiously affected manner.

Shinran's New Understanding of Amida

Unlike Honen, however, Shinran in his later stage abandoned *nenbutsu* itself as a means to attain enlightenment. Based on the grace of Amida, Shinran was assured of the final enlightenment grounded in faith/trust (*shinjin*) in the Amida's vow. The religious life begins as trust in the

---

8. Keel, *Understanding Shinran*, p. 41.
9. Ibid., p. 3.
10. Bloom, *Shinran Gospel of Pure Grace*, pp. 28–9.

mercy of the Amida outside of us, and it is expressed in gratitude for his compassion.

Shinran introduced two types of deep faith. One type implies that a person is aware of spiritual ailment and incapacity (the subjective side of faith). Another is grounded in faith/trust in Amida's unconditional compassion and wisdom (the objective side of the faith). Sincerity, faith and aspiration are all in unity, which orginates from Amida Buddha's universal grace.

At the moment, Shinran's teaching is found in the *Tannisho*, which was recorded by Yui-en, one of Shinran's disciples. :

> Amida's Primal Vow … is directed to the being burdened with the weight of karmic evil and burning with the flames of blind passion. … And evil need not be feared, for there is no evil which can obstruct the working of Amida's Primal Vow.[11]

The *nenbutsu* is rooted in the Vow, and in recounting his experience of faith, he exclaimed: 'How Joyous I am, my heart and mind being rooted in the Buddha-ground of the Universal Vow, and my thoughts and feelings flowing within the dharma-ocean, which is beyond comprehension.'[12]

The grace of Amida is universally applied to everyone, whether their moral life is bad or virtuous.

Historical Encounter: Christianity and Pure Land Teaching

Valignano, one of the Jesuits in Japan, noticed that the Lutheran understanding of salvation remains an undercurrent in Amida's grace.[13] Even earlier on, there was a historical encounter between Pure Land Buddhism in China and the East Syrian church in the seventh century.[14] The Pure Land teaching arose in The Three Stage teaching of Hsin-hsing (540–94) in China who denounced traditional Buddhism as corrupt. This sect promoted the teaching of the *Nirvana Sutra*, insisting that all people possess Buddha nature and all are capable of attaining Buddhahood in an equal manner. It also emphasized selfless giving (*dana*) for the poor

---

11. *Tannisho: A Shin Buddhist Classic*, p. 5.
12. Ibid., p. 3.
13. Schütte, *Valignanos Missionsgrundsätze für Japan* 1, p. 387.
14. The inscription text dates to 781 CE, witnessing to the Church of the East in China. Yoshiro Saeki, *The Nestorian Monument in China*, p. 75.

Comparative Theology of Grace

and sick. The entire set of good deeds in selfless giving or donation offers the cause for rebirth in the Pure Land.[15]

The Pure Land teaching was furthered and embedded within the tradition of Shan-tao (613–81) in China, who was revered as an incarnation of Amida in the Japanese Pure Land sect. Shan-tao lived at the period when Christian religion flourished in China. During the time of the Emperor Gaozong (650–83), who was his patron, Shan-tao was on sympathetic terms with the Assyrian Christians in China, teaching salvation by faith in Amida and the doctrine of the Trinity. In the teaching of Shan-tao, everyone fails to attain Buddhahood in the age of spiritual decay and is incapable of spiritual growth. Those of weaker faith are encouraged to practise sincere invocation of Amida's name, but the more fervent practitioners are to perform better in combination between ethical conduct and meditation.[16] However, it can be argued that Shan-tao's teaching is not presented strictly in opposition to the self-disciplined path, leaving this contradiction open.[17]

Shinran and Faith in Amida

Shan-tao's teaching is characterized by faith in terms of sincerity, trustfulness, and a desire for rebirth in the Pure Land. This finds inspiration in Honen, but in Shinran's breakthrough, such teaching is radicalized to the point of faith and rebirth as gifts of salvation that come from the grace of Amida working within us.[18] The Other Power of Amida implies the basic Buddhist teaching of no-self. Faith is identified with the action of Amida, shining from within. Our Buddha-nature is shining forth from the grace of Amida. Faith as shining forth of the Buddha nature is rooted in the Amida as such.[19]

Buddha nature as no-self is integrated into the Other Power of Amida, who works outside us through his primal promise or vow, for us in a personal sense, and finally active and present in us.

This integrative model refers to the epistemological rupture from the prevailing mode in which the genuine path to Enlightenment belongs to spiritual practices and meditations in monastery life. Against this, Shinran insisted that even meditation and morality of the eightfold path

---

15. Tanaka, *The Dawn of Chinese Pure Land Buddhist Doctrine*, p. 176.
16. Pas, *Visions of Sukhavati*, p. 275.
17. Repp, *Honens religiöses Denken*, p. 134.
18. William, *Mahayana Buddhism*, p. 272.
19. Ibid.

should be regarded as *upaya* (skillful means), because all human efforts and self-awakening practices fail to fulfill the perfection in reaching Buddhahood.

Thus, Shinran argues that the salvation of sinful human beings becomes possible by Amida alone. Nothing is necessary on the part of the human being to contribute to the free grace.

2. Understanding Luther in a Historical Context

In the previous discussion of Shinran, there were some significant elements in affinity with Luther. There is a similar spiritual struggle in Luther's life in reference to Shinran's breakthrough to the grace of Amida. Luther's major concern is 'how can I find a gracious God?' The idea of the righteousness of God is a punishing righteousness, as taught in medieval scholastic theology. Luther's breakthrough towards the Reformation is made in his suspicion of the scholastic teaching during the medieval period. The righteousness of God refers to a passive righteousness, in which the merciful God justifies us by faith.[20] His breakthrough, later called the 'tower experience,' led him to the Reformation. Romans 1:17 became the open gate to paradise for Luther.[21] Indeed, the concept of God All Terrible is revealed as God All Merciful in Jesus Christ.

Historical Background: Medieval Teaching of Justification

Luther's discovery of the gospel mainly contradicts Thomas Aquinas (1225–74): according to him four requirements are necessary for justification. 'The infusion of grace; a movement of free choice directed towards God by faith; a movement of free choice directed towards sin; and the forgiveness of sin.'[22] In this scheme of interpretation, the infusion of grace is the source for the justification of the unrighteous. God's forgiveness of sin through Jesus Christ implies that we should change direction by faith toward God eternal and immutable.

At the first stage, God's grace from without is infused into the human soul, creating the spiritual quality and disposition (habitus) within it, and thus the human soul possesses this spiritual quality and capacity to realize itself through human effort; then to render him/her acceptable

---

20. *Luther's Works*, ed. Jaroslav Pelikan (hereafter LW). 34, pp. 336–8.
21. Oberman, *Luther*, p. 154.
22. Aquinas, *Summa Theologica* (hereafter ST). I:2 Q 113.6.

to God, the created grace is cooperative with human will, functioning as the principle and basis of meritorious action. For Aquinas, 'habit is a disposition of a subject which is in a state of potentiality either to form or to operation.'[23]

The successive cooperation between God's grace and human will, once infused, plays a substantial role in making human deeds acceptable to God's reward. Justification makes a difference and change in human nature in which one is involved, moving away from sin in terms of the continuation and ultimate perfection.

As Thomas writes: 'If we speak of grace in the sense of the assistance of God moving us towards the good … whatever preparation there might be in us derives from the assistance of God moving the soul towards the good. In this sense … The principal agent is God moving the free choice; and in this sense it is said that *our will is prepared by God*, and *our steps are directed by the Lord*.'[24] In this line Thomas concurs with Augustine's statement: 'God by co-operating with us, perfects what he began by operating in us, since he who perfects by co-operation with such as are willing, begins by operating that they may will.'[25]

In effect, for Thomas, justification is being made righteous from without. However, habitual grace infused within the human soul creates human spiritual disposition, driving human cooperation with God in the event and process of justification. As Thomas writes, 'Habitual grace, inasmuch as it heals and justifies the soul, or makes it pleasing to God, is called operating grace; but inasmuch as it is the principle of meritorious works, which spring from the free will, it is called co-operating grace.'[26] The habitual (or sanctifying: *gratia gratum faciens*) grace takes the form of habit of the soul as infused toward taking part in divine nature. The habitual grace operative is the formal principle of justification, while it cooperates in actualizing human goodwill in good deeds; it is the formal principle of merit requiring human cooperation.

Furthermore, Thomas distinguishes human meritorious work in two ways: first, congruous merit proceeding from free will; secondly, condign merit from the grace of the Holy Spirit.[27] In *De Veritate* or the *Summa Theologiae*, Thomas does not stress the importance of merits prior to justification. But in the *Commentary on the Sentences*, he argues

---

23. ST I:2 Q 50.1.
24. ST Ia2ae. II2. 2.
25. ST Ia2ae.III.2.
26. ST I:2 Q 114.3.
27. McGrath, *Iustitia Dei*, pp. 85–6.

that that an individual can prepare him/herself for justification based on natural abilities, apart from divine grace.

The main problem of Thomas' teaching of justification can be seen in his overemphasis on the created grace as something like a supernatural fluid or fuel and its effects on the human soul, the intellect and the will. His notion of created grace (*gratia creata*) is very impersonal, making over-complex distinctions, such that Luther sharply rejects Thomist-Aristotle philosophy as obsolete.[28]

In medieval times, the concepts of merit and congruity were in debate. Once a moral act is performed outside a state of grace, it is conceived as congruous or appropriate to accept the infusion of justifying grace. But, once a moral act is performed within a state of grace, it is worthy of divine acceptance in the sense of the confign merit; thus God is under obligation to reward individual merit. It is the real merit. God will not deny grace to one who does one's best (*facienti quod in se est*). God rewards those who do *quod in se est*, while punishing those who do not.[29]

Luther's Breakthrough: Forensic and Effective Justification

During Luther's study at the University of Erfurt, Ockham and Gabriel Biel were central fugures in Luther's preparation for ordination. In a significant step towards the Reformation, Luther directed his argument against the scholastic concept of original sin (the lack of original righteousness), which is yet endowed with natural ability and reason against concupiscence. It is different from Augustine's notion of sin as the absence of good (privatio boni) in the natural ability, which is to be removed and cured by God's grace.

For Luther, we are justified before God only *extra nos* (outside of us) through the alien righteousness of Christ; it is imputed (not infused in a habitual sense) by grace through faith alone. Thus we are *simul justus et peccator* (at the same time, righteous and sinner).

Taking into account Augustine's notion of *incurvatus in se* (being turned toward the self), Luther moved closer to the tradition of Augustine, who established that Adam's sin is inherited or transmitted at sexual reproduction by concupiscence or inherited guilt. Nevertheless, Augustine is considerably different from Luther. Augustine does not deny one's free will, while defending the need for grace. This contrasts with Luther's position of will in bondage to sin in his treatise on the

---

28. Küng, *Christianity*, p. 425.
29. For more details see Chung, *Martin Luther and Buddhism*, pp. 99–109.

Bondage of the Will (1525). For Augustine the sinner has free will, though it is taken captive. As he writes, 'The free will taken captive ... does not avail, except for sin; for righteousness it does not avail, unless it is set free and aided by divine action.'[30]

Furthermore, Augustine makes a distinction between operative grace in the act of justification and its cooperative mode in the process of justification; God operates to initiate the justification of the human being, who is given free will capable of doing good. Subsequently, God cooperates with one good will to perform good works, by bringing justification to perfection. Merit before justification is denied, but after justification it is affirmed as a gift from God to the justified.[31] Luther, on the other hand, affirms that Christ's alien righteousness runs counter to the human precondition or disposition for justification or human righteousness, which stands in cooperation with God's grace. To overcome a reality of human selfish perversion and inward distortion, Luther considers his theology of the cross; this is because 'the visible and manifest things of God can be comprehended and seen through suffering and the cross.'[32]

The alien righteousness of Christ becomes the basis and the source of all our own justification and actual righteousness; faith is formed by Christ (*fides Christo formata*) rather than charity or love (*fides charitate formata*). The believer, instilled with grace alone, continues to grow in the spiritual life by continually returning to Christ, ever to be justified anew.[33] Like Augustine, Luther was not concerned with distinguishing justification (as event) from sanctification (as progress), but integrated justification in a forensic sense (the alien righteousness of Christ) with an effective sense (the real presence of Christ in the believer).

In fact, Luther embraces the double aspect in the event and process of justification, which can be clearly seen in union with Christ (happy exchange). It expresses a dynamic relation of faith to love, namely faith active in love (Galatians 5:6). For Christian life, Luther insists that 'having been justified by grace, we then do good works, yes, Christ himself does all in us.'[34] Faith as the gift of the Holy Spirit refers to the reality of Christ present in faith, shaping and guiding faith. In *The*

---

30. Cited in McGrath, *Iustitia Dei*, p. 26.
31. Ibid., p. 28.
32. 'Heidelberg Disputation (1518),' Article 20.
33. 'Two Kinds of Righteousness (1519),' in *Martin Luther's Basic Theological Writings*, p. 136.
34. LW 34, p. 111. *Union with Christ*.

Freedom of a Christian (1520), Luther formulates Christian freedom: 'A Christian is a perfectly free lord of all, subject to none.' Then, this freedom and emancipation through the grace of Christ leads us to the following stance: 'A Christian is a perfectly dutiful servant of all, subject to all.'[35] Finally, in commenting on Ephesians (5:31-2), Luther takes the benefit of faith to mean uniting the soul with Christ as a bride is united with her bridegroom.[36] Through the exchange of human sin with the grace of Christ, the living Christ speaks, lives and works within us.

Luther's tripartite model can be illustrated by synthesizing the forensic moment of imputation (*outside us*) with the personal side of the grace *for us* in connection with presence of Christ *in us* (the happy exchange). Luther can then be distinguished from the traditional model of justification in Medieval Catholic teaching as well as the forensic model of imputation (Melanchthon). It is necessary to construct Luther's own thought prior to textual juxtaposition with Shinran. In doing so, Luther is shown to have some points of consonance with Shinran.

3. Comparative Theology and Textual Enquiry

In the project of comparative theology, Clooney holds, the Advaita Text or the *Summa Theologiae* is constituted in the entirety of commentarial tradition; the reader is featured as an active participant in realizing the significance of the text.[37] The semantic motion occurs in the intentional, creative skill of juxtaposition, and the metaphoric process entails meaning extended through comparison, while producing new meaning by way of juxtaposition and synthesis. An analogical procedure (similarity in difference) is related to the textual conversation.[38] In a purposeful superimposition, the superior tradition is imposed on the inferior one. Here, a grammatological strategy of deconstructing texts (collage) helps comparative theology to release the texts from their controlling contexts and produce new meanings through deconstruction; such a strategy of writing averts the traditional mode of intentionality which is bound to the ideology of communication.[39]

---

35. 'The Freedom of a Christian (1520),' in *Martin Luther's Basic Theological Writings*, p. 393.
36. Ibid., p. 397.
37. Clooney, *Theology after Vedanta*, p. 31.
38. Ibid., p. 155.
39. Ibid., p. 173.

The intentionality of the reader is influenced by life-world and its specific language. This problematizes the idea of superimposition in which the low or the irregular is subjugated into the hegemony of the superior. Communication is not merely ideology, but it is also imbued with the dialogical practice in which the reader is better situated in learning from the text in terms of appreciation, critical distance and semantic retrieval. A text has its own life setting, in which the semantic circle considers the relation between text and social condition, in which an analysis of religious discourse is undertaken in reference to material interests and power relations. Thus, an archaeological analysis of religious discourse remains central in comparative theology, which is concerned with explicating the way the religious ideas would be embedded with construction of social reality. It takes issue with the intratextual confine, which refrains from 'extratextual knowledge about the truth or status of the compared texts.'[40]

For a constructive side of comparative theology, a critical analysis or exegetical work of Shinran's model is first to be explicated in his life connection with the traditional Buddhist model of the self-power. There is the social condition of the text and religious ideas in its historical background. The same enquiry is done with respect to Luther's epistemological rupture in his own context and struggle. This critical exegesis considers semantic articulation with social environment and power structure. Such hermeneutical skill belongs to the first ranked level of the comparative theology in its mode of translation, interpretation and recovery of meaning.

Then, a textual coordination, or articulation, is made in dealing with comparative types (such as justification, grace, soteriology, moral practice and social justice) for conversation and reconstruction; it belongs to the second order in characterizing comparative theology and its religious construction of reality. Comparative types are produced in terms of pattern of identity, deferential, semantic retrieval, and synthesis, in the procedure of which a type of Buddhist theology can be appreciated.

In this procedure, the texts compared are not decomposed or deconstructed, but their limitation or problem in the historical context is under suspense (or problematization); the religious discourse in the hegemonic mode of representation is analyzed and clarified through critical exegesis for the immanent critique underlying emancipation, as released from prejudices, misrepresentation and obscurities.

---

40. Ibid., p. 169.

In so doing, the textually formed reasoning in the archaeological and hermeneutical frame takes issue with Buddhist constructive theology, which relates the social construction of knowledge (externalization, objectification and internalization) to describe the formation of basic Buddhist doctrines. The doctrine of non-self is experienced and articulated in language as religious idea (externalization), which finds a reality of its own (objectification) through religious discourse and dissemination; people who followed sought to comprehend it (internalization) through accommodation.[41] However, this perspective tends to undermine the way the religious discourse would be elevated to the dominant knowledge system through institutional support and power structure.

Pattern of Identity: Christ and Amida

Comparatively speaking, in Shinran's view, a forensic meaning of faith is based on the belief in the name of Amida *extra nos*; it is imputed universally to believers through the promise. This imputed power is grounded in Amida's grace for us and in us; this tripartite model brings believers to become effectual in participation in the Buddhist teaching of compassion and social justice.

For him Amida's name is the Buddha of Infinite Light, which shines on all sentient beings. Shinran exposes the essential unity between Amida Buddha (the Dharmakaya as compassionate) and the Dharmakaya as suchness (sunyata). Shinran writes:

> There are two kinds of dharmakaya in regard to the Buddha. The first is called dharmakaya-as-suchness and the second, dharmakaya-as-compassionate means. Dharmakaya-as-suchness has neither color nor form; thus, the mind cannot grasp it nor words describe it. From this oneness was manifested form, called dharmakaya-as-compassionate-means.[42]

If the formless dharmakaya is revealed in the form of the dharmakaya-as-compassionate means (Amida) in a personal sense, D.T. Suzuki comments, 'Amida performs in a sense the office of God and also that of

---

41. Unno, 'Constructive Buddhist Theology: A Response,' in *Buddhist Theology: Critical Reflections by Contemporary Buddhist Scholars*, p. 389.
42. Shinran, 'Notes on Essentials of Faith Alone:' *A Translation of Shinran's Yuishinsho-mon'I*, p. 42; see Keel, *Understanding Shinran*, p. 165.

Christ ... The Vow is mediator, and as it emanates from Amida's Love, it is just as efficient as Christ in its office of mediatorship.'[43]

A 'Buddhist' theology in this fashion maintains that Amida (Christ) is eternal Buddha beyond form and name. Amida becomes another name for emptiness as ultimate reality, which is wise and compassionate. In the Buddhist distinction between formless Dharmakaya and the Body of Bliss (Sambhogakaya of wisdom and compassion), the character of Amida is manifest in the vow of a legendary Dharmakara. However, Shinran does not acknowledge the subordination of Amida to the Dharmakaya.

Shinran writes further:

> Thus appearing in the form of light called 'Tathagata of unhindered light ...' it is without color and without form, that is, identical with Dharmakaya-as-suchness, dispelling the darkness of ignorance and unobstructed by karmic evil. ... Know, therefore, that Amida Buddha is light, and that light is the form taken by wisdom.[44]

Shin's position is identical with Luther's insight into the essential unity in the hidden God (*Deus absconditus*) and the revealed God (*Deus revelatus*). Christ reveals God's whole fatherly heart: 'But God had seen my wretched state/Before the world's foundation,/And, mindful of his mercies great,/He planned for my salvation./He turned to me a father's heart.'[45]

In the Trinitarian context, Luther distinguishes God the Father from God the Son with no subordination. In the beginning Christ as eternal word was with God. The Word became flesh. Christ as the revealed God became one with the soul in the pattern of happy exchange, as seen in 'The Freedom of the Christian' (1520):

> So Christ has all the blessing and the salvation which are the soul's. And so the soul has upon it all the vice and sin which become Christ's own. Here now begins the happy exchange and conflict. Because Christ is God and man who never yet sinned, and his piety is unconquerable, eternal and almighty.

---

43. Suzuki, *Collected Writings on Shin Buddhism*, p. 58.
44. Shinran, 'Notes on Essentials of Faith Alone,' ibid., pp. 43–4.
45. Luther, 'Dear Christians, One and All, Rejoice,' in *Lutheran Book of Worship*, no. 299.

> So, then, as he makes his own the believing soul's sin through the wedding ring of its faith, and does nothing else than as if he had committed it, just so must sin be swallowed up and drowned.[46]

According to Luther, the teaching of justification, when properly understood, is faith in Christ. Faith in Christ implies a double meaning of being declared righteous by God (*extra nos*) and of being acquitted, renewed in the gift of grace (Christ for us and dwelling within us, as well). Faith is not understood as human work or repentance in preparing the stage to receive divine grace. Rather, in Luther's account, faith is described as the reception of divine promise and grace. The grace of justification is received by faith, in which Christ is really present. The justifying faith 'takes hold of and possesses this treasure, the present Christ.'[47]

Differential

Nonetheless, methodological affinity does not necessarily marginalize or suppress the incommensurability between Luther and Shinran in their respective approach to Amida, grace and faith. Luther's experience of *Anfechtungen* (inner struggle) led him to experience God's wrath and love only on the cross of Jesus Christ. Such experience of God is alien to Shinran.

Stated in a phenomenological fashion, the term 'unrevealed' God is not replaced by the rational attributes of trustworthiness and love with which the element of fascination in Luther is interwoven. God is a consuming fire which is felt with *majestas* and *tremendum* in religious awe.[48] In the blissfulness of the experience of God, faith entails a numinous horizon, and unites a human being with God; it stamps the very signature of the mystical, because faith makes a believer 'one cake' with God or Christ, in other words, a ring holds a jewel. Faith in the bliss of the assurance of salvation comes to terms with the union of a believer with God.

A God of 'revelation' is intertwined with God's 'unrevealedness,' the awe-inspiring, non-rational character of deity in the awful majesty of

---

46. LW, 31, pp. 351–2.
47. LW 26, p. 130.
48. Otto, *The Idea of the Holy*, p. 99.

the very Godhead. The numinous side of faith remains an undercurrent in the meaning of holiness and the wrath of God.[49]

The phenomenological description of faith differentiates Luther from Shinran's spiritual experience with the Other-Power based on the myth of the bodhisattva, named Dharmakara in India. Unlike Luther's notion of God's judgment and grace in the life of Jesus Christ, the notion of Amida is more metaphysical, legendary, and more spiritual than historical, or factual. It has little to do with God's justice and righteousness in the sense of wholly other and feeling of *tremendum* and fascination.

Recognizing the difference as different remains crucial in the comparative study of grace and faith. This difference, when recognized as different and unique, constitutes particular identity and safeguards the Christian or Buddhist teaching of grace against syncretic hybridity. In recognition of the difference, comparative theology does not necessarily mean an obstacle to interreligious learning; but it sharpens and reinforces the dialogue and engagement in a sober and lucid manner.

Retrieval

Given the differential, it is important to note Luther's notion of the cosmic Christ, which is impressively formulated along with God's universal reign: 'We believe that Christ, according to his human nature, is put over all creatures (Ephesians 1:22) and fills all things. ... Not only according to his divine nature, but also according to his human nature, he is the a lord of all things, has all things in his hand, and is present everywhere.'[50]

Luther's notion of the Cosmic Christ creates a space for Amida Buddhism to speak of grace and faith in its own terms and right, which belongs to the irregular grace of God. Luther's notion of faith entails recognition of the Other, especially as seen in his reflection of Ishmael: 'For the expulsion does not mean that Ishmael should be utterly excluded from the kingdom of God ... The descendants of Ishmael also joined the church of Abraham and became heirs of the promise, not by reason of right but because of irregular grace.'[51]

Faith in the grace of God is not encapsulated in the individualist sense of salvation egoism or monopoly of the truth. Rather it can be articulated and reconstructed in the recognition of the Other. The

---

49. Ibid., pp. 99–100.
50. LW 36, p. 342.
51. LW 4, pp. 42–4.

semantic retrieval in comparative procedure facilitates a constructive synthesis in which faith-epistemology in Christ/Amida is deepened and enhanced in the recognition of the claim and validity of the other.

Synthesis

The term 'Buddhist theology' is an experiment in understanding the model of the Pure Land doctrine, its ritual, its religious discourse, its own institution, and its religious construction of reality, which is sociologically distinct from other Buddhist discourses. If Buddhist theology takes into account a social scientific type of critical reflection among contemporary Buddhist scholars trained in the Western academy, it is grounded within the Buddhist tradition; this entails a constructive side in elaborating the trans-historical and transcultural significance of Buddhism in relevance to the contemporary world from the Buddhist perspective.[52] A Christian bias should be suspended as much as possible, describing the ideal and significance of Buddhist theology in terms of adumbration, critical renewal, reconstruction, and synthesis in an approximate and open-ended manner, which stands in continual renewal and semantic retrieval.

Central to Buddhist theology is bracketing judgments of normative truth and value, free from the superordination of Christianity upon other religions; this phenomenological attitude facilitates creating a new space in the in-depth study of non-Christian religions. This suspension is not merely conflated with value neutrality, but it seeks to synthesize semantic retrieval with value relevance through problematization, immanent critique and emancipation. The comparative theology in this regard 'has generated a strong new interest in critical, constructive theology that fits neither within the established method of religious studies nor under the rubric of Christian theology.'[53]

Given this, Shinran remains a classic example for constructing Buddhist theology and its social engagement.[54] According to Shinran, we are under the dominion of our sinful condition, but Amida has already embraced all through his promise, no matter how sinful or evil. Beyond the subjective side of belief, the Other constitutes the faith of the

---

52. *Buddhist Theology*, eds. Jackson and Makransky, p. 2.
53. Ibid., p. 14.
54. Tanaka, 'Concern for Others in Pure Land Soteriological and Ethical Considerations: The Case of Jogyo daihi In Jodo-Shinshu Buddhism,' ibid., pp. 346–63.

self, completely letting the self go. Faith is the sincere way is completely letting the self go, as seen in the Buddhist sense of faith as truth.

A type of Buddhist 'Protestant' theology à la Shinran is assured of Amida's vicarious atonement as the faith is confirmed in Amida, who is completely beyond the sinful condition of karmic reality and reincarnation. It implies the dimension of 'not yet' eschatology in which one will be reborn in eternal life in the Pure Land. This paradigm shift takes issue with the complete or non-dual identity of samsara and nirvana (form is emptiness while emptiness is form). According to Shinran, there is no such potential of a Buddha nature inherent in every sentient being, which is capable of realizing the absolute or non-dual identity of Buddhahood in this present moment in the sense of realized eschatology.

This Buddhist theological perspective considers the pattern of identity between *shinjin* and faith. Luther's teaching of justification is purely grounded 'on the promise and truth of God, which cannot deceive,'[55] although it does not discard the significance of human good deeds in the sense of diakonia. Likewise, Shinran's teaching of Amida's grace finds its critical, liberating role, as opposed to the dominant model of Buddhism in the medieval Japanese context; it can be seen in parallel with the scholastic teaching in Luther's time. Shinran's teaching refers to an even more difficult way to realize it on the human side, because human beings are completely caught in the sinful condition and the perverted reality of selfish ego. This condition of human distorted inwardness (*incurvatus in se*) cannot be overcome through strenuous practice toward perfect enlightenment and Buddhahood. The type of the Other Power (in reorientation to Amida or Christ) is common to Luther and Shinran along their threefold understanding of grace.

Shinjin in Shinran's sense is the essence of faith, which embraces a believing heart and trust in the Other Power; this can be compared with Luther's sense of *fiducia*, complete trustworthiness in the grace. *Shinjin* (faith) is followed by *nenbutsu*, which is not necessarily accompanied by the former. Faith is given to us by Amida:

> The Tathagata gives this sincere mind to all living things, an ocean of beings possessed of blind passions, karmic evil, and false wisdom. This mind manifests the true mind of benefiting others.[56]

---

55. LW 26, p. 387.

56. 'True Teaching, Practice and Realization of the Pure Land Way:' *A Translation of Shinran's Kyogyoshinsho* 4 vols, vol II.30.

Shinran further writes:

> *With sincere mind entrusting themselves: Sincere* means true and real. 'True and real' refers to the vow of the Tathagata being true and real; this is what *sincere mind* means. ... *Entrusting* is to be free of doubt, believing deeply and without any double-mindedness that the Tathagata's Primal Vow is true and real. This *entrusting with sincere mind*, then, is that arising from the Vow in which Amida urges every being throughout the ten quarters, 'Entrust yourself to my Vow, which is true and real'; it does not arise from the hearts and minds of foolish being of self-power. *Aspiring to be born in my land*; Out of the entrusting with sincere mind that is Other Power, aspire to be born in the Pure Land of happiness!'[57]

Fiducia in the theological context comes from God's faithfulness, which is implanted upon the human heart and makes human beings justified before God (Romans 1:17; Habbakuk 2:4). Luther comprehends faith as God's work in us, and the real presence of Christ in faith gives new birth, changing our hearts, our spirits and our thoughts. Faith is a living, bold trust (*fiducia*) in God's grace, because the Holy Spirit makes this happen through faith.[58]

Luther in *The Large Catechism* (1529) states that 'it is the trust and faith of the heart alone that make both God and an idol. ... For these two belong together, faith and God. Anything on which your heart relies and depends ... that is really your God.'[59] Faith clings to the Word, in which the truth of God becomes alive in us. Faith let God be God.

According to Taitetsu Unno, Shinran's concept of *shinjin* as 'true entrusting', or a believing heart, cannot be comprehended without the Primal Vow of Amida. A person's complete entrusting of self to the Primal Vow becomes one with the person's total entrusting of self to the reality of one's karmic self. The latter being made possible by the former, these two directions form a single awakening which means *shinjin* as true entrusting.[60]

---

57. 'Notes on the Inscriptions on Sacred Scrolls:' *A Translation of Shinran's Songo shinzo meimon*, pp. 33–4.
58. *Dr. Martin Luther's Vermischte Deutsche Schriften*, ed. Johann K. Irmischer. vol. 63, p. 125.
59. 'The Large Catechism (1529),' in *The Book of Concord*, p. 386.
60. Unno, *River of Fire, River of Water*, p. 59.

In this correlation model, it is useful to examine this Buddhist insight into *shinjin* in terms of Luther's notion of the real presence of Christ in faith. To my reading, Amida may realize the true entrusting (in the sense of *fiducia*), while dwelling within the believing heart. This is more than historical knowledge of Amida or assent to him, but shining forth from within. A Buddhist theology finds its expression and application in the Christian concept of *fiducia*.

In John Cobb's comment: 'To have faith in Christ is to be open to all truth and to all reality – not to cling to one truth and one reality. To trust Christ is to abandon all prejudice. All defenses, and to receive all that can be received. The recognition that Christ is Amida will help us toward this faith.'[61] The Other Power in Shinran's faith is 'the true principle or depth of our own being' in the sense that faith is the realization of this Other; It 'leads toward an identity of that Other with the state of being which it promises and bestows.'[62] However, Cobb identifies faith with trust in view of Luther's thought, without regard to the real presence of Christ in faith.

Reconstruction

Textually formed rationality of interpretation enables one to conceptualize the constructive side of comparative theology in terms of explicating the connection between religious discourse, ethical attitude, and its religious construction of reality. Textual enquiry is a way of crossing over the terrain of the Other, then back to Christian tradition by interpreting it in a fresh and constructive manner. Such reading is undertaken for the respect and recognition of the transformative power of the Other to renew and enrich a reading of Luther.

This characterizes a constructive side of comparative theology, which articulates the sense of fusion of horizons underlying a Buddhist theology. In this regard, a retrieval of meaning in recognition of the Other is of special significance, such that it becomes a basis for prayerful exchange. Luther boldly appreciates the irregular grace granted to pagan authority, especially the Turkish state as a model of the task of secular authority. God grants a great deal of gold, silver, riches, dominions, reason, wisdom, language and kingdoms to those who live outside the Christian world.[63]

---

61. Cobb, *Beyond Dialogue*, p. 129.
62. Ibid., p. 103.
63. Ebeling, *Luther*, p. 189.

Luther's notion of the irregular grace of God helps deepen a recovery of meaning in terms of intertextuality, in which the grace of justification is shared in the invocation of the name of Amida and his Primal Vow in the *Larger Sukhavatiyuha Sutra*: '… any among the throng of living beings in the ten regions of the universe should single-mindedly desire to be born in my land with joy, with confidence and gladness.'[64]

In response, Luther affirms, 'God would rather hear the curses of the ungodly than the alleluia of the pious.'[65]

4. Comparative Enquiry: Religious Construction of Reality

Correlation

Faith is active in love and justice. Insofar as faith arises in us, we are being grasped by Amida's light and are destined to attain enlightenment, but we are beset by blind passions and doubts; the settling of faith is based on a special form of Amida's grace, the benefit of which is being grasped by Amida's light, never to be abandoned. The arising of faith (event) is bound to the settling of faith (process), which implies a separate grace of Amida; it grasps us, not abandoning us. The notion 'being grasped, never to be abandoned' (*sesshu fusha*) is grounded in the promise of Amida in the *Contemplation Sutra*: 'Each ray of Amida's light shines universally upon the worlds of the ten quarters, embracing and not forsaking those sentient beings who utter the *nenbutsu*.'[66]

This perspective entails the significance of morality in contrast to antinomian followers. Moral life follows naturally from a genuine faith in the Vow and Name of Amida. Likewise, as St Paul says, 'What then are we to say? Should we continue in sin in order that grace may abound?" By no means!' (Romans 6:1–2).

Faith undergoes a change of heart and is accompanied by a gradual transformation in one's moral life, which accords with the bodhisattva's activity to save others in suffering. Suspension of what is taken for granted in the Buddhist episteme returns to the meaning of Amida grace, and returns to the world to change its reality by benefiting and guiding others toward emancipation.

---

64. Gomez, trans. *Land of Bliss*, p. 167.
65. Cited in Bonhoeffer, *Ethics*, p. 104.
66. *The Tanni Sho: Notes Lamenting Differences*, p. 93; see Keel, *Understanding Shinran*, p. 106.

Solidarity

As previously seen in Shinran's explication, everybody can receive faith equally from the universal grace of Amida. What distinguishes his teaching from elitist Zen can be read: 'All people … In saying the Name of Amida are not restricted.'.[67]

In quoting a poem of Prince Shotoku, Shinran argues that in the case of a rich man at court, seeking justice is like throwing a stone into water. But in the case of a poor man, it is like throwing water into a stone. Shinran's rejection of *Kami* worship would be regarded as a rejection of evil in society, which would undermine the connection between religion and those in power.[68] The Shin sect teaching inspired numerous peasant revolts in the later Muromachi period (1392–1573). Shinran's insight into the issue of social justice, as seen in his critique of Buddhist institutions and hierarchical systems, finds inspiration for engaged Buddhists in the present time; they look after 'a voluntary association of people guided by exemplary leaders and a common vision of a society based on peace, justice and freedom.'[69]

In the *jogyo daihi* we read that the practitioner of Other Power *shinjin* is constantly encouraged in the spirit 'to realize shinjin and lead others to shinjin' for the 'mind to save all beings.' One constantly practises the Buddha's great compassion that is expressed as 'to realize shinjin and guide others to shinjin.'[70]

A study of Shinran's faith and justice leads on to the significance of faith and justice in Luther. Luther's prophetic critique of economic injustice deserves special attention in the seventh commandment of the *Large Catechism* (1529). The economic reality in his time was distinguished by misusing the market in an arbitrary, defiant and arrogant manner. It caused the poor to be defrauded every day, and imposed new burdens and high prices upon their life. 'You shall not steal' aims at transcending the reality of greedy money and rampant

---

67. Cited in Unno, *River of Fire, River of Water*, p. xiv.
68. Dessi, 'The Pure Land as a Principle of Criticism,' *Japanese Religions*. vol. 32 (1 and 2), pp. 75–90.
69. Queen and King, eds. *Engaged Buddhism: Buddhist Liberation Movements in Asia*, p. 19.
70. Tanaka, 'Concern for Others in Pure Land Soteriological and Ethical Considerations: The Case of Jogyo daihi In Jodo-Shinshu Buddhism,' in *Buddhist Theology*, p. 353.

accumulation of the wealth in his time, which was beset by usury, hoarding and speculation.[71]

For Luther, the trust and faith of the heart alone make both God and an idol:

> There are some who think that they have God and everything they need when they have money and property; they trust in them and boast in them so stubbornly and securely that they care for no one else. They, too, have a god – mammon by name, that is, money and property – on which they set their whole heart. This is the most common idol on earth.[72]

Luther takes issue with mammon as a system of totality to be worshipped through his critique of the devouring system and the process of capital accumulation. This perspective refers to an aspect of religious construction of reality, which calls for a critical dialogue with Weber.

Problematization: Religious Discourse and Economic Attitude

In his comparative sociology of religious idea (calling) and economic ethics, Weber analyzes Luther's economic attitude in terms of a type of economic traditionalism. He considered Calvinism to be the true religion of modernity through its inner-worldly ascetic ethics. Weber's own grand narrative of rationalization (coupled with Puritan ethics) remains a key concept in his sociology of the religious construction of modernity and capitalism. His thesis is bound up with the historical process of disenchantment of the world, which has been precipitated by Puritan Calvinism; however, in the critique of magic and superstition in the name of rationalization, capitalist modernity created an 'iron cage' and has been caught to its fate captured in technocratic and bureaucratic systems; finally, a polytheistic reality of impersonal forces has become a fate of humanity which has to surrender.

What is at stake in Weber's theory of a religious construction of reality is that the idea of professional 'vocation' was central for Luther's religiosity and its economic backwardness; yet the notion of 'disenchantment' is characteristic of the Puritan Calvinist worldview underwriting modernity and capitalism. However, in my study of God

---

71. 'Large Catechism' (1529), in *The Book of Concord*, pp. 417–8.
72. Ibid., p. 387.

against mammon, Luther is credited to a type of economic justice, in which he was keenly aware of the 'devouring' system of early capitalism. This prophetic voice is appreciated by Marx, who notices Luther's critique of the Christian character of capital accumulation in the colonial context.[73]

The type of Luther's economic justice is keenly aware of the absurdity and irrationalism of early capitalism in his sharp analysis and critique of usury, speculation and injustice. It runs counter to Weber's type of economic traditionalism. In Luther's notion of the calling (*Beruf*), Weber acknowledges that such religious discourse acquired a new meaning through the Reformation and has spread in daily speech and activity in the world of all Protestant people. Thus, Luther developed the concept of the calling in harmony with the tradition of the Middle Ages (represented by Thomas Aquinas), but he reacted against the Catholic version of the renunciation of secular duties and obligations in the monastic life. Luther maintains that every legitimate calling has the same worth and value in the sight of God. Luther's moral justification of worldly activity belongs to one of the most important contributions.[74]

Furthermore, Weber notices that Luther was critical of usury and undertook his campaign against the Fuggers, the great merchants of his time. But Luther's position remains backward as seen from a capitalist rationality, because Luther interpreted the idea of the calling, mainly in favouring a traditionalist line.[75] As Weber argues, 'The individual should remain once and for all in the station and calling in which God had placed him, and should restrain his worldly activity within the limits imposed by his established station in life.'[76] In Luther's attitude in its 'absolute acceptance of things as they were' as divine ordinance, he was not capable of constituting 'a new or in any way fundamental connection between worldly activity and religious principles.'[77]

Weber's sociological thesis remains questionable and defective, because he does not clarify a juxtaposition between Luther's prophetic critique of early capitalism and his absolute acceptance of secular things as divine ordinance. In effect, Weber is not capable of observing that Luther's prophetic critique of mammon is primarily grounded in the biblical confession of God as the source of life and emancipation. It has

---

73. Marx, *Capital*, I, pp. 649–50.
74. Weber, *The Protestant Ethic and the Spirit of Capitalism*, p. 81.
75. Ibid., p. 83.
76. Ibid., p. 85.
77. Ibid.

little to do with a type of backward traditionalism. A comparative reading strategy requires a meticulous exegesis of Luther's texts in dealing with elective affinity between religious discourse and material interests. How would Luther contribute to the religious construction of reality?

In his 'On Secular Authority,' Luther definitely preached against uncritical obedience to political authority and secular powers, when the latter deviate their course from God's reign. In the theory of three estates (*economia, politia,* and *ecclesia*), Luther maintains that God's regiments oppose the power of evil through divine collaboration with human beings; thus the life arrangements are sanctified and organized around fairness, solidarity and justice. Stated sociologically, the three estates are important fields in a society stratified and structured in a hierarchical manner. Luther provides a critical insight into the reality of intersectional fields to renew and transform these spheres. He offers a responsible critique that can be a source of of justice and equality and emancipation.

This perspective contradicts Weber, who portrays Luther as indifferent to power politics and economic justice. However, Luther's ethics of fraternity belongs to one of his major considerations of God against the power of mammon, which Luther observes as a devouring system of totality. In 'Admonition to the Clergy to preach against the Usury' (*An die Pfarrherren, wider den Wucher zu predigen*), Luther writes: 'capital invested to gain more money by interest "eats" human beings and "estates" up to and including the Emperor. ... With the use of their intelligence alone, the heathen could recognize a profiteer as fourfold a thief and murderer. But we Christians hold them in such honor that we worship them simply in virtue of their wealth.'[78]

Weber's major problem is seen in his incapability of articulating the correlation between the rational organization of the capitalist system (rationalization) and its irrational absurdity (commodity fetishism). A prophetic critique of this reality of idolatry or the devouring system of capitalism must be appreciated as the source of immanent critique concerning religious sanction of the reified system. Luther's religious discourse and its critical side remain fundamental in constructing social reality in accordance with fraternity, justice and solidarity.[79]

---

78. Cited in Duchrow, *Global Economy*, 176. See Luther, 'Admonition to the Clergy,' in Gunter Fabiunke, *Luther als Nationalökonom*, pp. 193–230.
79. I fully develop my previous argument about God and Mammon in Luther's thought in Chung, *Comparative Theology Among Mutiple Modernities*, pp, 213–219.

Pure Land Buddhism and Social Construction

Weber draws attention to Shin Buddhism in his comparison with Lutheran teaching. Perhaps for the first time a deliberate policy appeared in the identity of the priests with lay people in the Shin sect, and sermon, instruction and popular literature were developed in a similar way to the Lutheran manner. Likewise, the faithful devotion to the Buddha Amida is seen in its affinity to the *bhakti* religiosity of India, which grew out the cult of Krishna.[80]

The Shin sect had a great number of followers among the Burghers who belonged to the strata that were most favourable to the reception of Western culture. Nonetheless, Weber argues that the Shin sect 'developed just as little of a rational inner-worldly asceticism as did Lutheranism.'[81]

On the contrary, Bellah in his *Tokugawa Religion* seeks to analyze the role of Japan's premodern culture of the Tokugawa Period (1600–1868) in its modernization process, and he deals with Shin Buddhism. Shin Buddhism would be compared to the Protestant ethic with respect to economic rationality, because the rationalizing tendencies in Japanese religion had contributed to economic and political rationalization in Japan.[82] Shin Buddhism went in the direction of isolating or even liberating religion from magic, superstition and ritual, surpassing any sects of Buddhism in this regard.

It is unfortunate to read the statement in which 'Jodoshinshu has not yet worked through the crisis of the relation of history to faith. If this crisis must be faced, then in some respects its problems are more acute even than those faced by Christianity, for its basis is still further removed from the actual course of history.'[83] On the contrary, Jodo-Shinshu scholar Takamaro Shigaraki emphasizes a socially active dimension in the Jodo-Shinshu teachings, and he draws largely on the writings of the founder, Shinran.[84]

Religion in the sense of the ultimate concern (Paul Tillich) is connected with what is ultimately valuable and meaningful; in other words, ultimate value. Religion has a social function in providing a meaningful

---

80. Weber, *The Religion of India*, pp. 278–9.
81. Ibid., p. 279.
82. Bellah, *Tokugawa Religion*, pp. 7–8.
83. Cobb, *Beyond Dialogue*, p. 139.
84. Shigaraki (1992). 'Shinjin and Social Action in Shinran's Teachings', trans. David Matsumoto. *The Pure Land*, new series 8–9, pp. 219–49.

set of ultimate values on which the morality of a society can be built. When such values are institutionalized, they can be taken as the central values in a given society.[85] This perspective plays a substantial part in underwriting the social aspect of the religious construction of reality. What is core in the Shin belief was only faith in Amida, with an emphasis on salvation. The stress on human sinfulness in the bondage to evil is fundamentally related to wholehearted trust in the divine power of Amida. This 'faith alone' orientation has undergone transformation in the course of history, finding its culmination in Rennyo Shonin (1415–99), the so-called second father of Shin Buddhism. Extending the work of Shinran, Rennyo required the practice of the Confucian virtues, while at the same time emphasizing wholly dedicating one's inner life to Amida.

In Bloom's account, there seems to be a lack of moral 'ought to' in Shinran, because he tends to relegate compassionate action to the future. Shinran's view of altruism assumes a form of passive quietism. When it was connected with Rennyo's ethical theory, it turned into 'an acquiescence to the reigning social mores.'[86] In this transition or transformation Confucianism took the first rationalizing impact in the sphere of ethics in Japanese society, undergirding a process of rationalization.[87] This historical shift changed a traditionalistic action of a magical type imbued with Pure Land Buddhism in such a way that it would be analogous to Protestantism.[88] Religious action regarding deity leads to the theory of *on* (blessings), which is obvious in the Jodo Shin sect. 'Our whole life must be one long expression of gratitude: we must regard life as a service which Amida demands of us.'[89]

A strong sense of gratitude to the grace of Amida compels us to fulfill our duties faithfully in promoting Buddhism, the good of family, state and society. 'To work thus for the world with a sense of gratitude is the true life of the Buddhist.'[90] Jodo Shinshu was widely disseminated among the common people in Japan. Rennyo was keenly interested in advancing the religious ethical regulation of everyday life with respect to occupational life. 'If we engage in business, we must realize that it is

---

85. Bellah, *Tokugawa Religion*, p. 6.
86. Bloom, *Shinran's Gospel of Pure Grace*, p. 84.
87. Bellah, *Tokugawa Religion*, p. 69.
88. Ibid., p. 70.
89. Ibid., p. 72.
90. Ibid., p. 78.

in the service of Buddhism.'⁹¹ Rennyo's stress on *on* (blessing) and his inner-worldly asceticism is striking:

> He always told his family members and followers not to waste anything necessary for everyday life, because by doing so one would commit a sacrilege to creation. Once he found a piece of paper thrown away in the hallway. He picked it up and, reverently, raising it before his forehead, observed with a sigh, 'How can they be so sinful as to waste what has been given in blessing!'⁹²

Unlike the universalism of faith alone in the early period Shinshu, Rennyo emphasised the significance of the ethical demand in the Shin sect. Salvation and ethical action had come to be united by middle Tokugawa times, and ethical action became the very sign or proof of salvation. Improving one's bad heart refers to a sign of one's 'having attained a believing heart (faith).'⁹³

Diligent work in one's occupation has come to occupy the central place, and ethical duties were required among the members of the religious community. Religious ethical action and an ascetic attitude would be best expressed, according to Rennyo, in dealing with one's occupation in regard to divine protection of Amida. In Shin tracts we read some of this acetic style of life: 'Cheerfully do not neglect diligent activity morning and evening. Work hard at the family occupation. Be temperate in unprofitable luxury.'⁹⁴

In the Confucian teaching, profit comes from human enterprise, and it is therefore not to be pursued. The worthy person should rather value righteousness. For Buddhists, greed or craving is closely linked to the merchant's quest for profit, and it is further denounced as one of the cardinal sins. Profit therefore has no value in both Confucian ethics and Buddhist teaching. What is central in reconciling such a contrast can be seen in the religious doctrine of *jiri-rita*. Profiting both self and others is religiously justified in business profit. The religious discourse of *jiri-rita* affirms receiving profit for benefiting others in the business of merchants and artisans. 'The spirit of profiting others is the Bodhisattva spirit. Having a Bodhisattva spirit and saving all beings, this is called

---

91. Ibid., p. 117.
92. Cited in ibid., p. 118.
93. Ibid.
94. Ibid., p. 119.

Bodhisattva deeds. Thus Bodhisattva deeds are just the deeds of merchants and artisans. In general the secret of merchants' and artisans' business lies in obtaining confidence through bodhisattva deeds.'[95]

The religious ideal of Bodhisattva moves into the material realm, because it is expressed in terms of profiting others through the semantic retrieval of the Confucian ethical ideal. This religious position was taught by Jodo Shinshu in the Edo Period and had come to disseminate its discursive formation and practice through *jiri-rita*; it gained institutional support and political power primarily in merchant towns. The merchants of Omi province were devout believers in Shinshu, and they made diligence, frugality, and an excessive partiality for saving into the core of their calling in the world of commerce.[96]

A synthesized doctrine of *jiri-rita* is done in the semantic retrieval through fusion of horizons has an impact upon the family system and economic motivation, and finds its affinity with the political system. Political motivation was imbued with the economic sphere of the merchant class. The Bodhisattva ideal and its practical, ethical style of life (*jiri-rita*) played a major role in shaping economic motivation and undergirding the economic development among the merchants; with political approval, religious discourse in power relations was disseminated widely and elevated to dominate the knowledge system. The feudal lord took an interest in the religious ethical injunction of Shinshu tracts, which would be reconciled with political value.

Obligation to Amida was combined with obligation to one's feudal lord, though such an intention was not actually of Shinshu. When his retainer, a devout Shin adherent, was asked to renounce his faith for the feudal lord, he was willing to die. Impressed by this religious commitment, the feudal lord replied: 'Now I fully understand the teachings of Shinran Shonin, to which I think no other teaching is preferable. He who is taught to break his bones for the grace of his spiritual teacher is most trustworthy because he also understands the grace of his lord and holds himself always in readiness to sacrifice himself for the lord's interests.'[97]

Given this divergent type of religious discourse, an elective affinity can be discovered between a religious idea and material interest, in which political motivation and the value system come to terms with each other. Power relations in the historical course of religious development would

---

95. Ibid., p. 120.
96. Ibid., p. 121.
97. Ibid., p. 122.

be more significant than economic motivation and value; the political obligation and religious motivation are completely merged, such that the religious discourse and its discursive practice became widespread and stratified among the merchants; it became part of the formalization of the ethical status of merchants, whose ethics are characteristic of the Edo or Tokugawa Period. According to Bellah, this type of religious discourse favourable to economic rationalization is actually analogous to the Western Protestant ethic.[98]

Nonetheless, the original idea of Shinran may become the source of immanent critique regarding the historical course of modernization in Japan, which had run against Shinran's prophetic ethics of religious conviction. His ideal of transcendent salvation becomes the basis of relativizing and criticizing the value of the present world and its materialistic attachment through faith, gratitude, and benefiting of others as grounded the grace of Amida and its bodhisattva's vision of altruism.

It is also analogous to Luther's prophetic critique of economic practice tainted with hoarding, usury and speculation. The grace finds its expression in prophetic diakonia taking issue with injustice, domination and violence in our midst. This religious construction of reality facilitates an alternative form of modernity in Asia, which cuts across Weber's unilateral metanarrative of Protestant modernity.

---

98. Ibid.

Chapter 4

Karl Barth, Religion and Comparative Theology

It is a task of theological audacity to analyze Barth's complex thought-form and appraise it in terms of comparative theology and religious construction of reality. The starting point is his dialectical view of revelation and religion. It is necessary to dissect Barth's complex mode of thought and irregular style by focusing on his forgotten insight of speech-act theology, which provides a basis for acknowledging religion and culture. A semantic horizon can be undertaken in the framework of speech-act theology, which helps me to appraise Barth as an inspiration for comparative theology and religious construction of reality.

Peter Berger's use of Feuerbach is considered, with his critical appraisal of Barth for Schleiermacher and his approach to Feuerbach in terms of analogical, dialectical enquiry. Attention is given to Barth as an exponent of comparative theology, to his theological reflection of Pure Land Buddhism and his comparative study of religion.

Based on this analysis and clarification, Paul Knitter's theology of religions, and Clooney's comparative theology are analyzed in their respective critical assessment of Barth. In response, Barth's reading of Pure Land Buddhism is examined in reference to the *bhakti* religion. As already discussed, Pure Land Buhhism is a unique 'Protestant' sect of Japanese Buddhism, which was developed and represented by Honen and Shinran within the context of Mahayana Buddhism. It therefore lends itself to this sort of interreligious study. Next, Barth's fragmentary reflection of world religions is introduced, and his speech-act theology for the constructive theology of comparative religions is evaluated.

Finally, Barth is compared with Troeltsch concerning their teaching of lights in the world and multiple modernities.

1. Barth and Religions

Barth's reflections on revelation and religion are investigated for a project on a Christian theology of religions.[1] Barth comprehends revelation as sublimation of religion, in which the latter is not to be abolished per se. Revelation is elaborated as the source of immenent critique in the dialectical sense of sublation, in which religion is singled out for analysis and also called into question. Then it holds in place by restraining or suspending religion, by undertaking critical analysis. Barth holds the meaning of religion in store by preserving it along with revelation. Through this polysemy of sublimation in a dialectical sense, Barth maintains that revelation takes up the religion under the reconciling grace of God.[2]

In fact, his dialectical mode of thought is not subsumed under the Hegelian triadic logic of thesis-antithesis-synthesis, but Barth's dialectical idea is framed in light of God's revelation in Christ, whose mystery is not reduced to historical movement and its logical immanence for a higher synthesis. For Barth, a higher synthesis is grounded and moved by the theological subject matter (*Sache*), which means self-revelation of God the *totaliter aliter*; the latter guides our understanding of God concerning the relation between revelation and religion in a critical and constructive manner.

Barth argues that the revelation has significance as it relates to religious traditions: 'The Veda to the Indians, the Avesta to the Persians, the Tripitaka to the Buddhists, the Koran to its believers: are they not all "bibles" in exactly the same way as the Old and New Testaments?'[3] Barth does not intend to confine the majesty and sovereign lordship of God only to the ecclesiastical sphere, but he calls the Christian church to take into account the lights in the world reflecting the Light of Christ. In Barth's statement we read, 'In His revelation God is present in the world of human religion.'[4] At the same time, however, Barth chides religion as unbelief. Barth's argument is of a dialectical character in terms of

---

1. Ensminger, *Karl Barth's Theology as a Resource for a Christian Theology of Religions*.
2. Ibid., p. 45.
3. Barth, *Church Dogmatics* I/2 (hereafter CD), p. 282.
4. CD I/2, p. 297.

appreciation, critical distance, and a recovery of new meaning. His dialectical method and argument can be primarily comprehended in his theological confrontation with the liberal theological preoccupation of religious consciousness or religious a priori; it is seen as his engagement with theological tradition from Schleiermacher through Ernst Troeltsch. According to Barth, 'The religion of revelation is indeed bound up with the revelation of God: but the revelation of God is not bound up with the religion of revelation.'[5]

Revelation and Interreligious Context

According to Barth, the revelation of God as the theological subject matter is not reduced and narrowed down to the *religion* of revelation as a human projection and institution. Rather the latter is bound to and guided by God's revelation. This dialectical position can be further articulated in Barth's reflection on Israel, because Barth's theology of Israel presents a paradigmatic example to Jewish-Christian dialogue. His position has undergone different stages, though, and culminated in his affirmation of God's faithfulness to Israel in his appraisal of the Vatican II document *Nostra Aetate*.[6]

Barth's dialectical position in the interreligious context can be characterized by a faithful self-examination, while challenging Christian arrogance toward other religions. It leads the Church to consider a humble attitude by listening attentively to the strange and profane voice of God; the latter remains an undercurrent in his teaching of divine speech-act outside ecclesial walls. This perspective circumscribes any assessment of Barth as sublime bigotry without having real interest in or awareness of the wider religious life of humankind. Rather Barth would be fitting to the position of 'particularity' in faithfulness to God's revelation and reconciliation in Christ, in which his particularity stance does not necessarily mean the exclusion of religious others. His particularistic stance runs counter to a triumphalist position in the encounter with people of other faiths, in which Barth is not convinced of the ecclesial triumphalism over against world religions. His position

---

5. Ibid., p. 70.
6. Barth, *Ad Limina Apostolorum*, pp. 36–7. Barth understands the Old Testament as the original form of the one revelation of God; this helps him recognize the natural proof of God in dealing with the contemporary Judaism. For more, see Pangritz and Chung, eds., *Theological Audacities. F.W. Marquardt Selected Essays*.

differentiates itself from the exclusivist model of conversion in the case of Hendrik Kraemer (1888–1965).[7]

Kraemer was born in Amsterdam and worked in Indonesia as a missionary; he became an influential figure in missionary circles worldwide, representing a so-called exclusivism in the name of Karl Barth. Kraemer's attitude to Islam sounds quite negative: 'Islam in its constituent elements and apprehensions must be called a superficial religion. … Islam might be called a religion that has almost no questions and no answers. In a certain respect its greatness lies there: … Islam, that is, absolute surrender to God, the Almighty Lord.'[8]

Unlike Kraemer, Barth does not downgrade the place of other religions. As the sublimation of religion, however, Barth asserts that 'we have not to become Philistines or Christian iconoclasts in face of human greatness … in this very sphere of religion.'[9] Barth's particular stance is grounded on the grace of God *extra nos* which is characterized by a self-critique of Christian arrogance; it summons a call to spiritual poverty before God's mystery, and to taking a humble attitude toward God's mystery to be heard in alien voice in the reconciled world.

God's Speech Act in Universal Horizon

Barth's theology of word cannot be adequately understood without considering its universal horizon of the speech act. God's revelation refers to an aspect of God speaking in person, which embraces the Church and the world. According to Barth, 'God may speak to us through Russian Communism [Leninism], a flute concerto [Mozart], a blossoming shrub [Moses' Torah], or a dead dog [perhaps jargon in the left-wing Hegelian circle aimed against Hegel's philosophy after his death].'[10]

God's speech act occurs in all media and has an analogical-political character. It finds an import in his reflection of God's kingdom, social justice, and democracy in his article 'The Christian Community and the Civil Community' (1946).

Likewise, Barth's stance in 'openness' to religious others is biblically grounded in dealing with the case of Balaam, or Cyrus. It entails an analogical character in scrutinizing the similar relation between God's speech act and religious others, despite its dissimilarity. Meanwhile,

---

7. Kraemer, *Why Christianity of All Religions?*, p. 15.
8. Kraemer, *The Christian Message in a Non-Christian World*, pp. 216–7.
9. CD I/2, p. 300.
10. CD I/1, p. 55.

Barth does not sidestep the gloomy reality of the unreconciled world, which is characterized by nothingness beset by lordless powers; these refer to political absolutism, the dominion of mammon, idol worship or ideology, and chthonic forces, which are imbued with scientific, technological change and consumerism.[11]

Given Barth's position, his theology is guided by God's revelation and embraces people of other faiths and culture in light of God's reconciliation in its universal horizon. His theology of speech-act forms a reality of intertextuality between Church and world in which God may address the Church through figures outside the Christianity. Nonetheless, he does not sidestep a reality of unreconciled regimes in politics, economic fields, and the cultural sphere – the phenomenon of impersonal forces, which is analogous to Weber's characterization of resurgence of value polytheism. This perspective becomes an undercurrent in his contribution to comparative theology and religious construction of reality through political challenge to power structure; it also recognizes the other religious ways as the semantic realm to be deciphered and interpreted for reconstruction.

Analogy and Sematic Procedure

Barth's dialectical theology is refined and sharpened in his analogical approach to God's speech act. Analogy can be a hermeneutical way of struggling with God the *totaliter aliter*, who appears to us as a speech event through secular occurrences, political realms and religious others. There are different varieties of dialectical method: one focussed on dialogue and critique for a higher synthesis is associated with an analogical enquiry, which expresses the mystery of God in terms of similarity-in-difference; one focussed on critical thinking is enhanced in an analogical semantic retrieval of God's speech act. Barth's analogical-dialectical enquiry facilitates the problematization of the unreconciled reality of lordless powers or impersonal forces by way of critique, suspending the problem of identity between God and secular occurrences, and undertaking an analogical synthesis of meaning in an approximate and open-ended manner.

It is a well-known fact that Barth repudiates National Socialism as a false gospel in his reflection on the Word of God. His problematization is seen in his analogical critique of the identity principle between God and National Socialism on the part of pro-Nazi German Christians.

---

11. Barth, *Christian Life*, p. 216.

His prophetic critique regards National Socialism as a form of an unreconciled reality beset by impersonal forces of brutality and violence. We discern line and direction in Barth's critical reflection in dealing with elective affinity between God (*analogans*) and secular forms of parables (*analogatum*), especially in his letter to Bethge discussing the latter's biography of Bonhoeffer:

> Ethics – co-humanity – servant church-discipleship – democratic socialism – peace movement – political responsibility.[12]

Barth's language of analogy is not merely reduced to a scholastic teaching of analogy or dialectical method; it is rather socially engaged and culturally refined by enhancing a critical mode of dialectical method for theological construction of social reality. This analogical language implies a semantic circle of intertextuality underlying God's relationality with the world, religion and culture.

Religion and Disgrace Effect

Religion, including Christianity, would be credited into analogical witness to the kingdom of God; but it would be reprimanded as unfaith when it falsifies and distorts the gospel of reconciliation. Sociologically relevant, religion may have the effect of solidarity as well as a disgrace effect, which should be placed under the critical scrutiny of the religious source of the Gospel (immanent critique). Revelation as the original source of the Gospel plays as sublimation of religion in terms of crisis, critical analysis, and incorporation of it into the grace of God.

2. Berger's Critique of Barth and Feuerbach

In Berger's account, however, the dialectical theology of Barth is reprimanded as anti-modernistic in his uncompromising 'No' to the subjectivizing and mediating efforts of liberal theology; it is especially seen in Barth's confrontation with Emil Brunner over the question of natural theology. Berger cites Barth's famous dictum in his struggle against Hitler; 'nothing can really happen.'[13] This formulation was embedded with Barth's resistance to National Socialism, having a strong political implication. Exegetical concentration on the Word of

---

12. Bethge, *Dietrich Bonhoeffer*; Chung, *Karl Barth*, p. 13.
13. Berger, *The Sacred Canopy*, p. 163.

God, as if nothing can really happen, implies a critique of German Christians' accommodation of the gospel to National Socialism. By expressing 'nothing can really happen,' Barth challenges an idolatrous form of German politics at his time, while forming the confessing church against it.

Berger takes issue with Barth's position of revelation, arguing whether the externality and non-subjectivity of God's grace in Christ or the objectivity of the tradition appear as a reliable foundation; it must be independent of all contingencies or in contrast to the shifting tides of an age in turmoil. It serves as an Archimedean point which may relativize 'all contradictory definitions of reality,' or 'against liberal religious individualism.'[14] Given this anthropological problem, Berger is suspicious of the way one can arrive at an Archimedean point in a world of socio-historical relativity. This is because an Archimedean point is located in a sphere, which is immune to historical relativization; it refers to the sphere of the Word or revelation, which is proclaimed in the kerygma of the Church and grasped by faith.[15]

Against this direction, Berger argues that if all religious propositions are regarded as projections which are grounded in human infrastructure, Barth's differentiation between revelation and religion does not make sense at all. Berger is convinced of Feuerbach's notion of projection for his anthropological consideration of religion and theology.

Barth: Feuerbach and Analogical Construal

Berger is not theologically astute in analyzing the dialectical method and analogical semantic in Barth's theology, but there is an affinity between Berger and Barth in their respective treatment of Feuerbach. Barth's dialectical view of religion includes in its form of unbelief Feuerbach's critical import.

In his thesis of sublimation of religion, Barth is concerned with analyzing the problem of religion in the theological context, especially in regard to liberal theology in nineteenth century neo-Protestantism in Germany. This liberal tradition has been lost in its theological anthropocentrism which replaces God's way to human beings through Jesus Christ. For Barth, Feuerbach rejects religion as projection in order to affirm the real essence of the human being, which is the most real being (*ens realissimum*); it has little to do with the ego of Kant and Fichte or the

---

14. Ibid., p. 163.
15. Ibid., pp. 182–3.

absolute identity of Schelling or the absolute mind of Hegel.[16] Feuerbach equates religion with the distinctive characteristic of the human being, self-consciousness. 'Religion, expressed generally, is consciousness of the infinite.'[17] Schleiermacher in Barth's view may become a mentor for Feuerbach, because 'if, for example, feeling is the essential organ of religion, the nature of God is nothing else than an expression of the nature of feeling.'[18]

For Feuerbach, to the degree that God becomes a human, the human person is the true Christ in the consciousness of the human species. The direct unity of species and individuality is the highest principle of Christianity. Feuerbach exalts anthropology to theology, making God real, while making God one with humanity; he suggests this can seen in the Christian understanding of incarnation, which '[lowers] God into man, made man into God.'[19] This refers to Feuerbach's concern of God in incarnation, in which human essence is expressed.

Barth recognizes Feuerbach's critique of the God of Christendom and utilizes the latter's position for his polemic against the humanization of God in the neo-Protestant theological tradition. Insofar as the critique of religion deconstructs idolatrous imagery, it is in service of the God of the Bible. For Barth 'the attitude of the anti-theologian Feuerbach was more theological than that of many theologians.'[20] However, for Barth, God in Jesus Christ is wholly Other and is not reduced to human consciousness or projection; rather God is immune from Feuerbach's theory of projection, in which the human being is self-apotheosis. Expressed in a phenomenological manner, God is an absolute being, totally different, who transcends the world as well as human consciousness. God *totaliter aliter* dethrones an attempt to elevate the consciousness of species in glorifying the apotheosis of humanity. Only God has a conception of God, because God is known to us through God's revelation.

Barth is keenly aware that the *revelation* of religion has been replaced by the revelation of *religion* in the liberal theological tradition. Neo-Protestantism means religionism, in which religion is not comprehended in light of *revelation*, but revelation by *religion*. For instance, Schleiermacher sought the essence of theology in religion as a feeling of

---

16. An Introductory Essay by Karl Barth in Ludwig Feuerbach, *The Essence of Christianity*, p. xiii.
17. Feuerbach, *The Essence of Christianity*, p. 2.
18. Ibid., p. 9.
19. Ibid., p. xv.
20. Ibid., p. x.

dependence upon God. Troeltsch attempted to explore the main task of the theologian as treating the phenomena of general religious history.[21] Revelation is apprehended by religious a priori in the universal history of religion, but history is not understood in light of revelation.

So Barth approaches religion in light of the revelation or God's reconciliation. It safeguards the uniqueness of God's revelation in Jesus Christ, while recognizing other religious manifestations and truth claims through reconciliation. In fact, Barth does not reject the phenomenology of religion and the historical study of it; rather he acknowledges that the voice of the deity has been heard and asserted in the world of religions. There are 'fundamentally unmistakable parallels and analogies in human realities and possibilities' in the other religions, which stand in consonance with Christian religion.[22]

Barth relates an expression such as God the *totaliter aliter* to Anselm's conception of God: 'that than which nothing greater can be conceived.'[23] Seen in this manner, all theological statements are judged under eschatological reservation, because they are incomplete, broken and inadequate in articulation of God's truth. Human language is undertaken in dialectical thinking and analogical construal in dealing with the relation between divine reality, humanity and the world, namely in terms of similarity in greater dissimilarity.[24] Barth respects Anselm as an important theologian standing in solidarity with the world, because the latter considers that God transcends the ecclesial sphere and boundary. The quest of the unbeliever is treated in Anselm's thought as identical with the quest of the believer. '[In Anselm] there is a solidarity between theologian and the worldling ... because the theologian is determined to address the worldling as one with whom he has at least this in common – theology.'[25] God as the source of analogy (*analogans*) makes secular realms (*analogata*) into predicates of the gospel, as well as the realm of divine semantics requiring our construal. Worldly realms can be made secular parables as analogical witness to the kingdom of God. Barth's analogical theology becomes an alternative to overcome Feuerbach as well as Schleiermacher.

Barth incorporates his dialectical method into an inherent part of analogical construal and undergirds a semantic circle in openness for and

---

21. CD I/2, p. 290.
22. CD I/2, p. 282.
23. Barth, *Anselm: Fides Quarens Intellectum*, p. 68.
24. Ibid., pp. 80, 117.
25. Ibid., p. 68.

solidarity with the world. God in revelation is known and apprehended analogically in human faith (analogy of faith); but our knowledge of God is self-critical and dialectical to the degree that it consists only in approximation, always remaining incomplete and open-ended, in need of correction at every point.[26] Barth's fundamental thesis of revelation is 'God speaking in person' in which God the Insuperable makes human language into a constructive import in analogical expression and hermeneutical experience of divine word and truth. Human engagement in the experience of the Word of God takes place in the whole of existence through ongoing renewal and orientation to new faith.[27]

This said, Berger remains limited and even defective in his critique of Barth, because he is not capable of comprehending Barth's theology of speech act and his dialectical, analogical mode of thought; this perspective helps to comprehend Barth's relational theology, to be accorded with socio historical relativity of religion. It integrates the cultural realm as a semantic field through which God may speak in a completely different manner from the ecclesiastical sphere; it correlates his theological starting point from above with God's grace of reconciliation from below.

3. Barth's Study of Buddhism

As I have elaborated elsewhere, Barth is concerned with Jodoshinsu Buddhism, a unique sect of Japanese Buddhism, or Pure Land Buhhism.[28] He discerns a parabolic character of justification in Jodoshinsu Buddhism, and seems to understand well the major difference between Honen and Shinran Buddhism, characterised by their contrasting emphases when discussing salvation. Honen (1133–1212) once stated: 'Even sinners will enter into life, how much more the righteous.' His pupil Shinran (1173–1262), with emphasis on grace alone, reacted: 'If the righteous enter into life, how much more in the case of sinners.'[29] This is because 'faith is for everyone … an unheard of invocation in the world of Buddhism.'[30]

In Barth's view, Shinran focuses on the human goal of radical desire for redemption, which implies 'the really controlling and determinative

---

26. CD II/1, p. 202.
27. CD I/1, pp. 220, 225.
28. CD I/2, p. 327. Cf. 'Barth, Comparative Theology, and Multiple Modernities' in Chung, *Comparative Theology among Multiple Modernities*, pp. 159–176.
29. CD I/2, p. 341.
30. CD I/2, p. 341.

power.' Thus, 'Amida, and faith in him, and the "pure land" are related to this goal only as the means to the end.'[31] Shinran's radical desire for redemption can be seen as a secular parable of the kingdom of God; in other words, it is an example of true words and lights in their own right and validity. As we read in his later doctrine of reconciliation: 'We may think of radicalness of the need of redemption or the fullness of what is meant by redemption if it is to meet this need.'[32]

This refers to religious longing for the *totaliter aliter*, which can be found in the world of religion in its radical desire for redemption, especially in the Pure Land teaching of radical grace. The conception of a religious a priori in Schleiermacher or Troeltsch is not strictly rejected, but it is integrated into the universal spectrum of God's reconciliation, which reinforces the meaning of other religions as a radical longing for redemption.

In his interpretation of Amida Buddhism, Barth focuses on human desire for redemption. If Amida Buddhism entails a symptom of grace and truth which originates in Jesus Christ, Barth argues that the Christian Protestant religion of grace is not the true religion, but a religion of grace. For Barth, 'we could quite reasonably say the same of Yodism, and with a rather more blunted sensibility, of the *bhakti* religion' in reference to 'a whole range of religions.'[33] Symptoms or lights of grace and truth as discernable in the world of religions become an extraordinary means of God's communication grounded on God's grace of reconciliation with the world.

Barth and God's Speech Act in Comparative Religions

Although the name Jesus Christ is not conflated with Amida, one can find and recognize the symptom and sign of divine grace within Amida's primal vow and solidarity with those in difficulty. God may speak through Buddhist compassion and solidarity, in which the name Jesus Christ does not refute its soteriological significance and radical desire. The living Word of God refers to the name Jesus Christ in his irregular mode of thought. The clarification of the Word of God in terms of irregular effect should remain central in shaping and characterizing Barth's initiation to comparative theology. Jesus Christ is not the

---

31. CD I/2, p. 342. For more detail on this, see Chung, 'Barth, Comparative Theology, and Multiple Modernities', pp. 159–61.
32. CD IV/3.1, p. 125.
33. CD I/1, p. 343.

principle of division in interreligious exchange, but the central principle in terms of reconciliation.

In Barth's account, *extra muros ecclesiae* (outside the walls of the Church),[34] there still exists the one true Word of God, which makes the other words true,[35] turning them into 'real testimony to the real presence of God on earth.'[36] I have discussed elsewhere how this informs the irregular style of actualism associated with Barth's speech-act theology (CD I/1: § 3).[37] This is summed up in his statement that 'God may speak to us through a pagan or an atheist, and thus give us to understand that the boundary between the Church and the secular world can still take at any time a different course from that which we think we discern.'[38]

For Barth, the truth of revelation, or *Aletheia* is associated with God the *totaliter aliter*, who still is in concealment during the self-revelation. It has little to do with Heidegger's notion of *aletheia* in terms of human ideas, concepts and judgments.[39]

Barth's dialectical theology is of a phenomenological character, and his notion of truth manifestation points to the revealer rather than conflating the revealer of the truth with truth manifestation in Heidegger's sense.

Barth's 'comparative' theology is formulated in the following statement: 'there can be no question, even in the future, of a real parallelism or coincidence between the doctrine and the life of the Christian and non-Christian religions of grace (however consistent). Instead, certain symptomatic distinctions will be visible here and there, in which the true and the essential distinction can always be preserved.'[40]

4. Theology of Religions and Comparative Theology

Enter Paul Knitter's critique of Barth's proclamation model.[41] Knitter calls into question Barth's affirmation of the finality of Jesus Christ, because here, 'salvation through faith is possible only in Jesus Christ.'[42]

---

34. CD IV/3.1, p. 110.
35. CD IV/3.1, p. 112.
36. CD IV/3.1, p. 113.
37. Chung, 'Barth, Comparative Theology, and Multiple Modernities', p. 163.
38. CD I/1, p. 55.
39. CD I/1, p. 270.
40. CD I/1, p. 344.
41. Knitter, *No Other Name?* p. 87.
42. Ibid., p. 91.

Against this, Knitter argues, 'God does offer answers, that there is the authentic revelation, apart from Christ.'[43] What is the authentic revelation of God apart from Christ? Is the revelation in Hinduism the same as the Christian meaning of revelation in Christ? Would Buddhist scholars be content with categorizing Amida Buddha in terms of the Christian concept of revelation?

Certainly, Knitter is aware that Barth has little to do with egotism or so-called 'better than thou attitude' in regard to non-Christian religions. But he has not managed to clarify Barth's theology of reconciliation in his teaching of words and lights through divine speech-act, which incorporates the realm of creation and world of religions into its universal effectiveness.

In Knitter's view, interreligious dialogue should be based on the recognition of the possible truths in all religions.[44] There are the truth claims of various religions, which are grounded in a deeper common ground about the same God.[45] This said, should we say that the Judeo-Christian concept of God is conflated with the Hindu notion of the unity between Brahman and Atman or its polytheistic manifestations? Would a logic of having the same God be accepted on the part of a non-theistic school of Buddhism? Such logic is vulnerable to totalization of other religious ways and their difference into a homogeneous framework. The difference vanishes only for the sameness underlying the double belongingness for a religious individual to pursue. The interreligious dialogue must be characterised by openness in order to fulfil its purpose for the possibility of genuine conversion to other religious systems, in other words, the double belongingness.[46]

In the relativization of Christ, Knitter's hybrid logic leads him to argue that 'without Buddha I could not become a Christian,' shaping himself as a 'Buddhist' Christian.[47] However, who knows whether Buddhists and Christians believe in the same God? Or without Buddha, shouldn't one become a Christian anyway? Knitter introduces the postliberal model, which deals with problem such as "exclusivism," "inclusivism," and "pluralism."'[48]

---

43. Ibid., p. 92.
44. Ibid., p. 208.
45. Ibid., p. 211.
46. Ibid., p. 212.
47. A problem lies in Knitter's own confession that he does not know Pali or Chinese or Tibetan. Knitter, *Without Buddha I Could not be a Christian*, p. xiv.
48. Knitter, *Introducing Theologies of Religions*, pp. 178–91.

The postliberal model is represnented by Clooney's comparative theology. He focuses on rereading the Christian texts after engagement in other religious texts (especially the Uttara Mimamsa Sutras or some particular Advaita commentary), in which he learns something new about God. A constructive side for the Bible and theological system can occur only in the event of juxtaposition with other religious texts through the inclusive textual reading.

A postcomparative theology of religions affirms that salvation takes place through Christ alone. But people of other religious traditions may be saved in their own traditions without Christ. This position is blended with the pluralist theology of religions, because salvation in Christ *alone* comes into tension with salvations in other religions. Furthermore, Hindu texts in their teaching of God are inscribed into rereading and comprehending the biblical narrative. An inclusive textual reading affirms that 'knowledge of Brahman is all that is required for salvation.'[49]

Thus, Clooney calls into question the exclusivism of Barth's theology and revelation, which begins with Jesus Christ.'[50] Barth is imbued with a 'mix of sympathy, keeping Christian self-critique, while having great disregard for other religions'.

Barth and **Bhakti** *Religion*

Clooney finds Barth's assessment of *bhakti* religion to be defective. Barth comprehends the *bhakti* as 'an act of utter surrender and resignation,' which 'can easily be intensified into a personal act of inward inclination and love.'[51] Although the supreme God can have any name in the *bhakti* religion, Barth argues, 'it is the emotion of love itself and as such which redeems man.'[52] The emotion of love enables a human being to take part in the answering love of God, which 'allows [him/her] to be sympathetic and kindly, unselfish, patient and serene.'[53] In the context of the *bhakti* religion, Barth does not see the aspect of forgiveness of sin and the rightcousness of God, which is central in the Protestant doctrine of justification. The justified sinner is a new creation in Jesus Christ.

---

49. Clooney, *Theology after Vedanta*, p. 190.
50. Clooney, *Hindu God, Christian God*, p. 132.
51. CD I/2, p. 341.
52. Ibid.
53. Ibid., p. 342.

In the Srivaisnavas tradition, Ramanuja did not provide a clear and consistent position in dealing with the 'necessary' role of the human self in the attainment of emancipation. In resolving this ambiguity among his followers, Vedanta Desika (1268–1369) in the northern school asserted the need of some human effort; he used an example of the young monkey clinging to its mother, who carries it to deliverance. Rudolf Otto characterizes this position in the term 'synergist'.[54] However, in the other school (under the leadership of Pillai Lokacharya), an emphasis is given to the unqualified superiority and the sole efficacy of divine grace. A type is used concerning the mother cat which carries its kitten by its mouth, without any cooperation. In the extreme form of its doctrine God is portrayed as an enjoyer of evil, because God, in loving the sinner, loves the sin as well.[55]

Informed by Otto's study of Indian *bhakti* religion, Barth argues that a very degenerate form of German Protestant Christianity 'felt that the *bhakti* religions could claim kinship with it.'[56] Against the degenerate form of 'German Christians' in collaboration with National Socialism, Barth chose Japanese Protestantism of Honen and Shinran for the comparative study.

In contrast to Barth, however, Clooney holds that in the Srivaisnavas tradition, there is nuanced theology, in which God is self-revealing in specific ways rather than God in general. Devotion has its own characteristics rather than equated with self-surrender. A Hindu theology of a personal God and divine love and mercy poses a great challenge by showing its similarity with Christian theology.[57]

The ideas of *bhakti* and *prapatti* (surrender) in Ramanuja and the other theistic writers are best understood as similarity with Christianity. '(Prapatti) is thus a direct and independent (adviiraka) means to *moksa*. The only requisite for *prapatti* is the change of heart or contrition [of] the *mumuksu* (the one who desires *moksa*) and his absolute confidence in the saving grace of the *raksaka* (saviour). It is not the possession of merit that is the operative cause of grace or *daya*, but the sense of one's unworthiness and the sinfulness of sin. The Lord is the only way and goal to the *mumuksu*, and *prapatti* is the act of self-surrender to

---

54. Otto, *India's Religion of Grace and Christianity Compared and Contrasted*, p. 56.
55. Kulandran, *Grace in Christianity and Hinduism*, p. 177.
56. CD I/2, p. 342.
57. Clooney's Foreword in *Karl Bath and Comparative Theology*, eds. Martha L. Moore-Keish, et al.

His grace. ...' It implies an intimate relation between the self-gift of the *mumuksu* and the flow of divine mercy of *daya*. Redemption is a justification by faith or *mahiivisviisa*, and not by works, and it is not won by merit as the result of a continuous process. It is the essence of the religion of *prapatti* that the Lord of grace seeks the *prapatpanna* (the one who surrenders) and draws him to Himself.[58]

Despite his limited knowledge of Hindu *bhakti* religion, Barth's criterion in comparison is grounded in the Protestant teaching of justification and grace (forgiveness of sin *extra nos*, divine righteousness, and new creation in Christ). If there is such a type in the *bhakti* tradition, Barth 'should be grateful for the lesson which it so abundantly and evidently teaches,' because 'the Christian religion cannot be the one to which the truth belongs per se.'[59]

Even if Barth could acknowledge a providential disposition in the *bhakti* tradition, Barth would raise some questions: (1) Is *prapatti* (utter human surrender) the basis to salvation or does it come from the divine operative grace? (2) Is it in accordance with 'a supplementary and auxiliary criterion'?[60] The other words and lights must be tested and judged in terms of Scripture, church tradition or doctrine; they would produce a positive effect and bear fruits to the faith community. (3) Is there a struggle for human justice in the name of the glory of God by transforming the oppressive structure in the social organization (caste system)?

For Barth, God the wholly Other is the one who changes completely (*ganz and gar Andernde*);[61] 'The fact that God is ... materially changes, all things and everything in all things.'[62] The name Jesus Christ refers to 'the partisan of the poor.'[63] The Church is fundamentally on the side of the victims of disorder, challenging the social disorder of the status quo.[64]

What characterizes Barth is his theology of speech-act which constitutes the intertextuality between the ecclesiastical sphere and worldly occurrences from the standpoint of God's reconciliation with the world in Christ. It would be controversial and even provocative if one could arrive at meaning through textual juxtaposition only, because the *Homo*

---

58. Srinivasacbari, *The Philosophy of Visintidvaita*, p. 383.
59. CD I/2, p. 342.
60. CD IV/3.1, p. 127–8.
61. KD IV/4, p. 161.
62. CD II/1, p. 258.
63. CD IV/2, p. 180.
64. CD III/4, p. 544.

lector (reading person) is also conditioned by social location and bound to material interests. It cuts across the intratextual reading at the level of mere abstraction, but invites the reader to the horizon of intertextuality between text, society and culture in terms of a symbol of reconciliation, critique, participation and emancipation. Barth emphasizes a prophetic awareness in his political responsibility, economic justice, and solidarity with those on the margin; a disgrace effect of religion is called into question and critically renewed in light of the subject matter of the gospel, the source of the immanent critique. This aspect remains an undercurrent in Barth's contribution to comparative theology and the religious construction of social reality in affirmation of other religious validity.

Barth and Comparative Religions

Barth's theology is structured upon the word of God in an analogical-dialectical frame of reference, along with its irregular horizon, such that his theology takes on a humble attitude and open character for God's speech-act through religious others in an extraordinary and communicative manner. In the discussion of the basic form of humanity (Martin Buber, Feuerbach, and Confucius), Barth argues, 'there are approximations and similarities; in this very fact we may even see a certain confirmation.' 'Even with his natural knowledge of himself the natural man is still in the sphere of divine grace.'[65] Barth particularly affirms the validity of the Jews: 'The Jew, even the unbelieving Jew, so miraculously preserved ... through the many calamities of his history ... is the natural historical monument of the love and faithfulness of God.' The Jew 'as a living commentary on the Old Testament is the only convincing proof of God outside the Bible.'[66]

I have also reported previously on his dialogue with J. Bouman from Lebanon, in which Barth holds, 'in theological appreciation of the situation there [in Lebanon] ... we were but completely in agreement that "a new communication about the relation between the Bible and the Koran is an urgent task for us."'[67] Barth challenges the Church to undertake the confession of guilt in dealing with 'the deplorable role of the Church in the so-called crusades.'[68] In his study of the sixteen Latin texts of Vatican II, Barth appreciates the Church's renewal of the

---

65. CD III/2, p. 277.
66. CD IV/3.2, p. 877.
67. Barth, *Briefe 1961–1968*, p. 504.
68. Barth, *Ad Limina Apostolorum*, p. 37.

relation with other religions, while problematizing the Church's fatal and deplorable role in the Holocaust and crusades.

Barth's interest in world religions (*Nostra Aetate* in the Second Vatican Council) makes it meaningful to appreciate his study plan on 'The general history of religion', in which he takes into account the relation between Christianity and Judaism, the relation between Judaism and Islam and finally, the relation between Buddhism and Hinduism.[69] In Barth's speech-act theology we see that the ontological connection plays a significant role in characterizing the relation between Jesus Christ and all people. This contrasts with Rahner's notion of the 'supernatural existential' linked to God's self-communicative attribute. I have explored this in more depth elsewhere,[70] but the key difference is between the possibility in Rahner's thought for 'anonymous Christianity', and Barth's insistence that Jesus Christ as the royal Representative is 'their Lord and Head as well, whether they have known Him or not, are only provisionally and subjectively outside Him and without Him in their ignorance and unbelief.'[71] Jesus Christ does not make people of other faiths into anonymous Christians nor prospective Christians, but 'they can be claimed as His de jure.'[72]

They may remain co-brothers and sisters who may inherit the kingdom of God through the grace of reconciliation. The Jew or the Buddhist may find their place in the mystery of God's grace in the reconciled world, serving as a medium of analogical or extraordinary witness to the in-breaking kingdom of God. Danger lurks in generalities *(latet periculum in generalibus)*.[73] In his later interview Barth affirms universal dimension of Christ working inside and outside the church. Christ is present even in the life of strangers such as Melchizedek, Cyrus, or even Balaam, heathens, atheists.[74]

But, Barth does not provide any explicit examples of true words and lights; this is in contrast to Zwingli, who had appealed explicitly to pagans having attained their salvation: Hercules, Theseus, Socrates, Cicero and others.[75]

---

69. Klappert, *Versöhnung und Befreiung*, p. 50.
70. Chung, 'Barth, Comparative Theology, and Multiple Modernities', pp. 169–70.
71. CD IV/2, p. 275.
72. CD IV/2, p. 275.
73. CD II/2, p. 48.
74. Barth, *Gespräche IV: 1964–1968*, p. 565.
75. CD IV/3.1, p. 135.

Because of the radical character of such investigation, it is important to keep the freedom of the enquirer intact, when exploring a relationship between Jesus Christ and other words and lights.[76] Barth's comparative theology safeguards him from falling into a grey zone of exclusivism (Kraemer) or relativistic, syncretic configuration, which is discernable in the theology of religions (Knitter).

Constructive Reflection: Barth and Troeltsch

It is necessary, then, to review a modernist interpretation of Barth in reference to Troeltsch. According to Rendtorff, what is crucial in Barth's theology is that it articulates 'the present status of the history of Christianity under the condition of modernity.'[77] The modernist interpretation comes to terms with Troeltsch, who affirmes human autonomy as the principle of European modernity. Such an interpretation makes it possible to examine Barth in terms of the European modernity. What matters is to analyze the extent to which Barth would appropriate the modern problematics such as freedom, subjectivity and autonomy in his theological working through the legacy of enlightenment and modernity.

Nevertheless, it is still important to consider Barth's strong criticism of the Enlightenment: '… a natural self-understanding of man was adopted as the norm of Christian thinking. In the sphere of this understanding the assertion could not, and never can, be made.'[78] Barth's analysis of alienation and injustice in the capitalist society is seen in his appraisal of the reality of lordless powers, which can be an alternative to Weber's surrender to impersonal forces imbued with polytheism of value. Barth is suspicious of what has been brought by rationalization and modernity in terms of disenchantment of the world. A rationally structured society is not clear of idol-faith and reification.

Rationality, according to Barth, is grounded in the relation of covenant between God and humanity and measured to the point of the rationality of reconciliation history. Alienation and reification of human thinking and action lead to comprehensive bureaucratization of human existence.[79] Barth conceptualizes the history of reconciliation in terms

---

76. CD IV/3.1, p. 133.
77. Rendtorf, 'Radikale Autonomie Gottes,' in Trutz Rendtorff, *Theorie des Christentums*, p. 180.
78. CD IV/1, p. 479.
79. CD IV/2, pp. 680–1.

of the history of the prophecy of Jesus Christ, which is in struggle against the domination of the lordless powers. It refers to the fight against the power and principalities of alienation, bureaucracy and reification, which are seen in the pathology of the iron cage as well as under proletarian dictatorship in state socialism. This refers to what Barth seeks in the religious construction of social reality through his theology.

Having said this, Barth can still be called a post-Eurocentric thinker. For him, there is no sphere in the reconciled world which is abandoned by God or withdrawn from God's control. He affirms dangerous modern expressions like the revelation of creation or primal revelation;[80] he contends that the divine work of reconciliation did not negate the work of creation, or deprive it of meaning. Words and lights in the world are accepted 'as free communications of the will of its Lord.'[81] As Barth provocatively writes:

> We recognize [that] the fact that Jesus Christ is the one Word of God does not mean that in the Bible, the Church and the world there are not other words which are quite notable in their way, other lights which are quite clear and other revelations which are quite real. … Nor does it follow from our statement that every word spoken outside the circle of the Bible and the Church is a word of false prophecy and therefore valueless, empty and corrupt, that all the lights which rise and shine in this outer sphere are misleading and all the revelations are necessary untrue.[82]

Christianity as a religion must also be relativized in favour of revelation, which means a crisis even for the religion of revelation.[83] It is relocated in the wider spectrum of reconciliation, which includes godless people and their religions. Barth asserts Christianity as a true religion only in the sense of a justified sinner. This discussion cannot be accepted as a primary polemic against non-Christian religions.[84]

Likewise, Troeltsch conceptualizes the teaching of divine lights. 'There are still other circles of lights, with other sources of light, within the great divine light of the world … there may arise new circles of light

---

80. CD IV/3.1, p. 140.
81. CD IV/3.1, p. 130.
82. CD IV/3.1, p. 97.
83. CD I/2, p. 331.
84. CD I/2, p. 327.

of this sort out of depths of the divine life. The eternal truth of God has its particular historical form for every circle and for every general stance. ... Every epoch stands immediately before God, and we stand immediately before God precisely as gathered together in the circle of light radiating from Jesus.'[85]

If the other lights radiate from God's self-manifestation in Jesus, a European synthesis of normative value culture has to be relativized by this radiating light of God's revelation in Christ. Troeltsch does not regard historical criticism as an end for itself, but as a means to clarify the social cultural condition of Christianity against its absoluteness. For him 'the historical connection of faith is attached all the more to "the religious personalities of Jesus and Paul, of Augustine and Luther."'[86]

In recognizing the other religious ways, Troeltsch's theocentric theology has much in common with Barth, though in their different theological epistemologies and orientations. What is common in them is their comprehension of Christianity against its absoluteness. 'In the world of religions,' Barth holds, 'the Christian religion is in a position of greater danger and defenselessness and impotence than any other religion. It has its justification either in the name of Jesus, or not at all.'[87] Barth's teaching of lights is framed within the divine speech-act in revelation underlying God's reconciliation with the world. It is of an analogical and dialectical character, interpreting the secular realms as parables in witnessing to the kingdom of God. Religious longing for redemption is fully integrated into this direction, as shown in its parallel with Troeltsch.

Troeltsch conceptualizes other circles of lights and sources, and his theological epistemology is based on the transcendence of God, in which his historical critical program is undertaken in the universal history of religion. Religious a priori and analogical construction of divine transcendence are at work in the whole of historical correlation within the universal history of religion. Troeltsch can be incorporated into the theology of reconciliation in which religious a priori finds its significance in religious longing for the *totaliter aliter*.

A constructive reading of Barth and Troeltsch does not eliminate their great difference, but provides a modernist interpretation of Barth in reference to Troeltsch. What differentiates Barth from Troeltsch is finally seen in their respective approaches to theological themes such as

---

85. Troeltsch, 'On the Possibility of a Liberal Christianity (1910),' in *Religion in History*, p. 350.
86. Troeltsch, 'Faith and History (1910),' ibid., p. 142.
87. CD I/2, p. 356.

confessional doctrine, historical critical method, biblical hermeneutical enquiry, and the relation between revelation and religion. But these two scholars are the ones who pursued a post-Eurocentric configuration of comparative theology in engagement with the world of religions in its universal history.

Concluding Remarks

This study of Barth's views on non-Christian religions and comparative theology has elaborated his insight into the elective affinity between religious ideas and material interests, while taking into account the religious construction of reality by semantic retrieval of his speech-act theology, in its irregular mode and in light of a theological symbol of reconciliation. Other religious ways are appreciated as the extraordinary ways of communication of God's mystery. His notion of God the *totaliter aliter* is central in his theology of revelation in a dialectical and analogical manner, in which he advances the relevance between God, the Church and the world.

In the post-Eurocentric character of Barth's theology, his speech-act theology contributes to a new project of comparative theology, which can be seen by examining his study of Amida Buddhism. Scrutiny of several critics (Berger, Knitter, and Clooney) shows how his work relates to Troeltsch.

It is significant to see how Barth's theology of the word is of comprehensive character, because it enriches source of epistemology, dialectical method, religions, political theology, and analogical mode of thinking, in his confrontation with the theological tradition of neo-Protestantism. His theology has been reinterpreted in a phenomenological frame of reference, elaborating the semantic realm of culture and religion through the divine speech act, which underwrites the constructive theology of comparative religions. Barth has little time for an acultural theory of modernity, which is beset by the iron cage of hubris and its pathology grounded in unlimited confidence on human reason. This aspect of modernity is undertaken in Weber's sociology of capitalist spirit and Protestant ethics.[88]

However, we don't need to reduce the modern project to one single pakage of Enlightenment. In contrast, it is important to conceptualize a concept of multiple modernities with postcolonial significance. There are many resources in culture and religions, which help to explore

---

88. Taylor, 'Two Theories of Modernities,' in Gaonkar, ed. *Alternative Modernities*, p. 174.

life-world as the source of immanent critique for a new practice and innovation.[89]

Despite his critique of Western modernity, Barth may appreciate traditional sources of culture, morality and other religious achievements in light of God's grace of reconciliation. What is decisive in Barth is to develop a theological project in emphasizing problematics such as sociality, solidarity and co-humanity in the discussion of comparative religions, since these are social critical categories in cutting across limitations of Western bourgeois subjectivity and its neo-Protestant theology. Barth transcends the asocial and ahistorical brutality of subjectivity and consciousness of modernity through God, who loves in freedom as the wholly other and changing.[90]

This perspective helps to develop Barth's thought form for comparative theology through sociological enquiry into multiple modernities. Barth's theology, seen in his speech act perspective, initiates a paradigm shift in radicalizing God as the *totaliter aliter* in Christ along with social critical consciousness and political significance.

In effect, theology and religion don't occur in a vacuum. Comparative theology focuses on how the texts have been historically tied to material interests and power relations, and it explicates the way the religious discourse would contribute to the construct of social reality. It is a project of theological audacity to locate Barth within a sociological hermeneutical framework, in which other religions and cultures are conceptualized as the semantic realm, which can be an extraordinary form of divine communication; it should be articulated in dealing with the elective affinity between religious discourse and material interests for a theological construction of social reality by taking issue with symbolic power, domination, and violence built in by lordless powers.

---

89. Ibid., pp. 183–4.
90. Schellong, *Bürgertum und christliche Religion*, p. 109.

Chapter 5

Islam: Religious Discourse, Power and Modernity

A religious construction of reality is of special significance in the discussion of Islam, its rational thinking, and its relation to modernity. This chapter deals with a historical, comparative analysis of religious discourse and types of political dominion in the context of Islam. The research is descriptive, historical and analytical in discussing Islamic discourse and its construction of social, political and cultural reality. It begins with Samir Amin's tributary theory and his historical, materialist interpretation of Islam and modernity. After clarification of Amin's theory, it focuses on exploring Islam and its Renaissance, *Nahda*, in the social, cultural and political context.

It then draws attention to the source of Islam, religious discourse, and the historical development of political power. It facilitates an endeavour to distinguish the Mecca model from the Medina model in order to cut across debate between political Islam and secularism. In a hermeneutical mode of enquiry, the Meccan model is elaborated as the source of immanent critique in relating the historical development of Islam in reference to modernity and civil society.

Islam is appreciated next in its symbiosis with Jewish culture and Christianity, as involved in its civilization in Baghdad and Spain. The Islamic contribution in this regard becomes a source of further development in terms of rational thinking, philosophy and theology.

Next the chapter focuses on Weber's comparative study of religious belief in predestination, delving into comparative theological reflection of Islamic predestination, Weber's sociology of the Calvinist position, and Calvin's own idea of predestination. A comparative theology entails a confessional character, which is enriched by semantic retrieval, improving on the limitations of the Puritan position through reading Calvin as the source of the immanent critique. Finally, the chapter demonstrates a constructive potential regarding Islamic Protestantism and reform movement, appreciating the Islamic source underlying ethical universalism, religious humanism, democracy, and civil society. The Excursus provides a brief reflection of Islam as a living faith inheriting from the axial religions.

1. Eurocentrism and Islam

In the sixteenth century the Islamic empires dominated sea trade in the Mediterranean and the Indian Ocean, flourishing culturally. In 1453 Islam accomplished the downfall of Christian Constantinople, but Spain's *Reconquista* (beginning in 718) was completed with the capture of Muslim Granada in 1492. This led to the merciless expulsion of all Muslims and non-converted Jews. The same year of 1492 saw the voyage on which Christopher Columbus (1451–1506) made the 'discovery' of the New World of the Americas. It resulted in the European colonization of America including the spreading of Christianity. Within a few decades, European powers became dominant in the field of science, technology, commerce and culture, leading to the European claim to a monopoly on modernity.

To unveil a myth of Eurocentrism over and against Islamic civilization, Samir Amin conceptualizes a tributary world system divided into core and peripheral areas; these are arranged from 500 BCE through Hellenism, the birth of Christianity, and finally the birth of Islam to 1500 CE. All tributary cultures are based on the pre-eminence of metaphysical and religious aspiration in the search for absolute truth.[1] In fact, Amin runs counter to the Marxist periodization of world history (Asiatic, slavery, feudalism, capitalism, socialism) in terms of the tributary (pre-capitalist) world system. In the course of history,, tributary ideology was already present in the accomplishments of ancient Egypt. Hellenistic, Eastern Christian, Islamic, and Western Christian cultures constituted the ideologies of the tributary mode of production.[2]

Given this economic system, it is out of the question to establish any opposition between Greek thought and 'Oriental' thought, because

---

1. Amin, *Eurocentrism*, p. 100.
2. Ibid., p. 111.

the latter does not exclude Greece. 'The opposition Greece = the West / Egypt, Mesopotamia, Persia = the East is itself a later artificial construct of Eurocentrism.'[3] Therefore, Edward Said's critique of Orientalism is inadequate, because he has not managed to propose another system of explanation. Said remains caught in his provincialism, leading to his analysis being 'inverted Orientalism.'[4]

In Amin's view, capitalism implies a more advanced stage of civilization rather than reduced to being a mode of production in a Marxist sense. Therefore, the social relations of capitalism are inseparably connected with other elements of modernity and its civilization.[5] Europe completely broke with the characteristic forms of tributary power that it had in common with the Muslim world, China and India. Major steps mark the history of this rupture: the Renaissance, the Enlightenment, the French Revolution, and the Industrial Revolution. This rupture is expressed by the claim that human beings make their own history, individually and collectively. This claim makes it possible to propose democracy and implies a separation between religion and political power: in other words, secularism.[6]

Renaissance, Modernity, and the World System

To reveal the global character of Eurocentrism, Amin suggests that modernity arising in Europe began in the Renaissance (covering the period between the fourteenth and seventeenth centuries), whose very first traces are found in Italy, but which came to cover much of Europe. Perhaps it would mark the transition from the Middle Ages to the modern age.[7]

The term 'Renaissance' is the product of an ideological construction that made a claim for Greco-Roman antiquity, and that was familiar with the principle of modernity. European intellectuals whose ideas were founded upon modernity and humanism (especially Lorenzo Valla and Desiderius Erasmus) claimed to go back to its past for the rediscovery of classical Greek philosophy, and thus to return to the sources

---

3. Ibid., pp. 112–3.
4. Ibid., p. 176.
5. Amin, 'The Implosion of Global Capitalism: The Challenge for the Radical Left,' 3. http://andreasbieler.net/wp-content/workshop/Amin20-20implosion20 and20 audacity 20E 20rev 20final20(2).pdf.
6. Amin, *Eurocentrism,* p. 65.
7. Ibid., p. 152.

(hence, the Renaissance); this humanist movement also influenced the breakthrough of the Reformation. European modernity was oriented forwards, though it was also in keeping with the Renaissance as oriented backward to Greco-Roman antiquity.[8]

The Renaissance was in some sense a precursor to the period of the Enlightenment in the seventeenth and eighteenth centuries. After the fall of Constantinople in 1453 to the Ottomans, many eastern scholars fled to Italy, introducing important books and manuscripts and a tradition of Greek scholarship. It is no coincidence that 1492 saw both the 'discovery' of the New World and the development of the Renaissance. This perspective articulates an Eastern influence upon the Western Renaissance and Christian development.

Even as early as the thirteenth to the fourteenth century, the market began to conquer in all spheres of life, in domestic as well as global connection. It drove the privatization of land by subjugating agriculture to the mercantile coordination of labour (foreshadowing the enclosures in Britain that took hold during fifteenth and sixteenth centuries).[9] From the late Middle Ages, European cities were the seedbeds of political capitalism in terms of the fusion between state and capital. The foundations of high finance in the modern, capitalist form were a Florentine invention 'during the trade expansion of the late thirteenth and early fourteenth centuries.'[10] In the late thirteenth century, Renaissance began as a cultural movement in Florence, Italy, especially with the writings of Dante Alighieri (1265–1321). With the formation of a European division of labour after 1450, capitalism found firm roots in the world economy. Those in north-west Europe successfully established themselves as the core states in relation to Spain and the northern Italian city-states as semi-peripheral, and north-eastern Europe and Iberian America as the periphery.[11] This perspective argues against an assumption in which the capitalist world system shifts its centre from the Mediterranean region toward the shores of the Atlantic in the aftermath of the Renaissance. Rather, the new European culture reconstructs itself much earlier, around a mythic view of a centre/periphery system, which functions as the foundation for Eurocentrism.[12]

---

8. Küng, *Islam*, pp. 406, 408.
9. Duchrow and Hinkelammert, *Transcending Greedy Money*, p. 16.
10. Arrighi, *The Long Twentieth Century*, pp. 11, 96.
11. Wallerstein, 'The Rise and Future Demise of the World Capitalist System,' in *The Essential Wallerstein*, pp. 87, 93.
12. Amin, *Eurocentrism*, p. 103.

However, Eurocentrism is many-faceted, rather than its origin being reducible to the Renaissance. It requires multiple explanations in critical analysis of European achievements, interstate competition, cultural civilization and Christianity in the sixteenth century to the nineteenth century. Certainly, the Renaissance had brought about the twofold radical transformation, which underlined the modern world. The first refers to the crystallization of capitalist society in Europe, while the second signifies the European conquest of the world.[13]

On the other hand, Islamic contributions to the European Renaissance cannot be denied. Its advent can be traced back to the translation of the works of Greek philosophers in Baghdad in the period from 750 to 850 under the rule of Abbasid caliphate. Cordoba, the capital of the caliphate in Spain, was the jewel of the earth in the tenth and eleventh century in terms of economic flourishing and cultural and intellectual aspects.[14] According to Marshall Hodgson, the term 'Islamdom', analogous to Christendom, is in one sense 'the society in which the Muslims and their faith are recognized as prevalent and socially dominant.' In other words, it implies 'a society in which non-Muslims have always formed an integral, if subordinate, element.'[15]

In sum, the Islamic world could hardly be thought of as assuming a subordinate role during this period of rejuvination, even up to 1869. However, after 1869, as the new Suez Canal was opened to navigation. European politicians, journalists and scientists began to perceive their power in drawing a radical line, with Europe as the bulwark of modern civilization over against the rest of the world (including the Islamic countries). Insofar as the year 1869 was a turning point in Europe-Islam relations, Oriental countries were to be judged exclusively by Eurocentric position within the structure of the imperial powers and colonialist discourse.[16]

Islam and its Renaissance, Nahda

Another key turning point in the relation between Europe/Christendom and 'Islamdom' was the French Revolution. This was not an isolated event, but set a precedent for the modern world system as a whole. Napoleon Bonaparte set out in 1798 to conquer Egypt, penetrating the

---

13. Ibid., p. 151.
14. Ibid., 376.
15. Hodgson, *The Venture of Islam*, 58.
16. Schulze, *A Modern History of the Islamic World*,15.

Muslim heartland both militarily and ideologically with the ideas of the French Revolution. After the Napoleonic wars (ending in 1815), the Islamic countries were also confronted with a new structure of trade, providing only raw materials for the European factories. They had become dependent on the rapidly industrialising European metropolis.

Muhammad Ali of Egypt and Sudan was the Albanian Ottoman governor, who was the real ruler of Egypt from 1805 to 1848. He sent a commission to Paris in 1826 in order to learn about scientific and technical progress and to introduce the cultural and intellectual achievements of France to Egypt. Rifaah at-Tahtawi (1801–73), the leader of this commission, is regarded as the harbinger of the Arab Renaissance. At-Tahtawi, after a five-year stay in France, wrote 'Travel Diary of my Stay in Paris,' which included a translation of the French Constitution of 1814. The Arabs have called their Renaissance the *Nahda*, i.e. rebirth. In imitation of the European phenomenon, a cultural renaissance began in the late nineteenth and early twentieth centuries in Egypt, Syria, and later Lebanon and others. In the course of history it was developed in terms of Pan-Arabism, which contrasts with the centuries of alien Ottoman rule and European colonialism.

The *Nahda* embraced Western society, holding that reforms should be undertaken in accordance with the values of Islamic culture. This combination of self-confident culture with open-minded modernism remains crucial in defining the creed of al-*Nahda*. Europe was admired, yet rejected, because of the arrogance of its conquest.

The *Nahda* enclosed itself in religious discourse rather than keeping its distance from it. Jamal ad-Din al-Afghani himself (1839–97) deserves attention. He was born and brought up in Iran, and his position is defined as standing between the traditionalists in returning to the Qur'an, the model of Medina, and the secularists in favour of European education. He favored representative rule against the authoritarian monarchies. Al-Afghani, a so-called 'Islamic Martin Luther,' acknowledged that European progress was made possible only through the Reformation. He stirred up Muslim nationalism and pan-Islamism for freedom, away from colonial pressure. He proposed an international union of all Muslim people for commitment to modernization, while fighting against traditional Islamic political institutions.[17]

However, in Amin's view, the *Nahda* did not fully grasp the meaning of secularism, the separation between the religious and the political, which is a requirement for modernity. The *Nahda* did not understand

---

17. Küng, *Islam*, p. 183.

the meaning of democracy as the right to break with tradition. The *Nahda* did not understand that modernity also gives rise to women's aspirations for liberation. Rather it reduced the meaning of modernity to technical progress.[18] Nevertheless, the *Nahda* can be comprehended as the significant moment in Islamic critical interaction with Western modernity and colonialism. The Islamic Renaissance can be seen as a historical bridge with Islamic civilization in its earlier period in Baghdad and Spain. This cultural enquiry can be developed by seeing the *Nahda* in terms of its Islamic source; the history of civilization may play a significant role in protecting the potential of Islamic source for democracy, civil society, and its own path to modernity.

2. Religious Discourse and its Construction of Power

In the study of religious discourse and power relations in Islam, it is important to investigate the religious source as an inspiration for the immanent critique in the historical development of Islam. A type of political dominion cannot be sufficiently comprehended in separation from the formation of religious discourse.

Muhammad was born around the year 579 into one of the less prosperous clans of the Quraysh tribe, in Mecca, a city in modern day Saudi Arabia; he received revelation from Allah at about the age of forty. At about age twenty, he had begun working as a merchant, and he is said to have made long journeys into Syria, where he supposedly met the Christian monk Bahira; the latter prophesied Muhammad's future greatness.[19] Later, Muhammad worked as a merchant for a rich widow, Khadijah, and married her; her wealth and status elevated his position in Meccan society. When he was about forty years old, an angel appeared to him and said:

> Recite in the name of your Lord who created – created man from clots of blood.
> Recite! Your Lord is the most Bountiful One, who by the pen taught man what he did not know (Q 96:1-5).[20]

Muhammad's monotheism came into conflict with polytheistic Mecca, in which the Kaaba, a shrine, was associated with numerous

---

18. Amin, *Eurocentrism*, p. 67.
19. Ayoub, *Islam*, p. 18.
20. *The Koran*, trans. Dawood.

gods. In the time of Muhammad the Kaaba was still full of images and statues of gods. In 619 the controversy reached a critical stage. Around 620 a group of six men from Yathrib were persuaded by Muhammad's revelation and became his steadfast companions. The next year, 622, an agreement was established between Muhammad and a group of converts in Yathrib/Medina. But in the same year Muhammad and his followers were forced to leave Mecca.

From 610 to 622 Muhammad had a ministry in Mecca, working as a teacher and a prophet of Allah. After being forced out, Muhammad became the ruler of Medina through tribal political alliances and ruled it from 622 until his death in 632. Muhammad's emigration from Mecca to Medina is called the *hijrah* in Arabic and hegira in English, marking the beginning of a new polity. 622 CE marks the official beginning of Islamic history and the beginning of the Muslim calendar. Living in Medina for ten years, Muhammad adopted a number of Jewish practices, including Yom Kippur (the Day of Atonement) and faced Jerusalem during the prayers. However, the Jews rejected Muhammad's claim as a prophet and the Qur'an as a sacred book. The fast of Yom Kippur was dropped in favour of the fast of Ramadan, the ninth month in the Muslim calendar. The *qibla* (direction of prayers) was changed from Jerusalem to the Kaaba in Mecca.[21]

His triumph over Mecca in the year 630 is marked by forgiveness of all his enemies, who, in turn, embraced Islam. Muhammad with his religious and ethical standards organized Islamic society in this city. He worked through persuasion rather than exercising political power. In the first Meccan period Muhammad developed his religion in pietistic urban conventicles in withdrawal from the world. He lived as a teacher and prophet and followed disciplines of prayer, fasting, and worship. In Medina, he was the political ruler and the military commander. In subsequent developments in Medina and in the unfolding of the early Islamic communities, the Medinian model of power and dominion continued to carry itself out in the course of Islamic history by means of conquest and subjugation of non-Muslims. The transition from Mecca to Medina represents a transition from peaceful rule by the underprivileged to power and dominion exercised from above. In fact, Muhammad's preaching in Mecca implies the abolition of slavery and all forms of social oppression, in particular those of which women are the victims. However, Muhammad's preaching which occurred in the setting of Medina was quite different; there the Prophet makes an

---

21. Ayoub, *Islam*, p. 24.

alliance with the ruling classes who rallied to Islam. The Meccan period of revelation had been undermined.[22]

However, in Quranic sources the more tolerant approach is affirmed: 'We have bestowed [honoured] blessings on Adam's children and guided them by land and sea. We have provided them with wholesome things and exhaled them above many of Our creatures' (17:70). Because there is no compulsion of religion (2:256), non-Muslims have freedom and rights to practise their religions. The modern Arabic term for human dignity or rights is derived from the verb 'honoured.' Human beings are defined to serve as God's representative on earth (*khalifa*) (2:30), because they are offered God's trust (*amna*) (33:72).

Islamic Faith and the Meccan Model

Given the sources of Islamic faith, it is indispensable to keep the Five Pillars of Islam. The first rule is to testify: 'There is no god but God and Muhammad is His messenger.' The second is to worship God five times a day, praying in the direction of Mecca. The first worshipper (muezzin) was a black Abyssinian slave (known as Bilal), who was tortured by Muhammad's enemy, but rescued by Abu Bakr, the Prophet's companion. Then Bilal converted and lived in Medina, becoming one of the Prophet's close companions. This story shows that Islam accepted people of all races from the outset. The third rule is to abstain from food and drink (also smoking and sex) between sunrise and sunset during the month of Ramadan, the ninth month in the Muslim calendar. The fourth is to give alms to the poor as charity every year, to establish schools, hospitals, libraries and mosques. One of the most distinguished charitable activities established a public drinking fountain in medieval times, which distributed water freely to all passers-by.

The Muslim's *zakat* (almsgiving, or a tax for the needy) may characterize Islam as the religion of orthopraxis together with belief, good deeds, and prayer. 'Those who have faith and do good works, attend to their prayers and render the alms levy, will be rewarded from their Lord and will have nothing to fear or to regret' (Q 2:277). An Islamic framework for economic development is driven by favouring the use of material resources for the public and collective welfare. This principle seeks to eradicate poverty as its primary objective, emphasizing redistributive justice; it challenges all forms of inequality

---

22. Nasr, *Islam*, p. 185.

and exploitation. This Islamic principle encourages solidarity and collaboration in all phases of life.²³

The fifth rule is to undertake a pilgrimage to Mecca at least once in one's lifetime, which is connected with the prophet Ibrahim (the biblical Abraham) and centres on the Kaaba.²⁴

The Prophet Muhammad undoubtedly enjoyed considerable authority. This refers to his charismatic power rather than the power of a warrior religion. Muhammad accepted the full legitimacy of all the authorities that guaranteed the reproduction of the social system. The authorities that managed the societies in question can never be reduced to religious leaders. These religious leaders (the *ulama* among Muslims) had the responsibility to see that the 'true religion' was respected. A sociological thesis of God and society can be comprehended in the sense that God did speak through the prophet Muhammad. An Islamic society cannot be separated from their faithfulness to the divine will of Allah.²⁵

Muhammad sought to bring all people together into one single monotheistic community (*ummah*) for the service of the one God in terms of teachings and practices. The special significance of the *ummah* has nothing to do with race or nation: 'You are the noblest community ever raised up for mankind. You enjoin justice and forbid evil. You believe in God' (Q 3:110). In chapter 112 of the Qur'an one of the first verses was assumed to have been revealed in the early Meccan period. 'Say: "God is One, the Eternal God. He begot none, nor was He begotten. None is equal to Him."'

The Meccan model shows that the Prophet was dependent only upon the power of persuasion and preaching the faith in the one compassionate God. In distinguishing between the Meccan model and the Medinian model, David Marshall focuses on the Meccan stage of Muhammad's life and the corresponding Meccan passages of the Qur'an. The Medinian paradigm, Marshall holds, necessarily involves and emphasizes Muslims in power over non-Muslims; it shares and shapes its model in God's triumph over them.²⁶

---

23. Duchrow and Hinkelammert, *Transcending Greedy Money*, pp. 88–9. See further Knitter and Muzaffar, eds. *Subverting Greed*.
24. Bloom and Blair, *Islam*, pp. 35–8.
25. Durkheim, *The Elementary Forms of Religious Life*, p. 208.
26. Marshall, *God, Muhammad and the Unbelievers*, p. 195.

Authority in Conflict and Political Development

However, ambiguities arose place about the nature of authority during the years of the Medina caliphates (so-called 'rightly-guided' caliphs, Abu Bakr, Umar, Uthman, and Ali); the ambiguities were quickly cleared up by the victory of the Umayyads in the conquest of the area that now makes up Syria, Egypt, Iraq and Iran.

From the very beginning there was a faction who felt that Ali, the Prophet's cousin and son-in-law, was qualified to serve as his successor. Ali's supporters maintained that Muhammad himself chose Ali as his successor, and they cited prophetic traditions (Hadith) to back up this claim. This undergirds the genealogical-personal principle for Shiites, the spiritual descendents of Ali. In 661 Ali was attacked at the door of a mosque in Kufa with a poisoned sword and died a painful death. By virtue of his marriage to Muhammad's daughter Fatima, his followers believed that his son would also keep authority within the Prophet's line. In the year 680 Ali's son Husayn and his supporters were killed by Umayyad forces. He was on his way to Damascus to reclaim the caliphate. Husayn's martyrdom left an indelible mark on Shiite Islam. From its outset, the Shiite community was led by a series of rulers known as imams, who all traced their lineage back to Ali. In the community of the Shiites, an eschatological faith in the twelfth imam finds its culmination, in which the twelfth imam went into hiding in 940 and will reappear on the Day of Judgment. This eschatological belief is characterized as Twelver Shiism, and it constitutes the largest group of Shiites in modern Iran.[27]

Others were resistant to this idea and ultimately took control of the caliphate and established the Umayyad dynasty. This is the Sunni branch of Islam, constituting the overwhelming majority group within the religion today.[28] This Islamic Arab Empire was founded by the governor of Syria, Muawiyyah from the Umayyah clan, who revolted against the fourth caliph Ali. Damascus, the Syrian cultural city, became the political centre of a new Arab dynasty in the Umayyad Period (661–750). The Sunnah, defined as a path or a manner of life, was collected in order to promote a faith in the verbally transmitted record of the Prophet's teachings, deeds and sayings, while including various reports about Muhammad's companions. The Qur'an (a direct message from Allah) and the Sunnah became the two primary sources of Islamic

---

27. Bloom and Blair, *Islam*, p. 52.
28. Ibid., p. 53.

theology and law. The Hadith (report or tradition) includes authoritative statements about ritual, moral and religious concerns about which the Qur'an has no statements.

After the death of Muhammad, the Qur'an in its final official version was taken up by Othman (the third caliph, 644–55). The Meccan passages were delivered in Mecca before 622, while the Medina passages belong to Muhammad's activity in Medina (622–32). In the ninth century the great collections of Hadith came into being as authored by al-Bukhari (d 870), then five further canonical Hadith followed. It became the second source of Islamic jurisprudence. Sharia (the Islamic law) derived from religious precepts, particularly from the Qur'an and the Hadith. In the Sunni world, Hadith refers exclusively to a saying of the Prophet, whereas in the Shiite tradition 'a Prophetic saying' is distinguished from 'a saying of one of the Imams.'[29]

Religious, Virtuous and Social Organization

During the period of the Umayyah (661–750) the scholars of the Qur'an, the Hadith and the law, and theologians, had gained public recognition with an autonomous authority in dealing with religious matters. Thus in the *ulama* (from *ulema*, a learned man) both theologians and legal scholars formed law schools which were supported by patrons and adherents rather than the state. They sought to avoid challenges to the authority of the caliph in matters pertaining to political affairs. Muslim civilization would be a civilization of *fiqh* (the Arabic term for theological and legal science). The religious discourse cannot merely be explained by military coercion or national 'warrior religion.' The religious leaders like the *ulama* played a substantial part in shaping and influencing everyday life. In consideration of the influential role of the leaders, Islam is defined as a religion of power, having little to do with a warrior religion tainted with violence and plundering.[30]

Considering Islam as a religion of power, a type of *ulama* demonstrates legal rational authority in search of legitimacy. Islamic sources entail modern, political associations through legal authority. This legitimation constitutes the rules, orders, or commands as rationally established by enactment, by agreement or by imposition in which they are given in the name of the impersonal norm and authority. As formalist juristic rationalism gains in prominence, the ideal type of domination is the

---

29. Nasr, *Islam*, p. 56.
30. Ayoub, *Islam*, p. 228.

bureaucratic rule as the purest one. Religious scholars (*ulama*), together with the Sufis, played a substantial role in Islamization in the Middle East, but capable of transforming its society and the underlying Islamic civilization. The Sufis (mystically inclined spiritual adepts) influenced the masses of the population by their sectarian association. Both religious scholars and the Sufis 'attempted to insinuate Islamic values and identities into an already complex civilization and to reshape that civilization in accord with their own ethos and interests.'[31] The caliphs sought to transform the existing imperial institutions in accordance with the idea of Islamic states. Political leaders attempted to create political structures in projection of religious ideals throughout newly occupied territories. Sociologically expressed, three realms – the community of *ulama*, the Sufi orders, and the pious endowments (*waqfs*) – constituted a public sphere of autonomy in its initial stage, which could promote a measure of diverse opinions within Islamic societies.[32]

However, three elements require a historical analysis with their distinctive development along with the political type of power and domination. Unlike Weber's evaluation of Islam as a warrior religion,[33] an *ulama* type of legal authority plays a major role pertinent to the social and economic structure in the context of Islam. All imperial types of domination are represented in a combination of several such types or in transition, such as in an expression like patrimonial bureaucracy. This perspective takes issue with Weber's type of Islamic rule simply as patrimonialism or Sultanism, in which all of the subjects are directly connected to a system of rulership; the ruler personally pays his subordinates.[34] Nonetheless, Weber's theory of patrimonial bureaucracies may find some support and evidence in recent historical research which deals with the institutionalization of rulership under the Mughals of India.[35] Stratification by status group was most decisive in Islam, as can be seen in the Islamic *ulama* type of legal rational discourse; it characterizes Islamic society in terms of a civilization of *fiqh*.

Sociologically expressed, the pious and learned scholars (*ulama*) developed religious activities by cultivating Sharia-mindedness as the

---

31. *Max Weber and Islam*, eds. Huff and Schluchter, p. 5.
32. Ibid.
33. Weber, *The Sociology of Religion*, p. 88.
34. *Max Weber and Islam*, eds. Huff and Schluchter, p. 32.
35. Turner, 'Revisiting Weber and Islam,' *The British Journal of Sociology 2010*, p. 162. https://www.onlinelibrary.wiley.com/doi/pdf/10.1111/j.1468-4446.2009.01285.x.

major religious piety in Islam; it would sometimes be in a different direction from the consequences of bureaucratic state power. Sharia-mindedness requires discipline to produce a special type of personality, thus Sharia-consciousness involves a technology of self-understanding. Especially in modern reformist Islam, a bio-political enquiry draws attention to the subjugated body of women and to gender differences, as well as the role of women in the transmission of religious piety from generation to generation.[36]

However, in the course of time, a universal Islamic state came to be organized in accordance with the Medina model, which finds its embodiment later in the Muslim Brotherhood in the Arabic-Islamic world by means of political and military authority. In imitation of the Medina phase, Abul Ala Mawdudi (1903–79) sought to bring the whole of South Asia or the whole world under Islamic authority and also that of Sharia.[37]

Islamic Traditionalism and Mamluk Model

In the thirteenth century, the Turkic Mamluks, who were originally military slaves, seized power in Egypt and Syria. In 1260 they established a rule in the Middle East that lasted for over two centuries (1250–1517). There were military slaves recruited to serve caliphates during the Umayyad dynasty (661–750), then this military slave system appeared in the Mamluk ruling system, in which former slaves became leaders, usurping political power and taking control in Egypt.[38]

The Mamluk system began in the era of Saladin (1137/8–93), who was Kurdish and Sunni. In his greatest triumph over the European Crusaders in 1187, he became the liberator of the occupied territory by enabling the Islamic reconquest of Jerusalem and other Holy Land cities in the Near East. Subsequently, the expanding power of the Ottomans in the Seljuk tradition had conquered Constantinople in 1453, and they were both conquerors and colonizers of Byzantine Anatolia (today the Asian portion of Turkey). The Ottoman Empire was most exclusively engaged in military conquests. It produced and accumulated wealth derived from local and regional production, trade and commercialization; it became more urbanized and wealthier than Europe. Mamluk traders from Egypt and Syria were the first obstacle to the Ottoman Empire in

---

36. Ibid., p. 164.
37. Troll, *Dialogue and Difference*, p. 113.
38. *Max Weber and Islam,* eds., Huff and Schluchter, p. 6.

its South Asian trade.³⁹ Under the established dynasty of sultans, Sultan Selim I (1512–20), the real founder of the Ottoman Empire (1281–1924), defeated the Mamluk Empire in Egypt and Syria.⁴⁰

It is not surprising that contemporary populist and nationalist authorities always evoke Saladin with respectful admiration, asserting an Islamic identity. Ethnic nationality and 'political Islam' would lead to collective identity, tending to downgrade the Qur'an and Muhammed's life as an example. However, the Mamluk model of administration and social reproduction has been called into question through Muhammad Ali (1805–48). In Napoleon Bonaparte's expedition to Egypt and after the brief occupation of it, Muhammad Ali had been nominated governor general and came to power. Unlike the Ottoman sultans, he boldly shaped Egyptian society based on European law and economic practices and sought independence from the Ottoman Empire. At the climax of European modernity in the nineteenth century, the so-called Pan-Islamic movement took the initiative in calling for the alliance of all Islamic peoples, in distinction from Pan-Arabism, which is grounded in the glorious period of the Arab Empire under the Umayyad Caliphate.⁴¹

Internal Conflict: Political Islam and Secularism

Democratic openings took place and culminated with the 1919 revolution in Egypt against the British occupation of Egypt and Sudan. Arab socialism developed in Egypt, and King Farouk was overthrown by the Revolutionary Council headed by General A.M. Nagib, who was then succeeded by Gamal Abdel Nasser (1918–70). However, opposition came from the Muslim Brotherhood spread across the Middle East. This movement was founded in 1928 by Hasan al-Banna (1906–49), a pupil of Rashid Rita, four years after the abolition of the caliphate by the Ottoman Empire. It has been known as political Islam, or Islamism, and has sought to re-Islamize Egypt. In practice, this entails a return to more devout religious obedience, a programme of mass education, and social and economic reform. In its initial stage the principle of the Muslim Brotherhood was non-violent and legalist, working within the framework of the law. They were opposed to extremist Zionist groups.⁴² However, a more radical 'political Islam' was formed by Sayyid Qutb

---

39. Frank, *ReOrient*, pp. 79–80.
40. Nasr, *Islam*, p. 174.
41. Küng, *Islam*, p. 238.
42. Rogan, *The Arabs, a History*, pp. 248–50.

(1906–66) within the Brotherhood, which was considered to be modern Islamic extremism. A former member of the Brotherhood, Sayyid Qutb, began to suppress the community of the Brotherhood, executing several of its important leaders. In 1966, he was executed for plotting the assassination of Gamal Abdel Nasser. The political Islam founded upon the initial Islamization has filled a void of depoliticization that Nasserism violently created in suppressing the moderately liberal democratic position, as well as the communist popular movement.[43]

In the conflict between the Muslim Brotherhood and the regime, the former advanced only a single demand: the application of Sharia law. Sharia offers no method for organizing the government and public administration that is capable of meeting the requirements of the modern world. In this respect, Sharia is indifferent to democracy, and it has never called into question the autocratic forms of power.[44] Nonetheless, Tariq Ramadan argues that Sharia can be seen in a broader context and corresponds to higher goals of humankind. It is not a timeless legal code, but a summons to social justice and respect of the rights of education, housing, employment and well-being.[45] Furthermore, he considers that the Brotherhood incorporates an anti-colonial resistance, particularly in the form of an agrarian reform movement in southern Egypt, and the critique of capitalism.[46]

Taking these ideas together, Abdelwahab Meddeb, the Tunisian Muslim scholar at the University of Paris X-Nanterre, provided a diagnosis of *intégrisme* for 'the sickness of Islam,' like intolerance as the sickness of Catholicism. The word integralism preserves the root *integer*, intact in the integral interpretation of the Qur'an and Sunnah. This is bound up with anti-Western resentment. This integralism can be seen in the twentieth century in political Islam such as that of Rashid Rida (1865–1935; the leader of the early Salafi movement), Hasan al-Banna, Abu A la al-Mawdudi and Sayyid Qutb.[47]

In stark contrast to the situation in Egypt, in the 1920s Turkey saw the imposition of secularism by Mustafa Kemal Atatürk, and a single party (the Republican People's Party) was created in 1924. Although it was inspired by the French enlightenment model, the historical experience of secularism in Turkey has little to do with the European

---

43. Amin, *Eurocentrism*, p. 73.
44. Ibid., p. 74.
45. Ramadan, *Islam and the Arab Awakening*, p. 114.
46. Ibid., p. 101.
47. Küng, *Islam*, p. 392.

or American experience of secularization. A reliable combination of religious freedom and political democracy was not fulfilled in Turkey.[48]

3. The Islamic Alternative and Symbiosis of Civilization

In the historical, sociological approach to Islam, political power, and legal rationality, some questions arise. Will the Muslim world be able to get out of the impasse into which contemporary political Islam has been trapped? Isn't Islam, like other religions, a major source capable of making a reinterpretation of religious ideas and ethics to support the required social transformation?

Given the political and cultural complexity, it is important to consider the history of symbiosis and emancipation in the historical context of Islam. This historical legacy would play a significant role in underlying an alternative form of modernity in comparison with Eurocentrism. The concept of alternative modernities is philosophically elaborated in dealing with Western modernity as a wave, but it is acultural and technologically advanced, along with capitalist rationalization and progress. This acultural wave of modernity imposes a falsely uniform pattern on non-Western cultures. However, the latter incorporate their own history in terms of religion, politics, culture, science, technology and economic development. Without consideration of the multiple encounters of non-Western culture, 'we will fail to see how other cultures differ and how this difference crucially conditions the way in which they integrate the truly universal features of modernity.'[49] It is therefore necessary to consider the Islamic contribution to civilization and intellectual achievements. In fact, there were wealthy civilization and enlightenment in Bagdad and Islamic Spain for a model of symbiosis and cosmopolitan character.

A Culture of Toleration and Dialogue: Judaism and Christianity

Granted that Muhammad is the messenger of God as the seal of the prophets (Q 33:40), the Islamic source of religious humanism affirms the dignity of Israel and Christianity: 'Children of Israel, remember the favour I have bestowed upon you, and that I exalted above the

---

48. Ramadan, *Islam and the Arab Awakening*, p. 76.
49. Taylor, 'Two Theories of Modernity,' in *Alternative Modernities*, ed., Gaonkar, p. 180.

nations. ... We gave Moses the Scriptures and knowledge of right and wrong, so that you might be rightly guided' (Q 2:47, 54). 'When Mary's son is cited as an example, your people laugh and say: "Who is better, he or our gods?" ... He was but a mortal whom We favoured and made an example to the Israelites' (Q 43:59). 'People of the Book [Christians], do not transgress the bounds of your religion. ... The Messiah, Jesus son of Mary, was no more than God's apostle and His Word which He cast to Mary: a spirit from Him' (Q 4:171).

There is a continuity between the Jewish religion and Jesus, as seen in a Quranic perspective, though the divinity of Jesus Christ is relativized. In fact, Muhammad's mission in the middle of the Meccan period is described as a mercy for the world. 'We have sent you forth but as a blessing to mankind, Say: "It is revealed to me that your God is one God"' (Q 21:107). 'We have sent you forth to all mankind, so that you may give them good news and forewarn them' (Q 34:27). During the period of the Abbasid caliphate, religious toleration was guaranteed to the Jewish community, with judicial autonomy and exemption from the military, which accepted the supremacy of the Islamic state. Codified by the Pact of Omar (dating from 800 CE), Jewish life flourished despite its restrictions.[50]

Under the rule of the Moors in Spain (from 711), the majority of the Christian population converted to Islam, while the Christian minority was Arabized, and called Mozarabians. Muslims and Jews were close in relationship on the basis of monotheism and Islam's legal tolerance for the Jews. At the beginning of the eighth century a mixed army of Arabs and Muslim Berbers began to conquer the Iberian Peninsula. When Abbasid caliphs conquered the Ummayads in 750 CE, Spain remained independent under an Ummayad ruler. In the tenth century, the Jewish statesman Hisdai Ibn Shaprut (915–70) was employed as court physician, administrator and diplomat in the Spanish Ummayad caliph court. Acting as head of the Jewish community, he became patron of Jewish scholarship. Cordoba, the capital of the Ummayad caliphate became a centre of Jewish civilization.[51]

The most important philosopher in Spain at the time was Ibn Rushd (1126–98), often Latinized as Averroes, born in Cordoba. He was influential in Christian scholasticism as well as the Jewish philosophy of

---

50. The Pact of Omar is a treaty between Muslims and Christians, listing privileges, agreement and limitations; it applied to Jews, too. Cohn-Sherbok, *Judaism*, p. 140.
51. Ibid., p. 151.

Moses Maimonides (1135 or 1138–1204). Between 1169 and 1195 Averroes wrote a series of commentaries on most of Aristotle's works. These are incorporated in the Latin version of Aristotle's complete works. In Padua of northern Italy, which was the stronghold of Averroism, for three centuries rational philosophy together with a revived Neoplatonism became an important component in the early phase of the European Renaissance.[52]

By the tenth century, Islamic Spain was a fertile symbiosis of Muslims and Jews. The great symbolic figure of Spanish Judaism was Moshe ben Maimon (1138–1204), called Moses Maimonides in the West. He was born in Cordoba and spent his life as one of the court physicians in Cairo to Saladin, the Muslim ruler of Egypt. He was a leader of the Jewish community of Cairo and remained the greatest figure in the intellectual history of medieval Jewry. His intellectual background was grounded in the philosophers of Muslim Spain, such as al-Farabi, Avicenna and Averroes, in their Aristotelian endeavour to reconcile revealed religion with the philosophies of ancient Greece. Maimonides was convinced by the Muslim Aristotelians in their identification of Aristotle's Prime Mover with the Neoplatonic ideal of the One, from which all multiplicity emanates. This philosophical perspective would help purify the problem of Judaism, because Judaism should be logically and intellectually consistent, coming to terms with reason.[53]

In addition to the Islamic civilization of toleration and dialogue in Cordoba, the real origin of Islamic philosophy lies in the glorious epoch of Abbasid (750–1258), in which Islam reached its classical form. It is characterized by cosmopolitan Islam embedded in Hellenistic and Persian culture, or in the higher unity of world culture. It has a policy of great tolerance toward other religions (Zoroastrianism, Judaism and Christianity). Islamic philosophy has its origin in the translation of the works of Greek philosophers in cosmopolitan Baghdad in the period from 750 to 850. In Baghdad, the Persian lifestyle was more favoured and "its scientific and technical knowledge was taken over, above all from medicine, mathematics, astronomy, agronomy, and weapons technique."[54]

Islam was a long way ahead of Latin Christianity in philosophy and science. The court of al-Mansur (754–75) attracted a large number of Muslim theologians and traditionalists, including Christian and Jewish

---

52. Küng, *Islam*, p. 382.
53. Seltzer, *Jewish People, Jewish Thought*, p. 395.
54. Küng, *Islam*, p. 257.

scholars. Under the caliph al-Mamun (813–33), the House of Wisdom was the first institution of higher learning in the Islamic and Western worlds. Nestorian and Jacobite Christian scholars had already translated into Syriac many Greek medical, philosophical and theological treatises. They were able to carry on their work at the House of Wisdom.[55]

Around 780, the bishop Mar Timotheous (780–823) became patriarch, or *Catholicos*, of the Church of the East (Timotheos I), which was then based at the ancient Mesopotamian city of Seleucia. Under Timotheos' leadership, the Eastern churches had critical interactions with Islam, because most Eastern Christians had lived under Muslim political power. The initial transformation of Islamic society into a universal religion took place during the epoch from 749 to 1258 when the Abbasid caliphs ruled from Baghdad. This era symbolizes a long period of peace, property, learning and culture often called the Golden Age of Islam, or cultural Renaissance.

Through his good relations with the court, Timotheos I rebuilt several churches, and he was kept in high esteem by the caliphs al-Mahdi and Harun ar-Rashid. Some Christians were involved in the caliph's domestic policy, even earning high praise. In the account of the Christian monk John of Phenek, a contemporary of the first Umayyad caliph, we read: 'As soon as Muawiyyah had come to the throne, there was a peace all over the world unheard of and unseen either by our parents or our grandparents, of an unparalleled kind.'[56]

In the following period of the Abbasid caliphate (750–1258), Baghdad became the new cultural and political metropolis and focus of Islamization. Timotheous I was highly regarded by the Muslim caliphs such as al-Mahdi (775–85) and Harun ar-Rashid (785–809). His apologia of Christianity would be done before al-Mahdi (775–785), the third Abbasid caliph; it survives as a precious monument of civilized, intelligent religious exchange. His disputation with Caliph al-Mahdi is said to have occurred at court; though it is possible that this occurred, it is regarded as a literary fiction. At any rate, this dialogue was translated from the original Syriac into Arabic and reproduced in several editions.[57]

From the Islamic side, it is also important to mention an early example of dialogue and interaction between Christians and Muslims in the age of al-Mamun (r. 813–33). The most intellectual of the Abbasid caliphs, al-Mamun, transformed the caliphal library (founded as the 'Treasury

---

55. Bloom and Blair, *Islam*, p. 84.
56. Küng, *Islam*, p. 193.
57. Baum and Winkler, *The Church of the East*, p. 61.

of Knowledge' by his father Harun al-Rashid (r. 786–809) into the great 'House of Knowledge' in Baghdad. In this great institution, a remarkable intellectual work was undertaken through a staff of translators, copyists and bookbinders. Even a delegation of scholars was commissioned to go to Constantinople to look for philosophical and scientific manuscripts.[58] Al-Mamun promoted dialogue with Christian religion and also engaged with representatives of a wide range of religious traditions, including Manichaeans.[59]

The 'Nestorian' Christians managed to found important medical training centres in Syria and Persia. Galen and other classic Greek texts were translated into Syriac, then translated by Arabs in Damascus, Cairo, Antioch, and Baghdad. The age of al-Mamun represents an early example of the golden age for dialogue and interaction, and mutual perceptions.

Islam and Theological Development

From the ninth to the twelfth century an Arabic philosophy came into being and reached its zenith in the figure of Ali Ibn Sina, a Persian during the Islamic golden age (Latin 'Avicenna') (980–1037). Avicenna affirmed revelation and law as God's goal in terms of a rational exegesis of the Qur'an and Hadith. Reason is in accord with revelation within his Aristotelian Neoplatonic metaphysics.[60] In his major *summa* the healing (of the Soul from Error) (*ash-Shifa*') had a decisive impact upon European scholasticism. His idea of God as unchangeable primal ground may find a critical import in Thomas Aquinas (1225–74).

In the theological debate with Arabic philosophy, it is al-Ghazali (c. 1058–1111) 'the greatest Muslim after Muhammad,' who paved the way to a new philosophical mode of theology in terms of faith and revelation. Through the synthesis of traditional theology of law (*ulama*) and the mystical Sufism, he created the Ulama-Sufi model, which finally became widely normative for the Sunni majority. Al-Ghazali critiques twenty teachings of the *falasifa*, which was a loosely defined group of Islamic philosophers from the eighth through the eleventh centuries (most notable among them Avicenna and al-Farabi). In critique of the *falasifa*'s metaphysics and natural science, al-Ghazali's aim was to make room for the epistemological claims of revelation. Faith seeks understanding,

---

58. Bloom and Blair, *Islam*, p. 84.
59. Goddard, *A History of Christian-Muslim Relations*, p. 52.
60. Ayoub, *Islam*, p. 173.

but philosophical understanding should not violate the specific area of revelation. Al-Ghazali can therefore be compared to Thomas Aquinas.[61]

Besides those already covered, there are a number of other models or paradigms in the history of intellectual traditions in Islam. A complete list might run as follows: eighth-century Mutazilate, tenth-century al-Ashari, eleventh-century al-Ghazali, eleventh–century philosophical enlightenment in Cordoba (Avicena and Averroes), and fourteenth-century Ibn Taymiya. Indeed, Islamic intellectual tradition is not monolithic at all. In every critique or modification or revolution of a tradition, human consciousness is guided by critical rational thinking in dealing with history, tradition, and knowledge system rather than moved within effective-historical consciousness in a generic sense.[62]

The Islamic contribution that we have highlighted should be the historical route toward an Islamic alternative form of enlightenment and modernity. It requires us to reinterpret the Islamic idea of *Nahda* by bridging it with Islam's resource of symbiosis of civilization and its greatest achievements. Islamic sources help to renew the historical moment of *Nahda* within the Islamic civilization and intellectual tradition, which facilitates Islamic interaction with Christianity. The legacy of symbiosis and intellectual and scientific progress should be incorporated in our discussion of Islam, *Nahda*, and modernity.

4. Comparative Theology: Calvinism and Islam

For our exercise in comparative theology, the next idea to consider is the Islamic idea of predestination in relation to Weber's thesis of Protestant ethics and capitalist spirit. Comparative theology seeks truth in and through various religious and non-religious traditions. It holds that a believer in one tradition attempts to understand a measure of truth, in and through other religious traditions. Comparative theology is not directed to challenging a particular faith per se, rather it is concerned with creating new means of understanding the other, while renewing and deepening the self through that process of learning.

Through comparison with other cultures and traditions, it is valuable to develop new means of communication through the lens of comparative theology, in which a depth of understanding can be achieved; it could also be seen as an attempt to read God's signs, which the Qur'an

---

61. Küng, *Islam*, p. 355. Griffel, *Al-Ghazali's Philosophical Theology*, pp. 97, 99.
62. Rahman, *Islam and Modernity*, 10.

emphasizes on multiple occasions. In many ways, it would exemplify the Quranic claim that God has created us in different tribes and that we are supposed to get to know each other.[63]

Islam teaches that Allah is the creator of all things, and it is he who has ordained and decreed all that will happen. 'Every misfortune that befalls the earth, or your own persons, is ordained before We bring it into being. That is easy enough for God; so that you may not grieve for the good things you miss, or be overjoyed at what you gain' (Q 57:21). 'The Day of judgment is fixed; Good deeds or evil deeds will be properly judged according to human conduct at the end of life, and rewarded in terms of Paradise or Hell' (Q 78:17). In the course of his life, an individual may be tempted toward sin by *jinn*, which are spiritual beings. However, the individual's ultimate end has been decreed by Allah. 'We have predestined for Hell numerous jinn and men. … They shall receive their due for their misdeeds' (Q 7:177).

Predestination in Islam and Calvinism

If succumbing to sin or striving for good has also been planned and decreed by Allah, how do we understand human responsibility in connection with God's predestination? In the theological development of the Islamic teaching of predestination, the doctrine of *Qadar* has been discussed: the concept of God's sovereign control over all creation, even to the final destination of one's eternal soul. The Islamic concept of *Qadar* (predestination, or divine cause) shows that all things in life are under God's eternal decree (including salvation). Is there a human *qadar* in accordance with God's *qadar*?

However, the major Islamic view demonstrates that God appears to carry out the eternal decree and predestination, because it belongs to divine will; it is undertaken without any reason or motive for so doing, unknown to human beings. 'Thus God confounds who He will and guides whom He pleases. None knows the warriors of your Lord but Himself. There is no more than an admonition to mankind' (Q 74:31). Allah's intention is to give human beings eternal bliss, but we cannot know for sure the way Allah would work at the end.

The Qur'an leaves open the question how God's predestination would be embedded with human freedom and responsibility. In the course of history the Umayyad caliphs designated themselves as representatives of

---

63. Khorchide and Topkara, 'A Contribution to Comparative Theology,' *Religions* 2013, p. 69. www.mdpi.com/journal/religions.

God (*khalifat Allah*), who were rightly guided by divine predestination in matters of all affairs – good and bad. Against this ideology of political rule, a position occurred that human beings are responsible for evil rather than attributed to God. In recognition of God's predestination, but sins do not come from God, but from human beings (or from Satan)

An Islamic concept of 'natural inclination' in human beings is called *fitrah*, in which a person is endowed, at birth, with purity or freedom from erroneous ideas. However, soon after birth, this *fitrah* is corrupted by *jinn* (spirits that tend to lead a person to sin) and devils. Allah will intervene and protect and guide those he wishes to lead ultimately to Heaven, while leaving the rest to be led astray by the jinn and the devils. However, the God of Islam is the compassionate and the merciful, not a capricious God who sends a group of innocent people to Hell, and others to Paradise. There are numerous passages focusing on the importance of human will and responsibility. 'Every soul is the hostage of its own deeds.' (Q 74:38). 'This is indeed an admonition. Let him that will, take the right path to his Lord. Yet you cannot choose, except by the will of God. God is all-knowing and wise' (Q 76:22).

According to Weber, Islamic predestination does not incorporate the double decree of God in the sense that it does not attribute the predestination of hell to Allah in comparison with Calvinist double predestination. Allah may withdraw grace from those committed to inadequacy and transgression.[64] For Weber, Calvin and Muhammad felt that the certainty of their own mission derived from their situation in the world and from God's will; their certainty has less to do with their personal perfection. On the contrary, Islam's predestination determined the uncommon events of this world in battles; it has little to do with the fate of the individual in the world beyond in the Puritan sense. In fact, the religious fate of the individual was held in his/her belief in Allah and the prophet. However, salvation is not demonstrated in the ethical and economic conduct of life in the Puritan sense. Any rational system of ascetic life was so strange to Islam, that the doctrine of predestination and its power were demonstrated in the wars of faith and the Mahdi (an eschatological redeemer of Islam). As Islam became more urbanized, its doctrine was inclined to lose its significance.[65]

In Weber's treatment of Calvinist predestination, the Westminster Confession (1647) is central with its chapters III (God's eternal decree), V (providence), IX (free will) and X (effectual calling):

---

64. Weber, *The Sociology of Religion*, p. 203.
65. Turner, 'Revisiting Weber and Islam,' p. 204.

> Chapter IX (of Free Will), No.3. Man, by his fall into a state of sin, hath wholly lost all ability of will to any spiritual good accompanying salvation. So that a natural man, being altogether averse from that Good, and dead in sin, is not able, by his own strength, to convert himself, or to prepare himself thereunto.[66]

And:

> Chapter III (of God's Eternal Decree), No. 3. By the decree of God, for the manifestation of His glory, some men and angels are predestined unto everlasting life, and others foreordained to everlasting death.[67]

This doctrine entails a logical consequence according to which even Christ had died only for the elect, not for all. The genuine Puritan had no trust in the effects of magical and sacramental forces on salvation, and eliminated magic from the world. For Calvinists, the world exists to serve the glory of God and the elected Christian in the world lives for that purpose only to the best of their ability. Their social activity in economic rationalism is dedicated to magnifying the glory of God (*majorem gloriam Dei*). Weber diagnoses that the source of the utilitarian character of the Calvinist ethic is grounded on the Calvinist idea of calling, in reference to its predestination.[68]

In Weber's account, Calvin himself maintains that faith is to be proved by its objective results or fruits (a *fides efficax*), which becomes a firm foundation for the *certitudo salutis*. The elected Christian is capable of producing the *fides efficax* by virtue of regeneration and the resulting sanctification to increase the glory of God by real good works; 'they are indispensable as a sign of election. … In this sense they are occasionally referred to as directly necessary for salvation or the *possessio salutis* is made conditional on them. In practice this means that God helps those who help themselves'[69]

Weber argues that in the first generation of Islam, the belief in predestination helped the Muslim warriors to live in complete obliviousness to themselves. It was an undercurrent in faith and fulfillment of

---

66. Weber, *The Protestant Ethic and the Spirit of Capitalism*, pp. 99–100.
67. Ibid., p. 100.
68. Ibid., pp. 108–9.
69. Ibid., p. 115.

holy war for the conquest of the world. However, the Puritans produced ethical rigorism, legalism, and rational patterning of life through their belief in predestination. Their inner-worldly asceticism, which is in a vocation pleasing to God, was the source of the virtuosity which is characteristic of acquisitiveness.[70]

What characterizes the chief ordinances of Islam in its historical development is its religious and political character, and its required dogma is grounded in the recognition of Allah as the one god and Muhammad as his prophet. This was based on the asceticism of a military caste rather than monks or a middle-class ascetic systematization of ethical conduct.[71] Weber's image of Islam as a warrior religion stands accused of being tied to his putative method of violent propagation along with his Christian prejudice. By contrast, for example, the appeal of Islam in Bengal was the work of charismatic individuals, and its outcome was the result of the peaceful evolution of a pious ideal among the peasantry; the emergence of Islam in South East Asia was based on the work of itinerant traders and preachers.[72] Weber's study of Islam in comparative, historical, and sociological frames of references is therefore seriously and comprehensively challenged.[73] The historical development of Islam cannot be explained merely by military coercion.

Critical Exegesis: Calvin and Predestination

In Weber's reading of Calvin, in terms of later Calvinist doctrine and development, Calvin is severely distorted. Furthermore, Weber's caricature of Calvin needs to be discounted from the Calvinist doctrine of predestination. Weber dimly hints that the *decretum horribile* is not derived from religious experience as Calvin suggests, but that it is undertaken by the logical necessity of his thought.[74]

On the contrary, Calvin deals with the teaching of eternal election (Inst. III. xxi) in reference to Christ's benefit in the secret working of the Holy Spirit. This gives an important insight into articulating Calvin's doctrine of election in terms of union with Christ, which is imbued with

---

70. Weber, *The Sociology of Religion*, p. 203.
71. Ibid., p. 266.
72. Turner, 'Revisiting Weber and Islam,' p. 162.
73. *Max Weber and Islam* refers to the comprehensive critique of Weber's method and his evaluation of Islam. *Max Weber and Islam*, eds. Huff and Schluchter.
74. Weber, *The Protestant Ethic and The Spirit of Capitalism*, p. 102.

the Holy Spirit.. Calvin grounds election in Christ alone, by refraining from futile human attempts to solve the mystery of God's eternal decree outside Christ (Inst. III. xxiv. 4). Our election in Christ occurs *extra nos*, that means with no recourse to human merits or achievement (Inst. III.xxii.3). The grace of justification and sanctification, or faith and morality, is engrafted into Christ, implanting the believer into the body of Christ through word and sacrament. Thus, Christ dwells in our faith and our hearts in a mystical union (Inst. III. xi. 10). In this way reformed theology incorporates the vocation of the elect in terms of union with Christ.[75]

Calvin's teaching of the Holy Spirit provides theological acumen for reinterpreting his doctrine of election in a more genuine sense than later Calvinist scholasticism. He features the cosmic but hidden power (*arcana Dei virtus*) of the Holy Spirit that is at work among the pagans.[76] 'The reprobates are sometimes affected by almost the same feeling as the elect. ... This does not at all hinder that lower working of the Spirit from taking its course even in the reprobate. ... The reprobate are justly said to believe that God is merciful toward them' (Inst. III.ii.11). In witnessing to the sovereign initiative of God, Calvin's genuine concern is of inclusive character rather than of a Manichean dualistic dichotomy. As he writes: 'God is said to have ordained from eternity those whom he wills to embrace in love, and those upon whom he wills to vent his wrath. Yet he announces salvation to all men indiscriminately' (Inst. III. xxiv.17). Thus, Jesus Christ died for all without discrimination.

Given this, it is necessary to consider Calvin's paradoxical argument: 'God adopts some to hope of life, and sentences others to eternal death' (Inst. III. xxi.5). God has blocked the door of life 'by his just and irreprehensible but incomprehensible judgment' (Inst. III. xxi.7). However, Calvin formulates this negative view of reprobation only according to his personal experiences and empirical facts rather than grounding it in God's eternal decree in a rigidly fixed manner. However, Calvin does not promote the latter signs, which produce our election or certainty of salvation (*signa posterior*: Inst. III. xxiv.4). Election in Christ *extra nos* runs counter to a practical syllogism concerning election, which has little to do with authentic Calvinist thought.[77] In Calvin's

---

75. Barth, CD IV/3.2, pp. 551–4.
76. For more details see Chung, "John Calvin: Mission and Evangelism," in Chung, *Hermeneutical Theology and the Imperative of Public Ethics*, p. 29.
77. Wendel, *Calvin*, pp. 276–7. Cf. Chung, *The Spirit of God Transforming Life*, p.90.

exegesis of 1 Timothy 2:4, we read: 'There is no people and no rank in the world that is excluded from salvation; because God wishes that the gospel should be proclaimed to all without exception.'[78]

This clarification of Calvin's doctrine of election cuts across Weber's sociology of Calvinism and the spirit of capitalism. A comparative theology is involved in a critical conversation with Weber's sociology, while promoting the Calvinist teaching of election in comparison with Islam. It seems a truism in Calvin and Islam that they confirm that God is sovereign, merciful and all-compassionate, while human responsibility is kept intact for the glory of God. A semantic retrieval helps clarify each religious position, and it renews the self through the reading of the other. The comparative theology is of confessional character with constructive intention, in which a new synthesis of meaning can be attained.

Constructive Reflection on Islam and Predestination

Contrary to Weber's assumption, belief in the Mahdi is popular among both Sunni and Shiite Islam. This idea is not found in the Qur'an, but in the Hadith, in which the Mahdi will come with Isa (Jesus) to defeat the Anti-Christ. Twelvers believe that the Mahdi should be the son of the eleventh Imam. Its tradition is seen in the idea of representation by the Ayatollahs in Persia in the sixteenth century under the Safavids, as well as in the Iranian revolution of the twentieth century. This messianic occultation is in contrast to the Sunni who believes that the Mahdi has not been born.[79]

It is true that the members of the *Ummah* followed the belief in predestination and hoped to establish their illegitimate dominion through legitimizing the predestined will of Allah; however, they were denounced for their secularism. Actually, belief in predestination entailed an ascetic effect in the warriors of the early Islamic faith, but it was not rationally involved in everyday life. It even assumed a fatalistic character in the life of the masses – kismet – and so it did not eliminate magic from the popular religion. What distinguished the Muslim tradition from the Puritan tradition is that the former 'depicts with pleasure the luxurious raiment, perfume, and meticulous beard-coiffure of the pious.'[80] As Muhammad says, 'when God blesses a man with prosperity he likes to

---

78. Calvin, *Commentaries on I and II Timothy*, trans. William Pringle, pp. 54–5.
79. Küng, *Islam*, p. 200.
80. Ibid., Weber, *The Sociology of Religion*, p. 263.

see the signs thereof visible upon him.'[81] This saying would imply that a wealthy person is under obligation to live in accordance with his/her status; it corresponds with the feudal idea of status, which is opposed to any Puritan economic ethic.[82]

Weber's major argument is seen in the insistence that capitalism existed among world religions, but there is no development found in them toward modern capitalism. 'Above all, there evolved no capitalist spirit'[83] in the sense of ascetic Protestantism. However, Weber takes ethical prophecies to break through magical or ritual forms, especially in the economic realm; religious ethics penetrates into social institutions through its theoretical attitude toward the world. As a religious ethic organizes the world on the basis of a religious orientation concerning a systematic, rational order and a cosmos, ethical tensions occurred with the social institutions in a sharper and more principled manner.[84]

Weber comprehends the role of Muhammad as an ethical prophet with charismatic authority, who challenged the traditional values of Arab society through new revelation in the Qur'an. In taking on the relationship between religious and secular power, the prophetic Abrahamic religions of revelation in principle adopt a stance for promulgating an ethic of charity and solidarity with the needy. These values run counter to the current world, which is beset by violence, injustice and cruelty. There was a principled struggle in the context of Islam between ethical rationalization and the process of rationalization in the economic realm. However, capitalism does not offer support for any charitable orientation and activity, since a Puritan economic ethic in its rationally ascetic character leads to the accumulation of wealth. We read from Weber's provocative statement: 'One of the most notable economic effects of Calvinism was its destruction of the traditional forms of charity. ... Calvinism put an end to ... any benevolent attitude toward the beggar. ... Consequently, begging was explicitly stigmatized as a violation of the injunction to love one's neighbor, in this case the person from whom the beggar solicits.'[85]

In his comparative study of the doctrine of predestination between Islam and Puritan Calvinism, Weber maintains that the giving of alms in Islam is one of the five commandments underlying a universal and

---

81. Ibid.
82. Ibid.
83. Ibid., p. 269.
84. Ibid., p. 209.
85. Ibid., pp. 220–1.

primary component of its religious ethics. A universal communalism of love that Weber articulates in contrast to the Puritan ethics of unbrotherliness may indeed be seen in Islam; it is one that would promote the principle of the solidarity of brothers and sisters in the faith.[86]

There is an insight of an ethics of conviction in the Islamic community of brotherly love and charity in opposition to the brutal reality of everyday life; such a religious ethic becomes a principal religious leverage in undergirding social change in society. We may see the meaning of predestination connected with human responsibility for the action which would be formulated in terms of Islamic donation; this aspect is left aside in Weber's analysis. However, he still observes that a protectorate of the weak is created in the case of the Mosaic and Islamic prophetic religions. Their prophetic religions (Christianity included) extended protection even to the relationship between classes (including women, children and slaves). The prohibition against usury in Islam and in ancient Christianity applied at first only to fellow believers, later becoming unconditional and universal.[87]

Islamic Protestantism and Reform Movement

In recent decades, traditional Islam has begun to be more accessible to European languages, especially English and French and their modern thought. To understand Islam adequately, it is worth noting that the living nature of traditional Islam retains the powerful hold of the Qur'an on the souls and minds of the vast majority of Muslims. Traditional Islam is compared to the mountain in which various geological processes are created, such as weathering and sedimentation, in forming its slopes.[88] If traditional Islam takes seriously its religious source by reinterpreting it in a fresh manner, to be more relevant to the challenge of the contemporary world, it would not necessarily be an obstacle to its synthesis of a new meaning. The modernist impact on the Islamic world has made inroads through the introduction of more modern attitudes in education and the media.[89]

Islamic reform was initiated in modern time by Ali Shariati (1933–78), and his movement is given different titles: Islamic Protestantism, Islamic Humanism, or Islamic Renaissance. It can be seen as the path to liberate

---

86. Ibid., p. 212.
87. Ibid., pp. 214–5.
88. Nasr, *Islam*, p. 175.
89. Ibid., p. 185.

both Islam and Muslims from the bondage of reactionary hierarchy and the supremacy of clericalism. Ali Shariati was a lay religious intellectual, who was educated at the Sorbonne and laid the foundation for radical reform in religious discourse in Iran. He finds inspiration from Weber's study of the Protestant ethic and the spirit of capitalism. He argued that an intelligentsia in contemporary Islamic societies should start with reforming 'religion.' 'The intelligentsia should begin by an "Islamic Protestantism" similar to that of Christianity in the late Middle Ages, destroying all the degenerating factors which, in the name of Islam, have stymied and stupefied the process of thinking and the fate of the society, and giving birth to new thoughts and new movements.'[90]

Although Shariati died before the 1979 revolution in Iran, his ideas have remained very much alive and influential in post-revolutionary debates, when it comes to the conditions and the necessity of reform in Islamic discourse. For him, the Islamic Reformation is driven in terms of liberty, equality and spirituality. Islam must be reinterpreted in line with freedom of the individual, social justice, and constructive and progressive spirituality. This perspective takes issue with systems of power, which are embedded with political dictatorship, material injustice, religious alienation and clerical despotism. For Shariati, no one can represent God. He boldly argues that the very term 'God' should be replaced with that of the 'people' in all Quranic verses, especially in dealing with social issues. Opposing clerical authority, Shariati called for an Islamic Renaissance and Reformation.[91]

For the task of reform and democracy, it is important to elaborate on the formation of the Shura (consultation) in the modern struggle for social and democratic change. The Shura can be advanced in achieving the resumption of *ijtihad* (independent reasoning) and consensus (*ijma*). It is concerned with rational clarification, systematization, and the formation of free opinion, analogous derivation, or argument (*ijtihad*) in matters pertaining to theological and legal issues. The gap between law and reality could only be resolved through the legal process of reasoning and decision-making in dealing with the Qur'an, the Sunna and the Hadith.

To the extent that the Shura (consultation) is the Islamic form of democracy, the Qur'an and Muhammad encourage Muslims to decide their affairs in consultation with those affected by each decision. Shura

---

90. Cited in Mahdavi, 'Max Weber in Iran: Does Islamic Protestantism Matter?' pp. 9–10. https://www.cpsa-acsp.ca/papers-2005/Mahdavi.pdf.
91. Abrahamian, *Radical Islam*, p. 119. Ali Shariati, *On the Sociology of Islam*.

refers to a long history of establishing consultative assemblies which return to the time of the Prophet Muhammad. Muhammad had encouraged consultation between rulers and their constituencies in later periods of his life. The route to independent judgment requires navigating a middle course avoiding rigid dogmatism, reckless actionism, and fanaticism. As al-Ghazali writes, 'know that the mean is most highly desirable in all things and virtues.'[92]

Concluding Remark

In Wilfred C. Smith's study of *Modern Islam in India*, he maintains that Islamic modernism was carried on through a liberal Islam with British bourgeois values. In historical development, the Islamic movement has created a new and creative vision, as engaged in the very early period of Islam (Khilafat al-Rishidah); it refers to the last ten years of the Prophet Muhammad's lifetime and the first thirty years after his death.[93] A project of 'Islamic Protestantism' seeks to eliminate the spirit of imitation and obedience which is the hallmark of Islam; it endorses a critical, revolutionary, aggressive spirit of independent reasoning (*ijtihad*).[94] Islamic modernity requires critical and independent thinking, and it reinforces hermeneutical enquiry of multiple forms of morality, human rights and democracy.

Taken in this way, Tariq Ramadan proposes a civil state in terms of an ethical alternative and democratic rule. Radical reform entails a way of interpreting the texts through ethical goals. The state under the authority of religion would be corroded from within, if it neglects ethics. Islam should be understood as an open system, which entails a religious and cultural reference guiding ethical consideration.[95] Given this, a religious source for modernity and civil society can be furthered in the study of the Qur'an as the immanent critique for religious humanism, democracy and civil society. According to the Sudanese Muslim legal scholar, Abdullahi Ahmed an-Naim, 'this process of abrogation should be reversed in order to develop a modern version of the Sharia which guarantees the equal rights of women and non-Muslims. ... we must openly concede and identify the discrimination contained in

---

92. Cited in Küng, *Islam*, p. 364.
93. Smith, *Modern Islam in India*, p. 12.
94. Mahdavi, 'Max Weber in Iran,' p. 10.
95. Ramadan, *Islam and the Arab Awakening*, p. 107; Ramadan, *Radical Reform: Islamic Ethics and Liberation*.

the historical formulations of the Sharia ... ; it must also integrate the Sunnah and other sources of the Sharia, because that is the context in which the Qur'an is understood and used by Muslims.'[96]

This hermeneutical position comes from the teacher of an-Naim, the Sudanese Mahmud Taha who was executed by the dictator Numeiri in 1985. Taha and his followers (the Republican Brothers) have campaigned for a modernization of Islamic teaching and the Sharia. Taha distinguishes the Meccan period of the Prophet Muhammad's preaching from the Medina period. The Mecca surahs must be distinguished from the time-limited application of them to society in the Medina surahs. He challenged a fundamentalist and literal exegesis of Islamic law.[97] In fact, we see that man and woman are equally worthy of respect in the Qur'an, which recounts: 'a man hides from the people a birth of a female infant, feeling humiliated by the circumstance. But his decision is judged to be evil' (16:59).

Ad fontes (coming back to the source of Islam) does not necessarily mean a nostalgia for the origin and the power lost. But it is critical to rewrite the present history of Islam for the sake of the Islamic teaching of democracy, rational reasoning and emancipation in symbiosis and solidarity. This refers to the religious discourse and its construction of social, political and cultural reality. 'Such is the path of your Lord: a straight path. We have made plain Our revelations to thinking men. They shall dwell in peace with their Lord. He will give them His protection as recompense for what they do' (Q 6:127).

Excursus: Islam and Axial Religion

In the sociological study of axial religions the florescences of the Axial Age were seen in the articulation of cultural regions in the sense of Oikoumene which had constantly spread and interacted. New traditions of high culture refer to unparalleled cultural florescences, the period of which can be ranged roughly 800–200 BCE and called the Axial Age.[98] In the Axial Age we see Taoism and Confucianism in China; Hinduism and Buddhism in the Indian subcontinent; monotheism in the Middle East; and Greek philosophy in southern Europe. Common regional cultivation of the Oikoumene implies one major lettered tradition in

---

96. An-Naim, 'Quran, Sharia and Human Rights: Foundations, Deficiencies and Prospects,' *Concilium* 2, pp. 61–9.
97. Taha, *The Second Message of Islam*, pp. 49–50.
98. Jaspers, *The Origin and Goal of History*.

each region. The literary traditions, which were founded by the Iranian and Hebrew prophets, were largely Semitic and Iranian, referred to as Irano-Semitic.[99]

The Axial Age faiths focused on a single deity or supreme symbol of transcendence in critique of mundane reality fraught with injustice, economic inequality and violence. In the post-axial age context, Muhammad's prophetic critique of polytheism can be seen in continuity with the Axial Age prophets and reformers, sharing their commitment to social justice and moral characteristics with Judaism and Christianity. In Armando Salvatore's view, 'Muhammad's message was conceived as a restoration, completion and renaissance of the authentic Abrahamic faith through a final and unequivocal revelation of God's word and will to humankind.'[100]

A new type of religion in the Axial Age accentuates a transcendent God, by relating it to the axial transformations and strengthening the civilizational impetus. Transcendence matters here, sociologically, for facilitating the emergence of human agency to transition from mythos to logos (human reflexivity). The idea of transcendence projects a critique of and an alternative to the prevailing mundane system, by going beyond it to another possible world. The main novelty of the axial breakthrough is in the capacity of human beings to reflect upon and give expression to a critical image of the world.[101] The axial framework helps avoiding the anachronism of binary opposition or Eurocentrism in the comparative study of world religion. The religious idea of transcendence, a critical principle over and against the prevailing system, gave an unprecedented impulse for institutional change and social renewal. Axial theory breaks through the archaic unity between religion and despotism and reinforces the potential of a religious idea and its practice in transformations of political structures and its governance.

The Islamic contribution to axial vision can be seen in its concept and practice of value rationality of common good and non-hierarchical community building. Islam strengthens a crucial feature of axial civilizations in the reconstruction of the social bond and arrangement and in the overcoming of pre-axial ties of authority.[102] The (post-) axial principle in Muhammad continues to find its impulse in the modern development of Islamic humanism, common good, and civil society.

---

99. Hodgson, *The Venture of Islam*, p. 114.
100. Salvatore, 'Tradition and Modernity', in *Islam and Modernity*, p. 19.
101. Bellah, *Religion in Human Evolution*, pp. 268–9.
102. Salvatore, 'Tradition and Modernity', in *Islam and Modernity*, p. 19.

Islamic anthropology emphasizes the human being as God's vicegerent, who is created out of the mud and clay, but instilled with God's spirit. The constant striving and struggle take place among man and woman in a shift from the mud toward the exaltation of God's representatives. It affirms true humanism in the egalitarian definition of the human creature (man and woman) in two-dimensional aspects endowed with the free will.[103]

In fact, 'we have honored [*karramna*] the children of Adam' (17:70). The modern Arabic term for human dignity or rights is derived from the verb 'honoured.' Human beings are defined to serve as God's representative on earth (*khalifa*) (2:30), because they are offered God's trust (*amna*) (33:72). Dignity and responsibility are conferred on all human beings. The axial approach to the Meccan model facilitates galvanizing a project of 'Islamic Protestantism,' and its sociology can be embodied and furthered in the hermeneutical retrieval of the Islamic democratic spirit of independent reasoning, communal consensus, significance of the people, value rationality of common good, moral solidarity, and politics of recognition in the multicultural context.

---

103. Shariati, *On the Sociology of Islam*, pp. 74–5.

Chapter 6

Comparative Theology: Culture and Religion

Comparative theology in religious studies focuses on the relation between religious discourse and its construction of reality, in which cultural issues become a major part of underlying comparative theology. A comparative theology gains prominence in cultural diversity and religious pluralism, so a multicultural reality requires an interdisciplinary approach to religion and culture in reinforcing social scientific enquiry; it must seek to explicate the extent to which inequality and power relations in the field of race, gender, ethnicity and social status would be organized around social cultural stratification.

The first part of this chapter examines a theology of culture by analyzing its various types; they are ranged from H. Richard Niebuhr's typology via Tillich's existential enquiry, and finally to George Lindbeck's postliberal model. The second part explicates a theory of social stratification and power relations in order to advance comparative theology in dealing with cultural and religious issues such as domination and inequality, as involved in race, ethnicity, gender, sexuality and class. These cultural issues have been sidestepped in the context of a theology of culture in Niebuhr, Tillich, and Lindbeck. Incorporating such issues into the problematic theme of comparative theology, the chapter proposes a life-worldly enquiry in terms of the biblical symbol of reconciliation for reconstruction and synthesis of meaning. It then puts forward a type of Christ for culture and in solidarity with the marginalized in the world of culture and religion.

1. Theology and Culture

H.R. Niebuhr is an influential theologian who takes on the significance of culture for theology. He is considerably indebted to Troeltsch. Troeltsch sought to analyze the sociological significance of Christianity throughout its history, and brings it to contemporary relevancy. Niebuhr appreciates Troeltsch as a mentor who helps Niebuhr to conceptualize the multiformity and individuality of human beings and movements in Christian history. His concern is to supplement Troeltsch's work of social teaching, while correcting and updating some limitations.[1] Niebuhr relocates Troeltsch's historical relativism within theocentric relativism, in which Niebuhr places all relative history of the human being under the governance of the absolute God.[2]

As for a theory of culture, Niebuhr draws attention to Bronislaw Malinowski (1884–1942), whose functional theory comprehends that culture has developed in response or adaptation to human needs or environment. He takes issue with an unlinear and diffusionist attempt, in which the cultural traits of the non-West are viewed as undeveloped or uncivilized. Against this attempt, Malinowski maintains that all diverse customs and behaviours of cultures serve a function, satisfying people's needs and purposes. Culture refers to the artificial, secondary environment as superimposed by human beings on the natural; it also contains 'language, habits, ideas, belief, customs, social organization, inherited artifacts, technical processes, and values.'[3]

Culture is designed for an end, serving a good, and the world of culture is a world of values. This perspective characterizes Malinowski's functionalism in which 'an organized system of purposive activities' becomes a central concept in his theory of culture. Value-relation in cultural achievements is preserved for the sake of satisfaction or social harmony, in other words, the good for human beings in an anthropocentric sense.[4]

A structural-functionalism has been developed by Malinowski's colleague Alfred Radcliffe-Brown (1881–1955), who emphasizes the life of society over the individual in appreciation of Emile Durkheim's idea of the social function of religion. The concept of functions is used

---

1. Niebuhr, *Christ and Culture*, p. xii.
2. Ibid.
3. Ibid., p. 32.
4. Ibid., p. 35.

to articulate 'the interconnection between the social structure and the process of social life,' in other words, 'the relations of process and structure.' Function can be understood as supporting a social need for order and cohesion rather than meeting individual needs.[5]

Culture refers to human achievements, and is always social, organizing human beings into permanent groups; individuals utilize culture in their own ways, changing cultural elements. They receive and transmit culture as social heritage; thus social life is always cultural, because culture comes along with social existence. Niebuhr identifies social heritage or the reality *sui generis* with the world of which the New Testament writers spoke.[6]

Cultural diversity and pluralism are the most important features in all cultures. In other words, they refer to value pluralism; it is because culture is concerned with what is good for all the individuals with special claims and interests. For this direction Niebuhr draws attention to Ruth Benedict (1887–1948), who maintains that each society is of a highly complex character, comprising 'many institutions with many goals and interweaving interests.'[7] Culture as a human achievement has characteristics of diversity and pluralism.

According to Benedict, human culture ('personality writ large') is compared to individual personality, since individuals live in their culture and each culture has a personality and its own moral imperative. It can be compared to a style of personal life, art or architecture in terms of its distinctiveness and difference. If each culture must be seen on its own terms, Benedict rejects the view of seeing Western society as the best.[8]

Cultural tolerance in the patterns of culture contradicts American exceptionalism and American history of race, in which the core of US culture represents egalitarian value and assimilation of different races into the 'caucasian'mainstream. The problem of color-line is based on racial discrimination, in which 'America' is developed as a society with a history and culture of assimilative inclusion and racism. For her, 'Racial differences and prestige prerogatives have so merged among Anglo-Saxon peoples that we fail to separate biological racial matters from our most socially conditioned prejudices.'[9]

---

5. Radcliffe-Brown, *Structure and Function in Primitive Society*, p. 12.
6. Niebuhr, *Christ and Culture*, p. 35.
7. Ibid., 38.
8. Benedict, *Patterns of Culture*, p. viii.
9. Ibid., 40.

In Franz Boa's (1858–1942) account, cultural life in Benedict's theory should be seen in the interrelation between various aspects of culture, leading to diverse patterns of culture rather than generalization.[10] Boa remains an important mentor in Benedict's 'culture and personality' approach. He conceptualizes historical particularism, in which each culture entails creativity, innovation or adaptation, representing its history and context in a distinguished manner. It counters diffusionism, which comprehends cultural development as unilinear cultural evolution spreading from more advanced to less advanced societies. This diffusionist perspective has been critiqued for its ethnocentrism and racism. Boa's theory of contextualism affirms diversity of cultural forms in times and places and across their social lines; it makes the first plural use of the word 'culture' in a modern anthropological sense. Cultural forms are to be sought and investigated primarily in their own historical context prior to any generalization about commonalities among them.[11]

Types of Christ and Culture

Based on his understanding of culture, Niebuhr tries to construct the way Christians engage in the relation between Christ and culture through his typology: (1) Christ against culture, in which Christ is seen as opposed to culture in the case of Tertullian's sharp rejection of culture; (2) Christ of culture, in which Jesus appears as a great hero of human history of culture in contrast to Christ against culture; the former is aptly seen in Culture-Protestantism in Schleiermacher, especially in Albrecht Ritschl;[12] (3) Christ above culture in which a Christ of culture is also a Christ above culture; this synthetic type is best represented by Thomas Aquinas;[13] (4) Christ and culture in paradox, in which a Christian lives in the Church as well as in the world as a citizen; this dualism plays a significant role, but recognizes the authority of the state. It expresses a grace of justification beyond history which characterizes above all Luther.[14] Finally, (5) Christ transforms culture. Christianity expresses the gospel, concerned with its character of transformation in a cultural

---

10. Ibid., p. xxiii.
11. Tanner, *Theories of Culture*, pp. 20–1.
12. Niebuhr, *Christ and Culture*, pp. 93–4.
13. Ibid., p. 42.
14. Ibid., p. 45.

context. This type is built upon the conversionist model represented by Augustine and Calvin.¹⁵

In addition, Niebuhr adopts a theocentric stance through the idea of radical monotheism in dealing with types of religion and its faith. He introduces different types of henotheism, polytheism and pluralism. Henotheists in the form of social faith are loyal to one god among many, in distinction from the pluralists who have many objects of devotion: sectarian community, nationalism or civilization is taken as representative of the henotheistic, social faith, because it may constitute the centre of value for loyalty.¹⁶

Niebuhr employs the sociological analysis of religion, especially in reference to Emile Durkheim. The latter defines the idea of society as the soul of religion, such that the gods of religion are collective representations as religious ideas imposed upon individual minds. They express the things with a social nature. Religious experience is made by the religious representations, and the latter has represented reality as society. The form of faith in the actuality of henotheism composing society is expressed in moral behaviour through obedience to written and unwritten social laws or before social authority. The sociological theory of religion helps Niebuhr to analyze henotheistic faith in the form of nationalism or fascism, as well as in Marxist Leninism; the latter rejects all morality from non-class conceptions as a deception. It subordinates morality wholly to the interests of the class struggle of the proletariat.¹⁷

Niebuhr sees the great alternative to henotheism as pluralism in faith and polytheism among the gods. His choice falls on radical monotheism which refers to One beyond the many; all the many derive their existence from the One, and they live by participation in it. All being is acknowledged as absolutely dependent for existence upon the One as the Creator. A reasoning in faith characterizing radical monotheism is undertaken in rational efforts to comprehend the One beyond the many. It underlies the aspiring religion and morals of open society including every relative existence. In God we live and move and have our being as worthy of existence and in it. 'Whatever is, is good.'¹⁸ 'God the Father, Almighty maker of heaven and earth' becomes a point of departure for Niebuhr.¹⁹

---

15. Ibid.
16. Niebuhr, *Radical Monotheism and Western Culture*, p. 25.
17. Ibid., p. 27. Footnote 3.
18. Ibid., pp. 32, 37.
19. Ibid., p. 33.

Comparative Theology: Culture and Religion 161

Niebuhr's typology of culture and religion reinforces his theocentric principle in comprehending the way Christians have interacted with religious representations, their forms, social institutions, and cultural norms in different contexts and various times. In John Hick's account, Niebuhr's radical monotheism would find an affinity with Tillich, who conceptualizes in the theistic sense God as being-itself, the very being and ground of all being.[20] If Niebuhr is concerned with the relation between theology and sociology through typology, Tillich conceptualizes a theology of culture in terms of definition of the relation between religion and culture in an existential frame of reference.

Existential Enquiry

Tillich elaborates his theology of culture through existential enquiry, focusing on the relation between religion and culture. Religious aspects involve that which is ultimate, infinite and unconditional in human spiritual life. In the largest and most basic sense, he defines religion as ultimate concern; the state of being is ultimately concerned with itself taken as religion. Here, the gap disappears between the sacred and secular realm in every moment of life. The sacred and the secular are within each other, and the ultimate concern is present in all preliminary concerns, while consecrating and transcending these.[21]

God is the name for the content of the ultimate concern, and faith refers to the state of being grasped by God. Tillich's existential concept of religion maintains that religion is the substance, the all-determining ground, and the depth of human spiritual life; it bestows upon us the experience of the Holy as the ultimate meaning.[22] Tillich's definition of God and religion helps us to critique capitalism and consumerism. Capitalism allows for us to shop for meaning, and to have power be our ultimate concern.

In a religious analysis of culture, Tillich comprehends the relationship between religion and culture in the sense that 'religion as ultimate concern is the meaning-giving substance of culture.' 'Culture is the form of religion,' or 'the totality of forms in which the basic concern of religion expresses itself.'[23] Such a definition safeguards itself against any dualistic relation between religion and culture. Tillich's existentialist

---

20. Hick, *Philosophy of Religion*, p. 6.
21. Niebuhr, *Radical Monotheism and Western Culture*, p. 41.
22. Ibid., pp. 8–9.
23. Ibid., p. 42.

position encourages theology to utilize the rich and profound materials and sources of existential analysis in all cultural realms. For him existential philosophy may determine the form of the answer rather than providing the answer, but the gospel has the function of answering the question regarding the meaning of human existence.[24]

Tillich's enquiry is framed with a method of correlation, which seeks to explain and clarify the contents of the Christian faith in terms of 'existential questions and theological answers in mutual interdependence.'[25] God in the self-manifestation to human being depends upon the human way of receiving and understanding God's manifestation; thus a theological correlation qualifies the divine-human relationship within religious experience in human existence as guided through a mutual interdependence. In this way, Tillich's existential enquiry counters Barth, who takes the initiative of God in revelation; God the *totaliter aliter* elects, guides and changes human life[26] through dialectical-analogical enquiry into the relation between God and human being. Barth's theological language in dealing with the mystery of God is of an analogical character in terms of similarity in greater dissimilarity; it is also narrative and exegetical in comprehending biblical language as testimony to God, which is in contrast to Tillich's symbolic language.

However, for Tillich faith is expressed only in symbolic language, because God is Being itself; the symbolic language 'points beyond itself while participating in that to which it points. In no other way can faith express itself adequately. The language of faith is the language of symbols.'[27] Tillich's existential enquiry thus has a theistic character in which symbolic language safeguards the transcendence of God against an idolatry of thinking of God in the sense of anthropomorphism.

Tillich emphasizes that the gospel implies the conquest of the law, and a new healing reality of salvation appears as the ground and meaning of human existence. In its prophetic role, the Church takes part in judging the culture and itself, listening to prophetic voices outside its walls; people outside the Church can be called participants of a 'latent' church in which the ultimate concern is hidden in the cultural forms and deformations. The 'manifest' church has to recognize these voices, despite their hostile attitude to it, while safeguarding itself against

---

24. Ibid., p. 49.
25. Tillich, *Systematic Theology* 1, p. 60.
26. Ibid., p. 61.
27. Tillich, *Dynamics of Faith*, p. 45.

demonic distortions. The Church as a part of the culture judges culture, while including its own forms of life in a self-critical manner. The Church and culture are within each other rather than alongside. The biblical symbol of the Kingdom of God includes the Church and the culture, while transcending them.[28]

An existential type is convinced of the transcendence of God over the Church and culture, while defining God as the ultimate concern immanent within the culture; such a type refers to Christ over the Church as well as of the culture, because Christ is present within the culture. According to Hick, Tillich's existential enquiry holds the permissiveness between supranaturalism and naturalism and constitutes a third and superior standpoint, transcending naturalism and supranaturalism.[29]

In dealing with the history of religions, Tillich further elaborates the existential mode of correlation between theology and religion in terms of a dynamic typology. In his presuppositions, revelatory experiences are universally human, entailing saving powers. But revelation is received and understood in humanity's finite situation, which is biologically conditioned, psychologically grasped, and sociologically constituted; it implies the reality of humanity's estranged character in a distorted form; here religion is elevated to be an end itself rather than a means to an end.[30]

This limited reality of human life requires a critique in the three forms of the mystical, the prophetic and the secular. The history of religions does not exist alongside or beside the history of culture, because the sacred is in the depth of the secular. The Ultimate lies within the secular realm.[31] The sacred is creative ground, as well as a critical criterion of the secular. The religious must utilize the secular as a critical tool regarding religious self-critique. In the history of religions, Tillich holds, there may be a central event which makes a concrete theology with universalist significance.[32] There was a long preparatory, revelatory history in the universal history of religions toward the Kairos in the right and fulfilled time, making possible the appearance of Jesus as Christ.[33]

In his dynamic typological approach Tillich articulates the types of the sacramental, the mystical and the prophetic-ethical in dealing

---

28. Tillich, *Theology of Culture*, p. 51.
29. Hick, *Philosophy of Religion*, pp. 69–70.
30. Tillich, *Christianity and the Encounter of World Religions*, p. 64.
31. Ibid., p. 66.
32. Ibid., p. 65.
33. Ibid., pp. 68–9.

with the universal religious basis in the experience of the Holy; the Holy appears in a special, sacramental way among all religions. A critical movement occurs, leading through spiritual-mystical protest to the corruption of the sacramental. The particular embodiment of the Holy is denied and devalued for the sake of the Ultimate One. The ethical or prophetic component takes issue with the corrupt consequences of the sacramental basis or the mystical basis, as it comes to the denial of justice. However, Tillich argues that if religious experience dispenses with the sacramental and the mystical component, it would fall into a moralistic and secularized form in the sense of a quasi-religion.

Combined with the three components, Tillich characterizes 'the religion of the concrete spirit'[34] in terms of the telos of the history of religions. In the teleological history of religions, theonomy appears, from *theos* (God) and *nomos* (law), which implies a fight of God against religion within religion. Theonomy, in the relation between the sacred and the secular, appears in the religion of the concrete spirit in fragments, because its fulfilment is of an eschatological reserve.[35] There are moments of *kairoi* in history in which the religion of the concrete spirit is actualized in a fragmentary manner, here and now. Tillich integrates a phenomenology of religion in drawing attention to the self-showing of the phenomena (such as the religious symbols, the rites, the ideas, and the various cultural activities) in the universal history of religions. The historian of religions seeks to place the reinterpreted concepts within the framework of the dynamics of religious and secular history, which is necessary in dealing with our present religious and cultural situation.[36]

Tillich's theology of culture and religion analyzes religious symbols rooted in the totality of human experience, while including local surroundings in all their ramifications (political, economic and social); religious symbolism can be used as a language of the doctrine of human being, that is the theological anthropology in an experiential-expressive manner.[37] He is at the threshold of a constructive theology of comparative religion and culture, in which religious discourse can be articulated and analyzed in reference to the religious construction of social reality along with agent, institution and power relations in a sociological, hermeneutical framework.

---

34. Ibid., p. 72.
35. Ibid, pp. 74–5.
36. Ibid., p. 77.
37. Ibid., p. 78.

Postliberal Model

Lindbeck calls into question Tillich's existential definition of religion and culture. In Lindbeck's account, Tillich's definition – religion as the substance of culture, and culture as the form of religion – belongs to an experiential-expressive formula, in which religion as the ultimate concern 'is the vitalizing source of all significant cultural achievements.'[38] Lindbeck instead presents an alternative to the definition of religion as the ultimate dimension of culture, in which religion, like a Kantian a priori, provides shape and intensity to the experiential matrix, as well as cultural significance. Like a culture or a language, a religion is a communal phenomenon, in which the experiencing of inner attitude, feelings and sentiments is made possible, constituting the subjectivities of individuals.[39] Lindbeck is considerably indebted to Clifford Geertz's cultural anthropology, and he applies the context-sensitive description of culture to religion. Geertz argues against a generalizing approach, implying that there is a danger of locking analysis away from the proper object. Culture, like religion, is a context within which 'social events, behaviors, institutions or processes' 'can be intelligibly – that is, thickly – described.'[40]

Given this, Lindbeck emphasizes the task of theology like an ethnographer equipped with the skill of description. He distinguishes his cultural-linguistic approach from experiential-expressive enquiry, which is based on symbols of inner feelings, attitudes or existential orientations.[41] The experience is elevated as the source and norm of objectifications in most religions, in which different religions and cultures are taken as 'diverse expressions or objectifications of a common core experience.'[42] This resembles Schleiermacher's approach to the source of religion in terms of the feeling of absolute dependence,[43] which is an utterly existential matter; doctrinal statements or dogma are reflections on religious feeling. This counters to a propositionalist model, in which if a doctrine is once true or false, it is always true or false. Here, church doctrines, seen in the context of traditional orthodoxies,

---

38. Lindbeck, *The Nature of Doctrine*, p. 34.
39. Ibid., p. 33.
40. Ibid., p. 115. See Geertz, *The Interpretation of Cultures*, p. 14.
41. Ibid., p. 16.
42. Ibid., p. 31.
43. Ibid., p. 21.

adopt informative propositions or truth claims in dealing with objective realities.[44]

For the cultural-linguistic model, Lindbeck finds the work of Barth to be crucial, because Barth's theology of revelation is set up over against the human experience; it is in affinity with a cultural-linguistic approach. He also respects Barth's understanding of the Scripture in terms of the self-imposition of revelation in shaping the primary function of the canonical narrative. Barth's exegetical concern with biblical narrative is a chief source for Lindbeck to develop an idea of intratextuality; it is deemed to be an appropriate way of doing theology as consistent with a cultural-linguistic theory of religion, which is in accordance with a regulative view of Christian doctrine.[45]

In fact, Barth does not undermine the significance of culture for theological construction. The cultural realm, seen in light of reconciliation, can become the sematic texts through which God may continue to speak to the Church. A theology of culture may be built upon Barth's theology of speech act taking place outside the ecclesiastical sphere, in other words, within the context of reconciliation.[46] Barth does not defeat the constructive side of dogmatic theology, because theological language concerning the mystery of God is semantically retrieved in and through analogical procedure, which embraces the universal horizon of intertextuality in terms of the symbol of reconciliation.

Despite this, Lindbeck has not managed to articulate this linguistic-worldly side in Barth's theology of reconciliation in accordance with the regulative and narrative view. Rather, Lindbeck's postliberal concern falls on offering a cultural-linguistic approach to religion, in which religions are compared to languages embedded with the forms of life; thus religions are similar to cultures (Wittgenstein). Insofar as language games are correlated with a form of life, a culture has both cognitive and behavioural dimensions; it applies to religious tradition, in which religious doctrines, narratives and ethical directives are all related to religious performance of rituals, religious experiences and the institutional forms. This perspective (in the fashion of Emile Durkheim) is involved in elaborating religion as language game within a cultural-linguistic framework.[47]

---

44. Ibid., pp. 16–17.
45. Ibid., pp. 121. 135.
46. Barth, *Church Dogmatics* IV/3.1. § 69. P. 2.
47. Lindbeck, *The Nature of Doctrine*, p. 33.

The function of the Church doctrines in the sense of a regulative or rule theory becomes more prominent in their use 'as communally authoritative rules of discourse, attitude and action,' than in the experiential-expressive symbols.[48] A religion is not derived from inner experience, but the latter is viewed as derivative. The agonies of Grunewald's Crucifixion are completely different from an image of goodness on Buddhist soil.[49] Human experience is shaped and influenced by cultural and linguistic forms, in other words, an external word (a *verbum externum*),[50] in which the culture-forming power of religious experience is regarded to be derivative rather than primordial.

2. Comparative Theology and Social Scientific Enquiry

The theology of culture – whether theocentric, existential or postliberal – tends to belittle social scientific study in treating cultural issues such as race, gender, sexuality and ethnicity. Christianity does not exist apart from cultural context, because it interacts with culture and is influenced by it rather than becoming free-floating or neutral over and against cultural life. It transforms culture through involvement, while being affected by it. Sociological fieldwork of cultural context is needed from the inside, because it is indispensable to comprehend life history and orientation of others in their own terms. Cultures are internally diverse and relative in their own unique lives, and they are changing, moved, and conditioned by social location and power relations. Comparative theology is concerned with intercultural studies and cross-cultural fertilization in the systematic study of the Other. God's truth is comprehended through specific cultural forms and can be translatable rather than reduced to doctrinal form.

What becomes crucial in the study of culture is to explicate cultural problems from inside in terms of a critical theory of social stratification for reinforcing the significance of comparative theology and religious construction of reality. Cultural problems should be an important component of comparative theology, which is mainly concerned with analyzing sacred texts, religious ideas, symbols and practices in their affinity with social institutions, political systems and cultural order. Weber's social theory is used for this task; it is mainly concerned with three interconnected areas: economic status (wealth), political status

---

48. Ibid., p. 18.
49. Ibid., p. 83.
50. Ibid., p. 34.

(power), and social-cultural status (honour or prestige). The emergence of economically conditioned power is comprehended as the consequence of other existing powers, which would be conditioned by social honour. Social honour or prestige, Weber holds, can be the basis of political or economic power. It is distributed in a community, and status groups take part in this distribution, constituting the social-cultural order. Multiple forms of power in economic, political, and social-cultural spheres are to be secured in terms of the legal order as an additional factor, though the latter does not become the primary source of the power.[51]

In Weber's account, a specific complex of social relations is engendered and specialized, while the agents engage in their everyday practice. A bureaucratic authority or power requires administration by trained experts derived from socially and economically privileged strata on the basis of training and educational certificates. Differences in educational achievement have significant consequences for the occupational system of stratification.[52] However, Weber does not analyze the system of reproduction in family, the Church, and the educational system in reference to the role of the state, which charges institutions with managing and regulating everyday life through symbolic goods. Education is related to the value of social networks in producing and reproducing a social form of cultural capital or cultural knowledge in the sense of a non-financial asset. Multiple forms of capital can be classified in terms of the usable resources and powers, which are distributed into and organized around occupational stratification; here, cultural capital becomes efficacious as a power or a resource in social institutions and bureaucratic authority, along with economic capital.[53]

Class Situation and Status Situation

In Marx's view, classes struggle against each other for possession and control of economic resources, fuelling social change in social stratification. Social conflict is caused by inequality and alienation which are a key principle for understanding culture and its dynamic change; this idea of social conflict may apply to the relation between genders, ethnicities, races and other social statuses. In Marx's understanding of society as the ensemble of social relations, objective relations exist independently of

---

51. *From Marx Weber*, trans. and eds. Gerth and Mills, p. 180.
52. Ibid., pp. 192, 200. See Nolan and Lenski, *Human Societies*, p. 263.
53. Bourdieu and Wacquant, *An Invitation to Reflexive Sociology*, pp. 117–20.

individual consciousness and will; it is more than interactions between agents or intersubjective ties between individuals.[54]

Marx places the primacy of the economic, material base over against the cultural, ethnic superstructure. Class position is organized and narrowed down to means of production and division of labour. The guiding principle is class conflict in the context of economic relations and development, while culture and ideas are seen as superstructure as determined by economic production. Ethnic conflict is to be seen in light of the alienating structure of economy.[55] However, if superstructure is assumed to have a role in influencing the economic base in a dialectical sense, it is significant to comprehend the relation between base and superstructure in the way that human thought is founded in human activity or praxis; the world is produced and changed by that activity.[56]

This perspective facilitates an integration of reciprocity between the economic aspect and the cultural-symbolic aspect, bringing a theory of social class closer to a critical theory of social stratification. Class may become a cultural category based on economic relations, yet embedded within a broader spectrum of intersectional fields. A cultural perspective on social capital (social groups in interpersonal relationships with a shared sense of identity, norms and values for a common good) qualifies a reality of division of labour, including the spectrum of middle-class in occupational stratification; it also includes positions in public administration and the state apparatus (professions) as well as other cultural producers.

The implementation of a theory of social stratification enhances the relation between economic aspects and cultural-symbolic aspects in a mutually determined way; it takes into account a dialectical unity or reciprocity between social class in the economic order and social status in the social-cultural order, because they influence one another. Such mutual conditions include the legal order, which, in turn, influences these two related spheres. The political parties are oriented toward acquisition of social power, aiming at class and status; they integrate them into the political strategy and its programme, by representing their respective interests determined by class or status situation.[57] Marx's insight, within the social-scientific framework, into the dialectical relation between base and superstructure, is qualified in terms of a

---

54. Ibid., p. 97.
55. Malesevic, *The Sociology of Ethnicity*, p. 15.
56. Berger and Luckmann, *The Social Construction of Reality*, p. 6.
57. *From Max Weber*, p. 194; see Bourdieu, *Language and Symbolic Power*, p. 246.

symbolic dimension of the division of labour, rationalization, reification and power relations. Several important categories of reflexive sociology (Bourdieu) help to sharpen a theory of social stratification by cutting across the limitations of Weber's interpretive sociology as well as Marx's economic reductionism; a relation between religious ideas and material interests is elaborated in terms of cultural dynamism, power relations, and diversity of capitals in the study of religion and culture.

The unique forms of social or cultural life (or social or cultural facts), which is life-world, guide, create and influence individual life. To understand the interaction between culture and individual meaningful life, the social scientific experiment uses hermeneutical articulation, in which critical analysis centres around religious discourse, material interests and power relations embedded in the intersectional regimes in social stratification. Given this, multivariate enquiry is crucial in mediating the relation between culture (the symbolic world) and material interests, while articulating the significance of reciprocity in taking on religion and society. Cultures are internally diverse in stratification by diverse status groups, always changing over time through human agency, and affected by religious discourse and social institutions, while embedded within power relations. Social inequality relates specifically to the different points of access to economic resources, political power, education or occupation. Race, ethnicity, gender and class are all seen as important components in shaping and determining social cultural structures and systems of power relations through social-cultural diffusion.

This social stratification cannot be adequately comprehended without an analysis of the elective affinity between religious ideas and social-cultural life in influencing individuals, their cultural disposition, and institutions in regards to race, ethnicity, gender and the culture of patriarchy. It is of significance to call attention to the aspect of symbolic violence as manifested in power differentials between social groups; such violence or domination can be seen in an imposition of the norms and values of the group with greater social power upon the subordinate group. Power relations in symbolic violence – invisible and imperceptible even to its victims – can be analyzed in terms of unconscious enforcement or legitimation in domination through the symbolic channel of communicational cognition, recognition and even feeling; this symbolic reality is at work in different social domains such as race, ethnic identity, gender and sexual orientation.[58]

---

58. Bourdieu, *Masculine Domination*, p. 2.

Race and Ethnicity

If race is built upon a biological connection or 'blood' category within a group, ethnicity retains cultural connections more involved in a common language, religion and cultural practices within the community. Ethnic groups are expressed as human groups in a common identity, which are other than kinship groups (a genuine community); the former retains a belief in their common origins, providing a basis for the creation of community.[59] Ethnic identities are more complex in their definition than racial categories (such as black, white, American Indian, and Asian and Pacific Islander). It can be argued that the biological claim is based on the ideological justification for racial categories, while justifying the prevailing system of economic, political and cultural inequality.

Stated in Boas' anthropology, differences in the cultural values, customs and behaviours among different societies are attributed to differences in culture rather than biological capacity or racial stock.[60] In dealing with the relationship between culture and race, he therefore makes claims of innate racial superiority/inferiority, because he argues that the most significant differences among humanity can be seen as products of cultural rather than biological factors. Seen in the perspective of social stratification, race relations can be primarily explored in terms of ethnic relations, in which an analysis focuses on monopolization by social status and political power. Ethnicity is comprehended as the device of monopolistic social closure. Such a theory argues whether an ethnic basis for communal action would be dependent upon a belief in a blood relationship.[61]

Ethnicity as a form of cultural status group exists on the basis of a particular group belief and is rooted in the belief in a common descent. Ethnicity is determined by a social estimation of honour, which is expressed in a particular lifestyle. Ethnic groups become hereditary status groups, which are expressed in terms of ethnic honour.[62] It would cause ethnic conflict which finds its root in the idea of a chosen people; it is based on conviction about the excellence of one's own customs as compared to the inferiority of other people's.[63] In fact, racial

---

59. Weber, 'Race Relations,' in *Weber Selections in Translation*, p. 364.
60. Tanner, *Theories of Culture*, p. 23.
61. Weber, 'Race Relations,' in *Weber Selections in Translation*, p. 368.
62. Malesevic, *The Sociology of Ethnicity*, pp. 25–8.
63. Weber, "Race Relations," in *Weber Selections in Translation*, p. 366.

characteristics are significant as limiting factors in the formation of ethnic identity. Differences in a shared set of customs or ethnically relevant customs play a part in the unfolding of a sense of ethnic identity, as well as underlying blood relationships; along with differences in language and religion, such differences are a normal result of differences in economic or political conditions.[64]

An ethnic group in cultural formation is also dependent on social and political action and mobilization. Political community inspires a belief in common ethnicity and mobilizes an ethnic group to support the social and political strategy. When people are organized into ranked groups, social prestige or status in hierarchies, social inequality becomes crucial in access to resources and distribution of social and cultural capitals; the social structure constitutes the biological side of race in wider cultural characteristics underlying discrimination and injustice. Ethnic conflict occurs in the country (like the former Yugoslavia) in which various ethnicities have lived together, intermarried and spoken the same language. Race and ethnicity can overlap with each other yet retain their distinction. For example, a Korean-American would probably consider him/herself to be a member of the Korean or Asian race, but, if he/she doesn't engage in any practices or customs of his/her ancestors (like traditional costume), he/she might not identify with the ethnicity, while considering him/herself as an American.

Racial or ethnic categories can be used to explain social inequality and other phenomena of domination. Race or ethnicity correlates with social problems such as poverty, inequality, unemployment, violence and imprisonment. In the period of slavery, the white people of the American South without property felt a racial hatred against black people because of their social status.[65] Race matters, because culture is built as a structure rooted in family, faith community and social institutions; cultural values influence economy and politics, while the latter promote cultural ideals.[66] Matters of race are intertwined with the cultural creation of other categories of inequality and injustice in the system of social stratification (for example, sexuality, gender, class and status). In taking up political economy, sociologists have expanded the investigation of the material aspects of race by looking at sexual identities, values and exchanges. A critical theory of social stratification incorporates an intersectional analysis of the system of oppression

---

64. Ibid., pp. 366–7.
65. Ibid.
66. West, *Race Matters*, p. 19.

and violence, for instance with respect to black women's experience in comparison with the experience of white, middle-class women.[67]

A cultural ideology of race has influence on theological assumptions in which God created nations in a racially distinct manner. A shadow of racial ideology or a system of racism can be seen in the separation or segregation of individuals, families and communities. For example, there is the inclusion of Rahab (a Canaanite) and Ruth (a Moabite) into the line of Jesus. Paul articulates God's inclusion of all people, for example, when he spoke to the people of Athens (Acts 17:26-28). As Benedict argues, '… racism has no scientific basis for its claims of congenital superiority for any one race or nation … Then the anthropologist, who has probably spent years of his life patiently investigating racial differences, has to say again that to recognize Race does not mean to recognize Racism.'[68]

Racism functions like a religious dogma of biological superiority-inferiority, but such a biological position remains questionable. Instead, the cultural theory inherent in racist rhetoric should be critically investigated and culturally analyzed in terms of the historical and social formation of racism. At issue is a social scientific analysis of the epistemological underpinnings of racial thinking, pejudice and discrimination in the European modernity and colonialism. European colonial modernity 'set the stage of racist dogmas and gave violent early expression to racial antipathies without propounding racism as a philosophy. Racism did not get its currency in modern thought until it was applied to conflicts within Europe …'[69]

A black theology of liberation refers to the most distinctive contribution in challenge to racial injustice. It elaborates the important place of black experience and the wounds of racial violence in the struggle for justice and wholeness. 'I was black before I was Christian.'[70] Black lives matter, since racism is an issue of controversy in its systemic and systematic oppression, causing protest and moral outrage in society, which is racially divided through social enforcement (police treatment of black or other non-white ethic groups).

More than that, there is a combination between sexuality and the symbolism of blood, which are grounded in the regimes of power. Racism took shape in the type of political power in which the purity of

---

67. Collins, *Black Feminist Thought*, p. viii.
68. Benedict, *Race: Science and Politics*, v.
69. Ibid., 174.
70. Cone, *The Cross and the Lynching Tree*, p. xvii.

the blood is protected and the triumph of the race is ensured.[71] Sexual racism is experienced in its discrimination in terms of interracial marriage and its judicial system. Its discrimination can also be seen in sexual orientations and ethnic backgrounds. An act of discrimination is embedded with occupational systems, or positions of employment, in which privilege is organized in accordance with accepted gendered norms and heterosexual normativity. It refers to the sexualization of a racial gender norm, in which gender and race can be explicated by looking at heterosexual ways of normalizing, underwriting a diverse reality of social cultural formation.

Gender and Sexuality: Symbolic Domination

It is frequently argued that gender is socially constructed, because the sexual differences between being feminine and being masculine are assigned to the social cultural system. Gender is distinguished from sex, which is based on biological differences between male and female. Gender differences can be understood as a central feature of patriarchy or a social-cultural system of patriarchal dominion. Gender status is produced in the institutional context, and it is connected to a gender role in which sex and gender can be conceptualized as a spectrum of human diversity; such diversity can transcend biological dimorphism. For instance, the case of *bakla* is considered a third gender in the Philippines; a man is dressed as a woman in the workplace, on public transportation, or even in church.[72] Self-identity is female rather than male.

In Thailand, a lady-boy (*Kathoey*; male-to-female transgender person through sexual reassignment surgery), which makes a third sex or gender, is culturally accepted. Local terms in the Philippines and Thailand, such as *bakla*, tomboy or lady-boy, coexist in its social formation, along with Western discourse of lesbian, gay and transgender.[73] In this instance, a culturally produced gender transcends the congealed normativity of binary sex or binary gender, requiring us to consider gender in terms of diverse and different interpretations of sex. A free choice of sexuality is fused with cultural difference in transcending the binary opposition of sex.

---

71. Foucault, *The History of Sexuality* 1, p. 149.
72. Garcia, *Philippine Gay Culture*.
73. Ceperiano, et al., 'Girl, Bi, Bakla, Tomboy,' *Philippine Journal of Psychology*, pp. 9–10.

Gender differences or inequality can be understood as a central feature of a social-cultural system of masculine dominion in relation to women. As educational opportunities are increased, differentiated and specialized in an advanced society, its formation requires a gendered division of labour (or sexual division of labour) according to men's jobs and women's jobs; granted social stability and organic solidarity, this has a detrimental consequence. Women are rare in higher positions within occupations. This vertical division of labour will not bring equality for all women, though work is divided in gendered ways across occupations (the horizontal gender division of labour). This has implications for the way in which wealth is distributed between women and men, along with the cultural capital of education.

In the social construction of gender, medical and scientific discourse plays a significant role in constituting femininity and masculinity.[74] A notion of gender is produced and represented by the medical and scientific discourse about it; discourse formation and practice come to terms with institutional ratification and juridical authority in constituting femininity and masculinity, underwriting a bio-political power. This refers to the reification of life-world or civil society in the social structure through political society (political power, economic capital and the communication system of mass media) in which mass media, an important regime of discourse, proliferates gender, sexuality, race and class.

The current form of gender and sexuality is influenced and organized around media simulations of reality, in other words, media-saturated consciousness; configurations of sign-value (or culture-value) about gender and sexuality are heavy with meaning, and through them a hyperreality of society is simulated by means of images, information and signs.[75] The understanding of gender and sexuality depends on the way people interpret mass media's discourse about gender and sexuality, whether positive or negative. Through proliferation of social media, LGBT+ identities have become places of consumption. Within current capitalist society, one's identity becomes datasets in algorithms in order to become a better object for marketing. The more we confess through non face-to-face interaction, the more we participate in the hyperreality created by social media and information saturation.

We live in a gendered society organized by way of heterosexuality, marriage and the nuclear family, which is portrayed as natural, normal and the right way of living. The system of heterosexuality becomes

---

74. Holmes, *What is Gender?*, pp. 2–3.
75. *Baudrillard: A Critical Reader*, pp. 8–9.

a general framework in giving account of the way in which gender identities in society are divided into the two gender types. However, there is no core gender identity, because gender performances are modeled after images or models imposed upon a male and a female through family, education, social institution and religion. Social and political forces shaped and codified masculine and feminine gender identity into the gendered and sexual being. A gender asymmetry is produced and reproduced according to need and the interests of the sexual division of labour, its system of rationalization; it underlies masculine dominion in totalizing the identity of the feminine into the former projected category. A performative approach to gender, or performativity of gender, comprehends sexual identity as a process.[76]

Judith Butler maintains that juridical systems of power, regulating political power, engender the subjects by representing them. The judicial formation of discourse and politics represents women as the subjects. The political construction of the subjects operates effectively in a concealed manner. This position makes it impossible to separate gender from political and cultural intersection. Gender intersects with race, class and sexuality through discursively constituted identities. Butler offers a mapping of intersecting differentials in dealing with the category of women by looking at it in the multiplicity of cultural, social and political intersections in which a concrete category can be constructed.[77]

Michel Foucault takes into account the political, disciplinary function of power underlying knowledge systems and domination, in which the human body is a site of power imposed by the state 'as a means of social control and political subjugation.'[78] The regime of truth within the framework of bio-politics is built on scientific discourse and the support of institutions which produces it, circulating through education, information, and social media. The discipline system constitutes sexuality historically as a bourgeois sexuality based on class sexualities.[79]

Religious Construction of Reality and Sexuality

Sex is commercialized as a good in the commodity society, and the sexual division of labour is organized around economic power in an androcentric system. This perspective does not separate the class situation from the

---

76. Butler, *Gender Trouble*, pp. 18–19.
77. Ibid., pp. 3–4.
78. Foucault, *The History of Sexuality* 1, p. 123.
79. Ibid., p. 127.

status situation in the political economy of symbolic goods underlying sexuality and gender in their inequality and commercialization. More credence ought to be given to the power of religious discourse and its construction of sexuality in shaping value rationality, political motivation, moral dignity and social organization. A multivariate approach is undertaken in dealing with an elective affinity between religious discourse and its construction of reality in reference to cultural facts and power relations.

In dealing with the historical reality of sexuality it becomes crucial to take into account religious attitudes and morals. The body and sexual passion in ancient Greek culture were differentiated from modern understanding. Early Christianity excluded and even condemned relationships between individuals of the same sex, while Greece exalted such relations, and Romans accepted them.[80] This dual practice in the sense of bisexuality is based on man's free choice, with no distinction between heterosexual and homosexual love.[81] However, pedagogical pederasty in same-gender eroticism between Greek men and the freeborn adolescent was often corrupted and damaging to the younger party youth in regard to the aged lover. This activity was based on inequality, even including abusive penetration by the aged party, rather than being aesthetically and morally valuable, as Foucault idealizes.[82]

If an erotic life is a cultural practice, it can be seen by examining the relation between religion and sex in Greek culture. Sexuality beyond pleasure refers to a reality of social structure, in which the Greek's use of pleasure is bound to a culture of aristocracy and patriarchy in subjugation of women, boys or girls, and the bodies of slaves. Bio-politics cannot be properly comprehended without the cultural impact of the human body, or the cultural facts of sexuality, which entail the cultural side of bio-politics in networking with religion and society. Political-cultural interplay remains critical in articulating a religious construction of erotic life. Greek forms of religious life were not concerned to correlate a divine power with a code of laws for the regulation of sexual behaviour, which runs counter to Judeo-Christian ethics.

In Weber's reflection on religion and the erotic sphere, a conceptual framework considers religious ideas in terms of the economic sphere, the political sphere, the aesthetic sphere and the erotic sphere.[83] Profane

---

80. Foucault, *The History of Sexuality* 2, p. 14.
81. Ibid., p. 189.
82. Ibid., p. 196. See Hubbard, ed. *Homosexuality in Greece and Rome*, p. 1.
83. *From Max Weber*, pp. 331–50.

heterosexuality, together with homosexual prostitution, is very ancient and sophisticated. A historical transition occurred from such prostitution to legally constituted marriage. A conception of marriage, which includes an economic arrangement for the wife and legal inheritance for the child, is pre-prophetic and universal. Sexual life replaced asceticism.[84]

All rational regulation of life contrasts with magical orgiasticism, cultivating eroticism by turning away from veiling the naive naturalism of sex. Such historical evolution involves the universal rationalization and intellectualization of culture in the sense of disenchantment with the magical world. Thus eroticism has varied considerably throughout history and culture. The erotic life in the classical Hellenic period did not know the seriousness of sexual love, but celebrated the characteristics of Hellenic love, as seen in Pericles' speech and the well-known statement of Demosthenes during the fourth century BCE.[85] Demosthenes' pederastic relation would be mocked as scandalous and improper in the sense of selling one's body for money. The comrade boy was the object which was demanded with all the ceremony of love as central to Hellenic culture. Culture becomes fate within the hegemonic cultural discourse, because cultural meaning of sexual activity is inscribed in the male body. Weber's view of pederasty through life-fate is considerably different from Foucault's ethical appreciation of it as 'a rather delicate stylization of the use of the aphrodisiac.'[86]

Given the difference between Weber and Foucault, it is useful to analyze the historical development and social relation between religious discourse and sex with reference to the symbolic division of labour and power relations; the sexual relation is articulated in terms of a social relation of rational organization, power and domination; in homosexual relations, an eroticized subordination is sometimes undertaken for masculine domination which feminizes the other. In ancient Greece, the victim was condemned to dishonour because he was regarded as the one who lost the status of a complete man and a citizen. In ancient Rome passive homosexuality with a slave was considered to be monstrous. In fact, penetration and power were espoused with the privilege of the ruling male elite.[87]

To the extent that the Greek reality of bisexuality is seen in terms of free choice between the two sexes, it is ascribed simply to the appetite

---

84. Ibid., pp. 343–4.
85. Ibid., pp. 344–55.
86. Ibid., p. 229.
87. Bourdieu, *Masculine Domination*, p. 21.

as implanted by nature in man's heart for beautiful human beings.[88] If a life of bisexuality was accepted by public opinion and found support in military or educational institutions in ancient Greece, it was also validated by religious rites and festivals invoking divine power in protection of those living in bisexuality. This aspect characterizes a cultural practice in terms of aesthetic lifestyle with moral value.[89] Nonetheless, an aesthetic approach to sexuality and natural appetite tends to belittle the extent to which bisexuality was critically assessed in regard to victim, penetration and male domination.

St Paul's critique of homosexuality can be apprehended in the form of his social critique of pederasty based on masculine power and domination. This masculine culture and its symbolic violence was to be transformed into community of equality and solidarity in which 'there is no longer Jew or Greek, there is no longer slave or free, there is no longer male and female; for all you are one in Jesus Christ.' (Galatians 3:28) This perspective runs counter to the destiny effect which is produced by the scheme of masculine power in feminizing the male in symbolic domination.

Furthermore, the culture of homosexuality in the ancient world was not more or less a constant. Rather one is born, grows and dies in society, which is embedded with inequality, injustice and dominion through cultural sexualizing. Differentials of sexuality are intersected in the multiplicity of religious, cultural, social and political spheres in which a concrete category of sexuality can be patterned and interpreted. Sexuality is intertwined with the cultural creation of other categories of inequality (race, class and gender). Thus, types of sexual preference are invested with different levels of significance within multiple realities of social stratification, without discarding the 'essential' sexual differences in inborn equality.[90] The androcentric episteme is organized by constructing the male or female body in biological reproduction in terms of the division of sexual labour and the sexual division of labour; it justifies such a symbolic system of domination and its legitimacy through androcentric rationality, by localizing the relation of domination and legitimacy in a social construction.[91]

Science, law and bureaucracy formalized sexual essentialism as deployed in the service of political power and rationalization, which have

---

88. Foucault, *The History of Sexuality* 2, p. 188.
89. Ibid., p. 190.
90. Hubbard, ed. *Homosexuality in Greece and Rome*, p. 2.
91. Bourdieu, *Masculine Domination*, p. 23.

led to inequality over sexuality and gender in the social cultural sphere. A masculine episteme is instituted in the order of things, and power relations are produced and held through the schemes of perception, recognition and misrecognition, which is penetrated into and expressed in and through the symbolic order of things. It produces the destiny effect in terms of a scheme of perception which stigmatizes homosexual relations.

3. Theological Method and Life-world Approach

A critical theory of religious discourse and its construction of reality facilitates comparative theology at a methodological level in elaborating a multivariate perspective on culture and religion. In many worlds of culture and religion, comparative theology seeks to reinterpret Biblical narratives or symbols in critical analysis of a social cultural system and its structure of inequality and domination. It is useful to explicate culture as the ensemble of texts through which comparative theology becomes a form of intertextuality between religion and the world; a theological symbol of reconciliation remains an arbiter in underlying this direction of intertextuality and correlation. A scriptural world comes to terms with the world of culture through communication and dialogue in the sense of undergirding a fusion of horizons in the semantic retrieval between these two entities.

A theory of religious construction of reality is used here, in a phenomenological frame of reference. If sociology seeks to explain meaningfully oriented behaviour, meaningful action in the cultural realm could be considered as a text which is to be deciphered, described and interpreted. The text has a semiotic dimension by virtue of its meaning – in other words, its semantic dimension.[92]

This perspective becomes decisive in Geertz's phenomenology of culture. Geertz conceptualizes his theory of culture in terms of semantics, because 'man is an animal suspended in webs of significance he himself has spun.'[93] Culture, seen as those webs and the analysis of them, has an interpretive character in search of meaning.[94] The culture is comprehended as an ensemble of texts in which cultural practice in its symbolic structure becomes a means of 'saying something of something.' Cultural life is deciphered in dealing with an ensemble of cultural practices through thick description and interpretation. At

---

92. Ricoeur, 'What is a Text? Explanation and Understanding,' in Ricoeur, *Hermeneutics & the Human Sciences*, p. 164.
93. Geertz, *The Interpretation of Cultures*, p. 12.
94. Ibid., p. 5.

this point, this cultural hermeneutic is deployed in terms of Husserl's theory of life-world. Husserl undertakes a methodological enquiry of intentionality and suspension of the natural attitude concerning what is taken for granted. Human consciousness (*noesis*) correlates with the regime of meaning (*noema*). An ideal meaning is not of an ahistorical dimension, since it is transmitted and affected under the horizon of life-world, which is historically pre-given and culturally transmitted, and socially embodied.

Seen in the multiplicity of life-world, Europeans, Africans, and Asians have their own validity, meaning or world horizon in an entirely different manner. Despite all their relativity, the life-world (history, tradition, culture and language) has a general, non-relativistic, common structure, enabling human understanding and synthesis of meaning in terms of the confluence of different horizons and multiple realities into the dialectical movement and stream. It qualifies an apprehension of natural attitude or doxic experience in connection with the social condition stratified in a hierarchical spectrum which appears to be naturally justified. A social scientific experiment seeks to problematize arbitrary divisions of labour, social constructions of sexualization, and its epistemic systems of legitimacy embedded within deep seated mechanisms, in other words, 'the doxic experience of the social world.'"[95]

Considered in this perspective, religion can be objectively comprehended as the life-world, as seen in the dialectical dynamic process and structure concerning cumulative tradition in historical and cultural development (rituals, art, music, economic ethics, theologies, sexuality and ethnicity among other things) and personal piety or faith.[96] It implies a cultural semantic approach to religion. If religion is not easily definable, or rather it is a European construct of recent origin, then a concept of religion as a static concept does not adequately express and capture the complexity and flux of religious lives in the historical and cultural matrix. Alfred Cantwell Smith's view of religion can therefore be seen as dynamic dialectics between cumulative tradition and personal faith in terms of the life-world.

Religious phenomena are described and interpreted in religious experience of the *totaliter aliter* in its self-unveiling aspect; what shows itself can be formulated in religious symbols, narratives, and sacred texts in relation to a social cultural matrix; the appearance of the sacred has an analogical character in its relative concealment, as well as in its gradually becoming revealed in the historical unfolding. Religious

---

95. Bourdieu, *Masculine Domination*, p. 9.
96. Smith, *The Meaning and End of Religion*, p. 194.

experience is mediated and expressed in language, which turns it into hermeneutical experience of the living word of God. The divine Word continues to find its expression and application through exegetical, hermeneutical works in terms of translation, retrieval of the layered meaning, and reconstruction. Comparative theology considers the significance of historical, critical method within the universal history of religion; religious a priori underlying one's faith-life is historically conditioned, socially influenced and acted on by other different streams of cumulative tradition. Here, a hermeneutical enquiry plays a significant role in understanding religious experience, faith-life, and faith community, interpreting it in connection with social cultural stratification.

In a phenomenological approach to religion as cultural semantic text, it is of special significance to draw attention to the ethical in the context of intersubjectivity; the ethical is systematized in terms of correlation between ethics (as a practice) and ethics (as a theoretical science at a meta-ethical level) in communal manner. Ethics is a practical answer to a cultural social situation, while it requires a reflective analysis of our ethical decision to and conviction (heart and volition) of that situation. The ethical science is seen in its practical intentionality in clarifying the meaningful action of an agent for embodied ethics, while a human being as an ethical agent takes part in the ongoing flow and goal through the fusion of ethical horizons interacting with one's surrounding society. We as ethical beings share a common social world in its intersubjectivity, which is influenced under the transcendental-ontological reality of life-world.[97] The ethical subject comes to terms with epistemological attitude in terms of suspension of natural attitude, responsible critique, synthetic retrieval of meaningful action, and emancipation.

Comparative Theology and Reconciliation

Sexual culture retains the system of cultural meaning and ethical stance regarding sexuality and its social practices. Sexual identity is built upon sexual culture, which is imbued with life-world. Sexual life is culturally constructed in the expression of sexuality and gender roles.[98] In dealing with the problem of sexuality and gender here, a bio-political enquiry is used in its connection with cultural facts of life through the multivariate framework, in which a critique of a culture of patriarchy involves analyzing the body as the site of power and domination through docility. The scientific discourse about sexuality plays a crucial role in

---

97. Ferrarello, *Husserl's Ethics and Practical Intentionality*, pp. 11–12.
98. Herdt, *Sambia Sexual Culture*.

producing hegemonic power by marginalizing other discourses about it. The discourse of marginalized groups is suppressed by rationalizing discourse, and it then establishes sites of resistance.

On the other hand, the intersex counters a binary frame of sex, by making it difficult for biologically-given sex to be categorized in terms of biological dimorphism. Gender is made or even forced by political power of normalization and judicial authority, foreclosing a search for styles of existence as different forms. Therefore, scientific discourse of sex or society's notion of sex is mostly a social construct under scrutiny; society has differentiated between sex and gender, and intersex is left out of the discourse.

Social scientific enquiry appropriates the role of discourse in power/knowledge and bio-political analysis in order to promote ethics of resistance against totalitarian power in politics and sexuality. An entire network of social relations is gendered in the system of law, the economic sphere, religious symbols, and sovereignty. Seen in the scheme of religious construction of reality, it is necessary to elucidate religious discourse in reference to material interests on broader spectrums and meanings; this construction can be explored in connection with gender status, race, masculine culture, body politics and sexuality. A comparative study of religion and gender shows the extent to which religious traditions, beliefs and practices have been constituted and perceived from the masculine perspective of sexuality and gender.[99]

The scriptures of the major world religions were written and influenced in the world of patriarchy and slavery, in which sacred narrative or commandments would be misused to justify a patriarchal culture of domination and inequality. A symbolic scheme of interpretation within the bio-political frame requires a new and fresh exegesis of the Word of God and its gender-related dimension in the social, political and cultural sphere; it must take into account a critique of patriarchy, sexual hierarchies and the role of gender. The latter is not essentially nor permanently fixed, but is socially constructed; it is eschatologically to be changed in the biblical context: 'For I am about to create new heavens and a new earth; the former things shall not be remembered or come to mind' (Isaiah 65:17). The subject matter of the Gospel is expressed in critique of the masculine system of power and domination in ancient Rome, while transforming the culture of patriarchy into the culture of equality and of recognition of difference in status and class (Galatians 3:28).

Culture as a human universal can be referenced to the life-world in which comparative theology searches for constructing a life-orientation

---

99. *Religion and Gender*, ed. King, p. 2.

and meaning through the semantic retrieval of layered meanings for synthesis and reconstruction in struggle with the mystery of God. A comparative theology in a theocentric frame of reference can be advanced in terms of correlation with other cultural activity in different cultures and religions. If we are never outside tradition and history, we do not exist outside sexual division of labour, cultural influence, power relations, and rational organization in society. This perspective incorporates significant ruptures and discontinuities into the theory of social stratification, in which the comparative study of culture and religion problematizes the extent to which exclusion in the social system would take place along with domination, foreclosure and omission.[100]

The life-world enquiry of culture and religion comes to terms with the philosophical reflection of religious ideas, in which one's religious identity cannot be properly constituted without its universal significance in recognizing different horizons of other cultures and religions. The vertical way of revelation comes to us, allowing a human being to take part in it in a dynamic and approaching manner; the horizontal line of religion is of a cultural character in constituting society in stratification in terms of religious discourse and power relations.[101] We have the treasure only in an earthen vessel (2 Corinthians. 4:7).

This said, the biblical symbol of reconciliation has its own particularistic terms, while acknowledging its universal horizon in encounter with people of other cultures and religions. Reconciliation in its universal horizon is grounded in *theologia crucis*, which strengthens the critical implication of reconciliation in challenging the unreconciled reality of the world, in other words, the reality of impersonal forces reifying society, culture and religion. It sharpens the meaning of the gospel for the world, standing in solidarity with those in inequality and in a structure of violence framed by economic source, political administration and cultural distribution.

Comparative theology in the life-world frame of reference relocates a theocentric aspect within God's reconciliation, in which there is a type of Christ for and from those on the margins; it is heard in the prophetic voice of Dietrich Bonhoeffer, who adopts 'the perspective of the outcast, the suspect, the maltreated, the powerless, the oppressed, the reviled – in short, from the perspective of those who suffer.'[102]

---

100. Tanner, *Theories of Culture*, p. 132.
101. Van der Leeuw, *Religion in Essence and Manifestation*, p. 680.
102. Bonhoeffer, *Letters and Papers from Prison*, p. 17.

Chapter 7

Comparative Theology and Interreligious Dialogue

Comparative study of religion and culture is an indispensable project in featuring public theology. If public theology deals with problems of civil society, it cannot avoid the sphere of religious pluralism and cultural stratification, which requires interreligious encounter and mutual learning for collaboration, justice, and peace among religions. Churches and religious movements retain contributing factors in the political process in defending democracy and promoting human rights in the US civil rights movement, as well as in the European context. For Habermas, pluralism and the struggle for religious tolerance have become driving forces in shaping democratic society. They galvanize religious tolerance as 'politics of recognition' in democratic, pluralist society.[1]

Placing theology in the cultural way of life, comparative theology integrates the sociological study of religion and culture by involving an integral dimension of daily life. This perspective characterizes comparative theology in everyday life as a special cultural activity,[2] while enhancing religious construction of public reality.

For this task, there is a need to undertake a long tour in hermeneutical treatment, starting with Barth and Tillich in their respective contributions to Buddhist-Christian relations. Then it is important to critically enhance their insights toward a social scientific approach to religion and culture, referring to Troeltsch and Weber, who are concerned with

---

1. Habermas, *Between Naturalism and Religion*, p. 269.
2. Tanner, *Theories of Culture*, p. 69.

sociological analysis of elective affinity between religious discourse, material interests and power relations. Such epistemology underlies a cultural narrative approach to culture and religion as an ensemble of semantic texts in light of a proleptic conception of reconciliation. Comparative theology plays an indispensable part in interreligious dialogue for religious construction of reality in terms of common good, peace and interreligious recognition and solidarity.

1. Barth and Religion

Barth is called the representative of 'neo-orthodox,' emphasizing a trend toward a theology of repristination in Europe. However, Tillich acknowledges that Barth is keenly interested in social political situations; Barth's greatness is appreciated in his continual critical renewal of his position, in which he appears to be more than a merely kerygmatic theologian.[3]

As I have discussed Barth and religions in chapter 3, it is important at this juncture to elaborate the significance of Barth in the context of interreligious dialogue. Barth's theory of religion has been severely criticised because of a questionable translation of the revelation of God as the abolition (*Aufhebung*) of religion (*Church Dogmatics* 1/2. §17). However, the German term *Aufhebung* is of dialectical connotation in critique, exaltation and sublimation. Barth explains: 'The abolishing of religion by revelation need not mean only its negation: the judgment that religion is unbelief. Religion can just as well be exalted in revelation, even though the judgment still stands. It can be upheld by it and concealed in it.'[4] In the discussion of the problem between revelation and religion, Barth draws attention to God's hiddenness in the world of human religion, because God has actually entered the sphere of the human universal, such that there are 'fundamentally unmistakable parallels and analogies in human realities and possibilities.'[5] Barth affirms: 'In His revelation God is present in the world of human religion.'[6]

Barth acknowledges that Troeltsch considers the phenomena of general religious history, in which religion is not understood in terms

---

3. Tillich, *Systematic Theology* I, pp. 1, 5.
4. CD I/2, p. 326.
5. CD I/2, p. 282.
6. CD I/2, p. 297.

of revelation, but revelation in terms of religion.[7] If Barth affirms God's presence in the world of human religions, his position of God's universality does not contrast with Troeltsch, who affirms the mystery of God in the universal framework of history of religion. What is common between Barth and Troeltsch is the perspective that the Christian religion is not 'fundamentally superior to all other religions' in the sense of 'the fulfilled nature of human religion.'[8] Given this, his term 'religion as unbelief' is polemically applied to Christian religion first; it has little to do with a negative value judgment upon religious science or philosophy. Barth warns us not to 'become Philistines or Christian iconoclasts in face of human greatness as it meets us so strikingly in this very sphere of religion.'[9] For Barth the religion of *revelation* is not bound up with the *religion* of revelation. However, it is unfortunate that Barth has an unqualified understanding of other religions in his wholesale description of the aim of atheism as that of mysticism. 'The Chinese *Tao*, the Indian *Tat tvam asi*, Hegel's in-and-for itself of the absolute Spirit' – should all these be classified as the same category in which all cows in the darkness are grey?

Barth and Buddhist-Christian Exchange

In 1938 Barth initiated a comparative study of the Protestant teaching of grace and Japanese Shin Buddhism. He focuses on the difference between Genku-Honen, the founder of Pure Land Buddhism, and his pupil, Shinran.

Amida was named infinite light and life and regarded as the supreme and personal God, who is 'the Creator and Lord of Paradise, a pure land in the west.'[10] Honen emphasizes the primal promise of Amida in the Chinese Buddhist text, in which Amida made a primal vow to save those who sincerely believe in him and wish regeneration into his country, even with compassion for all, including the sinner. However, Honen does not undervalue good works and religious practice in the Buddhist traditional manner. His pupil Shinran systematically developed his teacher's teaching of Buddhist soteriology, while breaking through to

---

7. CD I/2, p. 290.
8. CD I/2, p. 298.
9. CD I/2, p. 300.
10. CD I/2, p. 340.

a new insight into the radical grace of Amida. Shinran rejected aspects of meritorious works and spiritual disciplines as the means to attaining the grace of Amida. He became the founder of the Yodo-Shin-Shu sect, and his doctrine affirms that 'everything depends on the faith of the heart.'[11]

In the Japanese Protestantism of Genku and Shinran, Barth finds a providential disposition, and he is grateful to this abundant and evident teaching.[12] In other respects, Barth argues that the Shin Buddhist teaching was a popular demand for an easier and simpler path to salvation, because there is no doctrine of the law and holiness or wrath of Amida. Nothing dramatic can be found in the redemption of the human being or to relieve the goodness and mercy of the Amida. Finally, Barth's appraisal can be definitively seen in his argument: 'In the Yodo religion it is not Amida or faith in him, but this human goal of desire which is the really controlling and determinative power.'[13]

At this point, Barth's approach must be challenged. Shinran's existential-spiritual struggle, which is analogously compared with Luther's *simul justus* and *peccator*, is not neatly taken as a popular demand for an easier and simpler way to salvation. In the Buddhist eschatological teaching, Amida would perform his primal promise for all, and this radicality is placed at the centre of Shinran's teaching. He affirms the sincere faith as a more difficult path than self-power. Those who are liberated from the primal promise of Amida are called into the critique of social injustice, promoting universal priesthood and serving social welfare. Shinran is appreciated as the classic example of engaged Buddhism in today's context.[14]

Faith in Shinran's term is not conceptualized as the human goal of desire through the practice of *nenbutsu* (invoking the grace of Amida) for salvation. Amida Buddha, infinite light and life, shines within one's heart, creating sincere faith and truth as a gift. Shinran's teaching initiates the paradigm shift in eliminating the traditional idea of Buddha nature residing within our capacity. The really controlling and determinative power is the infinite light and life of Amida, who dwells in us, as the sincere mind (*shinjin*) in the true and real quality of the primal promise.[15]

---

11. CD I/2, p. 341.
12. CD I:2, p. 342.
13. CD I/2, p. 342.
14. Bloom, *Shinran's Gospel of Pure Grace*.
15. Keel, *Understanding Shinran*, p. 86.

Religion as Parable of God

In his later teaching of true words and lights of the world, Barth provocatively argues that 'we will certainly be prepared at any time for true words even from what seem to be the darkest places. Even from the mouth of Balaam the well-known voice of the good Shepherd may sound, and it is not to be ignored in spite of its sinister origin.'[16] He argues that these 'true words' demonstrate 'God's free communications in the parables of the kingdom which come to it through the general history of the world around it.'[17] Barth even affirms that 'dangerous modern expressions like "the revelation of creation" or "primal revelation" might be given a clear and unequivocal sense in this respect.'[18]

This perspective does not necessarily contrast with Troeltsch's theory of religious a priori in the universal history of religions. Barth implicitly acknowledges that Shin Buddhism is classified as parabolic witness which is the extraordinary way of communicating divine mystery. Revelation is not mutually exclusive to religion, but elevated and concealed in God's mystery. As he writes, 'We may think of the mystery of God. ... We may think of the radicalness of the need of redemption or the fullness of what is meant by redemption if it is to meet this need.'[19] We may see such radical need of redemption in Pure Land Buddhism, but Barth's position is assertive and inclusive. He does not refine dimensions of religious symbolism in God's activity of speaking a free word through hermeneutical mediation.

2. Tillich and Religious Symbolism

If Barth considers religion from the standpoint of revelation imbued with God's speech-act, Tillich reacts against Barth's revelational approach to religion. In his later stage of life, Tillich still keeps in view the correlation between the religious socialist movement in the 1920s in Central Europe and the Protestant principle. It is expressed in his article on 'A View of the Present Situation: Religions, Quasi-Religions, and Their Encounters.'[20]

---

16. CD IV/3.1, p. 119.
17. CD IV/3.1, p. 130.
18. CD IV/3.1, p. 140.
19. CD IV/3.1, p. 125.
20. Tillich, *Christianity and the Encounter of World Religions*, pp. 1–16.

History might be portrayed as the theater or stage, which receives a qualified moment or fulfillment of time from the manifestation of the Kingdom of God. Tillich affirms: 'Kairoi are rare, and the great kairos is unique, but together they determine the dynamics of history in its self-transcendence.'[21] Tillich's theology of kairos imbued with the immanent critique reacts against a quasi-religious form, which assumes the character of rule of ideology or ideocracy.[22]

Theonomy and the Idea of the Holy

Tillich further examines the religious socialist concept of theonomy, by which religious socialism is understood as a move toward theonomy, as expected by the present kairos. Theonomy is demanded as the general goal of creating a new form of religion, culture and morality coming out of the kairos.[23] This denotes the state of culture under the influence of the Spiritual Presence by relating all cultural forms to the ultimate. For example, the Word of God, which is not restricted to the Scripture, is Spirit-determined. The Spiritual Presence can grasp one who speaks and elevates one's words to the state of bearers of the Spirit; the word of God under the Spiritual Presence expresses a union between the subject and the object by overcoming their divergence.[24] The theonomous principle addresses the whole history of religions as a fight of God against the demonic implication of religion. It is actualized in a fragmentary manner, appearing here and there in the critical moments of *kairoi*. This refers to the ideal type of religion in light of the holy, which is the ground of being.

In the phenomenology of the holy, Tillich integrates Rudolf Otto's *The Idea of the Holy* into his dynamic-typological framework. In describing the experience of the holy 'numinous,' the holy is defined in terms of the presence of the divine. In the description of the mystery of the holy as *tremendum* and *fascinosum*, Tillich argues, Otto remains limited to articulate the experience of the ultimate concern as the ground of being from an existential, personal perspective.[25] For Tillich, the holy stands in a profound dialectic with the profane, which implies 'to be

---

21. Tillich, *Systematic Theology* III, p. 372.
22. Ibid., p. 5.
23. Tillich, *On the Boundary*, p. 81.
24. Tillich, *Systematic Theology* III, p. 256.
25. Tillich, *Systematic Theology* I, p. 216.

before the doors of the sanctuary.'[26] The profane is embedded with the rational structure in the moral, the legal, the cognitive and the aesthetic realm; in other words, undergoing the process of rationalization and secularization.

Tillich embodies the idea of the holy with the secular realm (unlike Otto's transcendental referent), while keeping intact its eschatological side in connection with the Christian symbol of the kingdom of God. In his dynamic-typological approach, we observe how significantly a phenomenology of the Holy works within the finite realm in terms of typology in the threefold sense: the sacramental (or ritualistic) basis, the mystical (or spiritual) element, and the ethical or prophetic (or charismatic) element, which remain crucial in all religions.[27] This typology seeks to synthesize three different elements into the theonomous religion, which is called 'the religion of the concrete spirit.'[28]

Indeed, Tillich acknowledges that the Word of God is filled with and determined by the Spirit in the theonomous sense. But he does not follow through by conceptualizing a linguistic type in connection with the religious symbolism and textual dialogue in interreligious exchange. In fact, the thoughts or ideas penetrate into all spiritual activities of a human being, who could not be a spiritual being without word, thought and concept. The word in the sacred texts remains imperative, especially in the world of religion. The word retains an all-embracing function in spiritual and cultural life through narrative, communication and written codified discourse of the belief system. In fact, a linguistic dimension cannot be separated from religious doctrine, ritual performance and moral precepts.

Thus it is indispensable to include a type of *verbum* in its divine nature with personal, universal effectiveness. Linguistic type refers to God's activity in speaking or narrating a living word or narrative activity in a symbolic, verbal sense. Dialogical life in personal relationship remains central in shaping religious, cultural life in terms of mutual colloquium and consolation among religious members. It is connected with symbolic action and expression in God's activity of narrative in many and various ways in historical manifestation. This characterizes the universal meaning of Jesus Christ in creation and reconciliation (Hebrews 1:1). A narrative type of rationality reinforces kerygmatic

---

26. 'The Significance of the History of Religions for the Systematic Theologian,' in *Christianity and the Encounter of World Religions*, p. 74.
27. Ibid., p. 71.
28. Ibid., p. 72.

implication, while highlighting its action through veracity and moral validity, especially in the interreligious context.²⁹

Tillich and the History-of-Religions School

In his final stage of life at Chicago (October 1965), Tillich addresses the history-of-religions school in a public lecture in discussion of constructing systematic theology.³⁰ Tillich does not mention the name of Ernst Troeltsch in his last lecture, but he re-employs the history-of-religions thinking and attitude for developing systematic theology. Troeltsch explores one's theoretical horizon in connection with the totality of human religions. His method of correlation focuses on a historical comparative study of religions by grounding one's religious validity and truth claim in the universal development of the history of religions. It deals with 'the pluralism of rival analogous claims to truth.'³¹

Tillich does not share Troeltsch's sociological approach, but he appropriates a phenomenology of religion (Rudolf Otto and Mircea Eliade). He describes the extent to which the phenomena or regime of religious meaning could show themselves in the history of religions in terms of 'the symbols, the rites, the ideas and the various activities.'³² Tillich acknowledges the significance of reconstruction in the method of history-of-religions in synthesizing the dynamics of religion with secular history for a more present relevancy. The crucial thing for him is to comprehend religious symbols in terms of the social matrix or totality of human experience in examining all the ramifications of religious symbols.³³ However, he does not follow this argument through. Tillich's religious symbolism articulates the method of correlation in distinction from Troeltsch by using it in a threefold sense. First, it denotes correspondence between religious symbols and the symbolized. Second, it describes 'the logical interdependence of concepts' underlying God,

---

29. Marquardt, *Von Elend und Heimsuchung der Theologie*, pp. 160–1.
30. 'The Significance of the History of Religions for the Systematic Theologian,' in *Christianity and the Encounter of World Religions*, p. 68.
31. 'The Dogmatics of the History-of-Religions School,' in Troeltsch, *Religion in History*, p. 88.
32. Ibid., p. 77.
33. 'The Significance of the History of Religions for the Systematic Theologian,' in *Christianity and the Encounter of World Religions*, p. 78.

humanity and the world. Third, it refers to 'the real interdependence of things or events in structural wholes.'[34]

Tillich seeks to interpret the meaning of the holy and the meaning of the divine in terms of correlation, in which he presents a doctrine of God by analyzing the meaning of the ultimate concern. However, he does not undertake such a method in social scientific study of encounter, interaction, competition and mutual fertilization in the world of religions. In articulating religious symbols, Tillich initiates the Protestant principle as a prophetic critique, by analyzing the demonic power structure of quasi-religious forces. 'Religious symbols are not stones falling from heaven. They have their roots in the totality of human experience, including local surroundings in all their ramifications, both political and economic.'[35]

If the holy objects go beyond their role as mediums, establishing themselves as holy, they become demonic. The representations or objects of the ultimate concern take place as holy in the actual life of most religions, being transformed into idols. Justice becomes the criterion as prophetic critique in judging idolatrous holiness.[36]

Buddhist-Christian Dialogue

Tillich elaborates typological thinking in dialectical dynamism, that is, a dynamic typology in dealing with an encounter with other religions as living and evolving in parallel with Christianity.[37] Tillich engages in interreligious dialogue with Buddhism in a practical and existential sense. He seeks common ground in rendering both dialogue and conflicts feasible (even a serious confrontation included). A prophetic critique can be seen in the openness of both partners to criticism of self-religion and each rejuvenation.[38]

Tillich proposes several procedures underlying comparative theology in terms of interreligious intentionality and practice. (1) Religious experience of revelation is universally human, such that it implies revealing and saving power in all religions (universalist position, or life-world

---

34. Tillich, *Systematic Theology* I, p. 60.
35. 'The Significance of the History of Religions for the Systematic Theologian,' in *Christianity and the Encounter of World Religions*, p. 78.
36. Tillich, *Systematic Theology* I, p. 216.
37. 'Christian-Buddhist Conversation,' Tillich, *Christianity and the Encounter of World Religions*, p. 35.
38. Ibid., p. 39.

of each religion). (2) Revelation is received in a distorted form and comprehended in humanity's limited character and historical, social condition: human understanding of revelation restrained in biological, psychological and sociological environment (existential principle). (3) In a revelatory process in the history of religions, adaptation and distortion are subject to critique in terms of the mystical, the prophetic, and the secular (Protestant principle). (4) A central event in the history of religions makes possible a concrete theology with universalist significance. The sacred is the creative ground as well as a critical judgment of both self-religion and the secular, because it is the depth of the secular rather than lying beside the secular. But the secular has the formative role as a tool of self-critique of one's religion. The Holy or the Ultimate is within the secular realm (the ontological reference).[39]

In Tillich's interreligious epistemology, there is no possibility of a fusion between the Christian and the 'Buddhist' idea of God. In the discussion of the controlling symbols between Kingdom of God and nirvana, Tillich argues, the biblical symbol of the kingdom of God is identified with the expectation of God in which the telos of *everyone* and everything will be united. But in the Buddhist symbol of nirvana the telos of *everything* and everyone is fulfilled. Nirvana is an ontological symbol as expressed in 'the image of the blessed oneness of everything,' in the sense of 'the ultimate Ground of Being,' whereas the kingdom of God is implicated in social, political and personalistic terms.[40] However, the basic difference between the two symbols is immense, because the Ultimate in Christianity is symbolized in personal categories (participation principle), whereas in Buddhism it is in transpersonal categories such as 'absolute non-being'[41] (identity principle).

In the symbol of the Kingdom of God Tillich emphasizes a revolutionary character in a radical transformation of society, which has no analogy found in Buddhism, despite its emphasis on the great Compassion.[42] However, Tillich's reading is met with Buddhist criticism. Masao Abe affirms nirvana or Enlightenment as the subjective realization, in which 'everything and everyone are respectively realized as they are.' 'Nirvana is nothing but a person's realization of the existential true Self as the

---

39. 'The Significance of the History of Religions for the Systematic Theologian,' ibid, pp. 65–6.
40. 'Christian-Buddhist Conversation,' ibid., p. 40.
41. Ibid., p. 41.
42. Ibid., pp. 45–6.

ultimate ground.'[43] Everything in samsara and everyone is fulfilled. 'In short, Buddhist Nirvana is the realization of the human existential true Self in which, and in which alone, everything and everyone, including oneself, are respectively and equally fulfilled in its particularity.'[44]

Abe's explanation corrects Tillich's definition of nirvana in terms of the state of transtemporal blessedness. Abe affirms the Buddhist cardinal principle of dependent origination (Tillich misses this point), in which true nirvana (Sunyata) is the real source of both non-attached wisdom and great compassion. Nevertheless, in Abe's conceptualization of absolute nothingness as the true nirvana, there is ethical vulnerability in accommodation to social and historical evils. It requires a prophetic critique of quasi-religious force and its detrimental consequence of a Buddhist understanding of karma bound to the absolute nothingness.

3. Life-World and Elective Affinity

Enter Ernst Troeltsch, who argues that the history of religions can be used to refine the significance of comparative theology in the sociological frame of reference. I seek to elaborate Troeltsch's sociological position – as presented in chapter 1 – with regard to Tillich. In his sociological formation of Christianity, Troeltsch paves a new vista of historical critical approach to uphold a comparative study of Christianity and other religions. His sociological typology (sacramental, prophetic-ethical and mystic type) explicates the extent to which the Christian forces would be correlated with the political, social, cultural and economic spheres. This sociological clarification can be re-employed in the comparative study of other religions throughout history. This sociological type explicates the distinguished position and difference of religious ethics in terms of accommodation, involvement and new synthesis, and this perspective can be enhanced as the method of correlation in dealing with other types of comparative religions.

Troeltsch may relocate Tillich's dynamic-descriptive typology and relation between religion and culture within a social scientific framework. Troeltsch helps to widen the relation between religion and culture in a historical, sociological frame, and sociological clarification can be made of the elective affinity between religion and culture in its dynamic process of involvement, transition and transformation in terms of correlation. There is the causally adequate connection (or elective

---

43. Abe, *Zen and Western Thought*, p. 176.
44. Ibid., p. 177.

affinity) between religious thoughts and material interests in diverse social fields, out of which 'the peculiar form of religious thoughts gains concrete stimulus, force, movement, and aim, and social and even, finally, economic influences are at work.'[45]

Troeltsch considerably widens and enhances the casual connection by fresh attention to the cooperating elements of religion, culture and society. In fact, religious revelations unfold out of this casual connection, acquiring new development, synthesis and transformation.[46] His research sheds light on the extent to which the whole Christian world of thought and dogma is dependent upon the fundamental sociological conditions, while featuring similarity, combined articulation, fusion, difference, or rupture and transformation according to the ideal types of church (sacramental-institutional), sect (prophetic-ethical) and mysticism (spiritual-individual).[47]

Christian ways of life are not generalized as a logic of sameness, but a study of Christian life-world acknowledges distinctive features, difference, rupture, and transformation among faith communities. In his interpretation of Christian social teaching at a given period, such change and construction are undertaken in terms of correlation with the totality of society and culture, which are interlaced with political power, and the economic system. Troeltsch refines his sociology with his method of history-of-religions as a way of interpreting Christianity through 'the importance of analogy and the mutual interrelation of all historical developments.'[48] Troeltsch features analogy in terms of similarity of all historical events without leaving out the differences. This analogical imagination is imbued with the method of correlation, which underlies the interaction of all phenomena in the history of civilization and religions.

In this interaction, there is a yearning for the absolute, in other words, the religious a priori as expressed in the autonomy of reason, while grasped psychologically. The conception of religious a priori is grounded in the active presence of the absolute spirit, which is operative as the real ground of every a priori in the realm of the finite.[49]

---

45. Troeltsch, *The Social Teaching of the Christian Churches* II, p. 1002.
46. Ibid.
47. Ibid., p. 994.
48. 'Historical and Dogmatic Method in Theology (1898),' in Troeltsch, *Religion in History*, p. 13.
49. 'On the Question of the Religious a Priori (1909),' ibid., p. 41.

The historical critical approach such as analogy, religious a priori, and correlation can be a chief source in his sociological method of reciprocity between Christian ideas and political, social, economic formations.[50] It can be used to analyze difference, change, rupture and transformation in the interpretation of religious discourse and ethical attitude in accordance with material interests and power relations.

Troeltsch highlights the mystery of God the Absolute as transcendent referent, before whom every and each epoch exists directly in its religious and cultural achievements. The Christian symbol of the kingdom of God remains an inspiration, because it is within us proleptically, because 'the final ends of all humanity are hidden with His Hands.'[51] This perspective is of special importance in developing a comparative study of religions through the proleptic conception of the kingdom of God or God's future.

Life-World Critique and Historicism

Troeltsch characterizes history as life-world, but he fails to articulate the horizon of history of religions as an a priori reality. Religious a priori in the Schleiermacher-Troeltsch tradition should be integrated with or grounded in the life-world a priori, in which religious a priori (or religious way of thinking) may have its objective side with subjective-relative significance. According to Husserl, 'The life-world does have, in all its relative features, *a general structure.* This general structure, to which everything that exists relatively is bound, is not itself relative. ... And this includes ... everything objectively a priori, with its necessary reference back to a corresponding a priori of the life-world.'[52]

Religious a priori, apart from the life-world a priori, would be merged into the psychological, mystical, anti-intellectualistic and relativistic realm. The religious a priori can be critically renewed and widened through hermeneutical mediation of religious consciousness (*noesis*) with the meaningful whole of life-world (*noema*). This perspective breaks through Troeltsch's concept of the religious a priori combined

---

50. 'The Social Philosophy of Christianity (1922),' ibid., p. 218.
51. Troeltsch, *The Social Teaching of the Christian Churches* II, p. 1013.
52. 'Elements of a Science of the Life-World,' in *The Essential Husserl*, p. 374.

merely with the psychological, so that he seeks to form an irrational unity of life.[53]

Life-world in its linguistic-narrative character influences and moves one's consciousness and critical reflection. Understanding through language brings out history, classic texts, tradition and culture. In intellectual engagement with the regime of the meaning (*noema*), a critical reflection (*noesis*) enhances intelligibility and its advancement by participating in the text or meaningful world. It is undertaken through gradual adumbration of initial outlook, then widening and synthesizing intentionalities of horizon, finally synthesizing their fusion and semantic retrieval.

This position premises Troeltsch's historical criticism on the epistemological dynamism, while appreciating the latter's idea of prolepsis. It avoids epistemological relativism, which can be seen in the method of history-of-religion. A method of correlation is better placed within the life-world, which correlates with human experience of the religious world of meaning in a dynamic, progressive manner toward the future of God.

Weber and Religious Construction of Reality

Our deliberation of Troeltsch and Husserl is poised to include Weber's sociological approach to comparative religions. His classic study shows the Calvinist idea of election in its connection with economic attitude (a certain rule of adequate casual connection), which finds an elective affinity with a capitalist spirit of rationalism. In the historical process of rationalization, religious adherents 'elect' the features of the religious source of ideas to be in affinity or point of coincidence with their material interests, according to religious needs and adjustment. Ideas are selected and reinterpreted by the agent in dealing with the religious doctrine to the point of finding such an affinity with their material interests in their historical, social context.[54]

Weber uses the construction of types or models in explicating patterns of meaning. Ideal type is constructed by looking at a type of rationality influencing human action in a purposive, meaningful way (political type of capitalism or rational type of industrial capitalism). An ideal type enables the sociologist to understand the real action

---

53. 'On the Question of the Religious A Priori (1909),' in *Religion in History*, p. 39.
54. *From Max Weber*, p. 63.

in a meaningful manner, which characterizes 'a realistic sociological typology' in Weber.[55]

It is especially important to lay out a theory of elective affinity, which is explicated in critical reflection of empirical rules disclosing casual connections. A society is composed by analyzing a complex of causal relationships between religious beliefs, charismatic leaders, status group by education and occupation, and power structure of the group. Society is therefore stratified according to the principles of their consumption of goods by monopolization, and according to education and occupation. This is represented by special honour, prestige and styles of life, as seen in the Indian caste system.[56]

Every society is divided into several social strata, which are characterized by a specific way of life in political, social, economic and cultural spheres. In the status privilege by difference of education 'our society contains a very tangible element of stratification by status,' which 'influences the economic structure.'[57] A critical theory of elective affinity in its typological materialist regime can be applied to investigate social stratification underlying diverse public spheres (the economic sphere, the political sphere, the spheres of esthetic and erotic life, the intellectual, cultural sphere).[58]

In the comparative study of world religions, social groups are identified as an influential status group such as the Puritan divines, the Confucian scholars, the Hindu Brahmins, and the Jewish Levites and prophets. As the dominant carriers of culture, their distinctive styles of life are developed and established as the conventional ideal, undergoing the struggle with other religious groups (for example, the Hindu Brahmins against Buddhism and Jainism). Certain religious beliefs, such as the idea of duty in one's calling, gained widespread influence through charismatic leaders, and virtuous and religious adherents, while status group shapes the social structure in its strata and layers. It is taken for granted as a result of *domination with ethical significance*, in other words, morally inspired discourse instilled with reforming social structure.

Weber's sociological realism is not far removed from Foucault's archaeological analysis of discourse. Foucault sees the historical analysis

---

55. 'The Nature of Social action,' in *Weber Selections in Translation*, p. 15.
56. *From Max Weber*, p. 192.
57. 'The Social Psychology of the World Religions,' *From Max Weber*, p. 301.
58. Ibid., pp. 331–57.

of the continuous and accumulated discourse as the ideology of the past, while undertaking suspense or problematization of such a regime. He seeks to decipher the regime of the not-said, the discontinuity, or the subjugated, through a pure description of discursive event.[59] Religious discourse is practised and produces a corpus of knowledge in dealing with certain themes (such as sexuality, moral issues or social crimes) by participating in the process of rationalization with other experts; this discursive formation and practice are buttressed by institutional support and political policy.

Stated in Weber's fashion, ideas or discourse – religious, moral, cultural, practical – are carried by influential social groups which have powerful social, economic and cultural effects. They are institutionalized as contributing factors upon intellectual existence, while becoming a driving force in the course of material life. The material life is also a cooperative force along with the religious discourse. Weber reinforces Foucault's archaeology, to the degree that his analysis of elective affinity is re-employed to clarify the extent to which the discourse of representation or domination (episteme) would be capable of excluding and subjugating the different or the unfit at a given period. A type of representation can be an ideal type in accounting for religious discourse with power (church type), while a type of influence is of charismatic character (sect) in explicating the role of the religious carrier and status group underlying social stratification in diverse public spheres.

This epistemic perspective can be integrated into the sociology of history-of-religions by inventing several types in competition and interaction with social historical forces, institutional support, and political policy along with bureaucratic administration. Indeed, Foucault highlights the primary quality of the original text and its prominence as discourse in its permanence, which is capable of bringing out the multiple or hidden meanings. This text creates an open possibility for discussion, effect and development. However, commentary gives an opportunity to say something in the sense of reappearance and interpretation, which is other than the text itself as uttered, in some ways, finalized.[60]

Nonetheless, exegetical-hermeneutical significance is considerably undermined in Foucault's archaeological analysis of discourse. He focuses unilaterally on the representative type of discourse and its hegemony

---

59. Foucault, *The Archeology of Knowledge and the Discourse on Language*, pp. 7, 138, 191.
60. Ibid., p. 221.

invested in power relations. At this point, Foucault's archaeology can be considered to be hermeneutically inadequate, as it mediates the two different regimes between exegesis and archaeology for articulation. The interpretive frame of articulation problematizes the limitations of Weber, who is constrained to explore the original text as the source of correcting the disgrace effect, as would happen in the historical development of religious carriers according to their need, material interests and power strata.

4. Life-World and Hermeneutic of Narrative

A social scientific approach can be enhanced and reinvigorated by a hermeneutical theory of life-world, in which textual study (or com-reading) in comparative study of religious texts remains crucial. There is a need to undertake a hermeneutical revision of Troeltsch, in which several conceptual principles (analogy, critique, religious a priori, and correlation) are better relocated within the phenomenology of life-world. A critical theory of life-world embraces critical methodology and narrative in connection with historical time. There is no question of an epistemological rupture between history and narrative (sagas and ancient epics included), which becomes the underlying structure of a meaningful whole. Analogical construal of the textual world focuses on correlation between history and narrative.[61]

The narrative type of discourse is differentiated from Foucault's archaeological type of discourse as representation invested in power relations. Instead, a conceptual clarity can be used to take on the narrative form of religious discourse and its widespread influence imbued with spiritual, personal and moral significance. This strengthens moral, value rationality in the life of religious adherents, whose lifestyles can be effected and enriched with hermeneutical significance. The narrative perspective gives a new impulse to Weber's theory of elective affinity, while better conceptualizing it in the following patterns: causal adequate explanation, narrative influence, material interests, power structure, and social stratification. Ideas or thoughts are embedded with social fact, while influencing reality 'like a pure stream, critical-clear, and transparent.' But ideological ideas in quasi-religious forces run 'like a dirty river, muddied and polluted by the impurities that have flooded

---

61. Ricoeur, *Time and Narrative* 1, pp. 91-2, 151,

into it. From the one it is healthy to drink; the other is poison to be avoided.'"[62]

With this in mind, a critique of disgrace effect (ideological function of religious discourse) can be undertaken in terms of religious source and its narrative significance, which are not reduced to sociological functions of agent roles and their power relations in social stratification. Husserl's theory of life-world therefore mediates the narrative linguistic understanding with historical, critical explanation. Husserl's theory of life-world is re-employed in Gadamer's hermeneutical theory, in which history of effect is mediated by language for human understanding, dialogue, and interpretation. The life-world, or world horizon imbued with tradition and history, influences the interpreter's own thought in textual dialogue, while the latter plays a role in reawakening the text's meaning. Such an encounter takes place in a fusion of horizons between the text and the reader in a progressive, open-ended manner.[63]

Nonetheless, language can be distorted and misused as the discourse of representation justifying the status quo of reification under a symbolic system of violence and power relations. A distorted side of language becomes the regime of critique through internal colonization of the life-world under the system (steered by politics, money and mass media).[64] Of crucial significance in Husserl is his research into all limited intentionality of meaning which correlates with the meaningful whole of life-world or story. Everything is given as existent in terms of the life-world, bringing out the world horizon and life-story.[65]

A critical theory of life-world must be positioned in ideal significance in the structure of givenness (linguistically transmitted and narrated through history, tradition, text, and culture). It implies a structure of a meaningful whole which is correlated with intentional acts of experience, while overcoming prejudice of the logical psychologism.[66] A life-world approach includes break, rupture, and critique of the materials transmitted in culture and religion, which are embedded with 'exclusion, domination, and omission.'[67] All that has been accumulated or taken for granted should be put into responsible critique and emancipation. It implies depth philosophy in radical self-understanding, in

---

62. Cited in Geertz, *The Interpretation of Cultures*, p. 197.
63. Gadamer, *Truth and Method*, pp. 324, 388.
64. Habermas, *The Theory of Communicative Action* II, pp. 333, 389–90.
65. Gadamer, *Truth and Method*, p. 246.
66. Ibid., p. 225.
67. Tanner, *Theories of Culture*, p. 132.

communion with the reality of the ultimate transcendence through the meaningful world.

This perspective comes to terms with comparative theology, which is concerned with a critical analysis of givenness of life in culture and religion, in which religious construction of reality is examined through critique, semantic retrieval, and emancipation in reference to the proleptic position of reconciliation.

Life-world Clarification and Comparative Theology

The life-world concept clarifies Geertz's definition of religion. Religion is conceived as a cultural system. Religion, seen through life-world, 'denotes an historically transmitted pattern of meanings embodied in symbols, a system of inherited conceptions expressed in symbolic forms.'[68] Religious symbols function to synthesize a people's ethos with religious styles of life, motivations, and worldview. Religion establishes 'a basic congruence between a particular style of life and a specific metaphysic'[69] in the sense of a general order of existence. This religious metaphysic in the general order of existence equips an aura of factuality which would make people's moods and motivations uniquely realistic.[70]

Religion has objective reference as a life-orienting worldview, narrative, and reservoir of meaningful whole in regard to the general features of some universal cultural enterprise. Religious power is seen in its special and powerful message through revelation which gives, animates and awakens life. It opens life to the world of *totaliter aliter*, or the Holy. Given this, religion is public because meaning is.[71] It becomes a context or a life-world in construction of social events, behaviours, institutions, or processes to be intelligibly or thickly described.[72]

A phenomenology of thick description can be allied with a social scientific approach to religion as a cultural symbolic system in dealing with the elective affinity between religious ideas, narrative significance, material interests and power relations. The life-world clarification of culture or religion assumes that human thought is basically both social and public through linguistic interaction, narrative formation and significant symbols. Human existence is a cultural phenomenon,

---

68. Geertz, *The Interpretation of Cultures*, p. 89.
69. Ibid., p. 90.
70. Ibid.
71. Ibid., p. 12.
72. Ibid., p. 14.

implying an incomplete and unfinished being as driven by the meaningful whole of life-world.

This position cuts through the limitations of Lindbeck, who appropriates Geertz's idea of religion and culture through language game theory (Wittgenstein) by emphasizing religious truthfulness and its validity claim only through the intratextual world and its narrative.[73] In Lindbeck's regulative view of religion, we read: 'Intratextual theology redescribes reality within the scriptural framework rather than translating Scripture into extrascriptural categories. It is the text, so to speak, which absorbs the world, rather than the world the text.'[74] This cultural intratextual approach to religion and its regulative view of religious doctrine find significance in Clooney's comparative theology purely in a commentarial manner. In Clooney's definition, comparative theology focuses only on 'reading together' (*collectio*), while inscribing other religious texts within the Christian theological tradition. It rethinks and rewrites 'Christian theology only out of that newly composed context.'[75]

This type of comparative theology remains within the limits of intratextual truth only, while undermining the correlation of religious development in the universal history and cultural symbolization of religion as connected with verbal activity in narrating a story. The narrative implies the story or myth. It refers to narrative-symbolic correlation, which has analogical significance in the structure of symbolic meaning in religion and culture. The activity of narrating a story goes beyond the textually encoded world, while entailing the culturally transmitted narrative in daily life, biographical story, and dialogue. Conceptual reflection in linguistic formation receives its impulse and first order of meaning from the symbolic representation of the story in verbal symbolic representation.[76]

The language game can be situated within the social and cultural form of life in the realm of dialogue, communication and translation. Cultural narrative model in its symbolic structure strengthens historical explanation, narrative understanding of one's identity and cultural authenticity, and analogical construal of the Ultimate in the progress of fusion of horizons imbued with life-world.[77]

---

73. Ibid., p. 135.
74. Lindbeck, *The Nature of Doctrine*, p. 118.
75. Clooney, *Theology after Vedanta*, p. 7.
76. Bellah, *Religion in Human Evolution*, pp. 14, 174.
77. Gadamer, *Truth and Method*, p. xxxvi.

5. Prolepsis, Public Theology, and Culture

As we have seen, Barth affirms a common ground by reading 'the wholly providential disposition' between Protestant Christianity and Amida Buddhism. He does not sidestep the cultural dimension for theological construction. Barth affirms that 'The problem of culture is the problem of being human ... since theology is a specific activity of humanity. The problem of theology and dogmatics can also be seen as wholly set within the framework of the problem of culture.'[78]

If theology is a specific activity of humanity, it is imperative to refine speech-act theology within the cultural narrative framework, in which culture must become a context for shaping theology as a form of cultural activity. In other words, symbolic expression in the cultural narrative has a texture expressed in meaningful action before becoming a written text. It is embedded within a 'system of interacting symbols' and 'patterns of interworking meanings.'[79] This meaningful system is to be thickly described and analyzed in terms of elective affinity between cultural formation, material interests and power relations. This perspective improves on the limitations of Barth's revelation-centreed position and Tillich's existential approach to culture and religion.

In fact, Geertz credits Weber's sociological principle into his comparative study of religion and culture, because 'Believing, with Max Weber, that man is an animal suspended in webs of significance he himself has spun. ... I take culture to be those webs, and the analysis of it to be therefore not an experimental science in search of law but an interpretive one in search of meaning'[80] Such enquiry is an interpretive science in search of meaning in dealing with religion and culture in webs of significance and a symbolic meaningful whole. Furthermore, Geertz utilizes Paul Ricoeur's phenomenological hermeneutic, in which the event of speaking (*Sagen*) has its destiny to become the said of speaking: *Aus-sage* – the enunciation, the enunciated. We write the *noema* (thought, meaning, content, or gist) of the speaking in its intentionality (*noesis*); the *noema* is the meaning of the speech event, discourse and communication.[81]

Weber's scientific explanation of one's individual action can be appropriated in a phenomenological frame of reference, in which

---

78. CD I/1, p. 284.
79. Geertz, *Interpretation of Cultures*, p. 207.
80. Gadamer, *Truth and Method*, p. 5.
81. Geertz, *Interpretation of Cultures*, p. 19.

narrative understanding can be undertaken in dealing with an agent's meaningful action; it is distinguished from a type of representation with power relations. One's meaningful action is readable and decipherable in its cultural, symbolic expression, because it has public character in social intercourse. It is hermeneutically mediated in the system or patterns of interworking symbols and meanings. It reinvigorates social scientific analysis of elective affinity between religious symbolism, narrative significance, material interests, cultural stratification, and power relations in the public sphere.

This phenomenological elucidation finds its epistemological pivot in underlying comparative public theology, which focuses on the differences and distinctive qualities of cultures in light of the Christian symbol of prolepsis with its meaning of reconciliation. Reconciliation has come as a gift of God by highlighting its penultimate reality in religion and culture.

Prolepsis, Reconciliation, and Semantic Text

In his conclusion of *The Social Teaching of the Christian Churches*, Troeltsch impressively writes: 'The life beyond this world is, in very deed, the inspiration of the life that now is.'[82] This thesis emphasizes the Christian symbol of the kingdom of God in its proleptic sense. It means that the Church awaits the coming of the kingdom, while it 'proleptically participates in its spiritual effects'[83] in Jesus Christ. In so doing, it is necessary to explore the religious phenomenon in its correlation with other religious streams and traditions. It characterizes the proleptic pluralism, which correlates reconciliation with creation. It does not reduce the living and emancipatory Word of God, or the prolepsis of God's future into intrascriptural categories. It is the living word of God, as it were, which embraces the Church and the world; it is not the text in its unilateral absorption of the world. It characterizes a cultural narrative model in its proleptic configuration, in which a critical theory of life-world is deployed with a social-scientific approach to elective affinity between religious discourse, material interests, and power relations in social cultural stratification.

This perspective does not separate Barth (speech-act theology) from Tillich (religious symbolism), but recasts their insights in Troeltsch's

---

82. Troeltsch, *The Social Teaching of the Christian Churches* II, p. 1006.
83. 'The Social Philosophy of Christianity (1922),' in *Religion in History*, p. 212.

proleptic historicism. There are even parallels between Barth and Troeltsch in their respective teaching of lights and words. In *On the Possibility of a Liberal Christianity* (1910) Troeltsch maintains: 'it is impossible to keep alive the distinctively Christian idea of God apart from seeing its life-giving embodiment in Jesus; ... This is why he himself will always keep on living wherever the Prophetic-Christian belief in God is alive.'[84] On the other hand, 'the immensity of the world leads us to assume an infinite plurality of spiritual worlds ... there are still other religious life-contexts with their own redeemers and paradigmatic figures. ... There are still other circles of light, with other sources of light, within the great divine life of the world. ... Every epoch stands immediately before God, and we stand immediately before God precisely as gathered together in the circle of light radiating from Jesus.'[85]

This perspective can be enhanced in linguistic narrative configuration of religion and culture (both spoken and written), which is to be thickly deciphered and elucidated in social scientific analysis of elective affinity and social stratification. Troeltsch is an exponent of Christian theism and personalism, which may find an impulse in Barth's theology of God's speech-act in the framework of reconciliation. Barth's reflection of speech-act embraces the Church and the secular realms as extraordinary ways of communications to God's mystery.

The symbolic expression stands for a transcendent referent, God's activity in speaking the living word in many and diverse ways with analogical significance. It emphasizes the public character in its meaningful articulation and with hermeneutical significance. Symbolic expression confers an initial readability on the texture, a quasi-text to be deciphered in its structural character of a symbolic texture.[86] This symbolic perspective, seen in the light of reconciliation, facilitates an attempt at strengthening a proleptic reading strategy in comprehending religion and culture as an ensemble of the texts in cultural narrative formation. Religion and culture refined as an ensemble of texts are to be deciphered and elucidated in the proleptic light and grace, which illuminates faith standing at the divine horizon.

A type of prolepsis elucidates Troeltsch's method of correlation in terms of life-world, in which its analogical imagination is undertaken in creative construal of religion and culture. The proleptic type rediscovers Troeltsch's genuine concern, which positions Christ dynamically in

---

84. Ibid., p. 348.
85. Ibid., p. 349–50.
86. Ricoeur, *Time and Narrative* 1, pp. 57–8.

relation to culture through recognition, self-rejuvenation, and dialogue. Such a position is grounded in the gospel of reconciliation, which is given as a gift, a prolepsis of what is to come. It comes to terms with creation by sharpening its horizon through anamnestic-ethical significance of *theologia crucis*. This perspective is obviously formulated in Luther's provocative dictum: 'Sin boldly!' – this has a radical meaning of justifying faith for fragile and broken souls. This ethic from God's future underlies the gospel of reconciliation in terms of created co-creator, which is instilled with Christian life-world of beatitude, restorative justice and divine agape.[87]

In a like manner, Bonhoeffer radicalizes the universal horizon of the gospel of reconciliation in deep solidarity with those who suffer in society and the world.[88] A proleptic stance takes into account a type of discourse as speech-event, which is always saying something about something in reference to the world. The meaning (*noema*) and the intention (*noesis*) are interlaced with each other under the influence of life-world. The symbolic function of language is performed and actualized in religious discourse, which says something of something to somebody in terms of cultural practice or symbolic action.[89] In fact, religion or culture under life-world appears to be an ensemble of the texts, which inscribes meaningful practice, rational behaviour, analogical construal of reality,[90] and moral significance into the life of culture.

In our comparative systematization of social phenomenology, several assumptions are brought into an epistemological procedure which lays out comparative public theology: (1) The interpretive explication of religious belief systems through exegetical-hermeneutical endeavour; (2) An analysis of elective affinity and its historical development undertaken in religious carriers according to ethical influence, material interests, power structure and social stratification; (3) A dominant discourse (a type of representation with disgrace effect) to be judged in light of the religious source (immanent critique); (4) A comparative

---

87. Peters, *Sin Boldly!*; *God – The World's Future*.
88. Bonhoeffer, *Ethics*, p. 104.
89. Geerz, *Interpretation of Cultures*, p. 449.
90. Ibid., p. 353. Analogical construal of symbolic meaning can be seen in the structural anthropology of Claude Levi-Strauss. The savage in totemism says something about something to somebody in a concrete metaphorical way. When he distinguishes his clan (descended from bear) from his neighbour (from eagle), such expression is based on analogical construal of reality rather than illiterate biology.

investigation undertaken to bring out the distinctive features and contributions among religions (a type of influence) in their widespread spectrum; (5) a critical historical approach taken in analogical construal of commonality in difference in terms of correlation and new synthesis in light of God's prolepsis in reconciled world.

This philosophical, sociological procedure helps lay bare what public theology endeavours to do in comparative reading of religion and culture, while undertaking critical deliberation of givenness of life and life-world in reference to the proleptic stance of reconciliation and anamnestic form of *theologia crucis*. Public theology becomes a culture-specific activity in the cultural narrative fashion, which correlates analogically with the living word of God. God's activity in narrating divine drama can be seen in its interweaving into the Church's realm and the secular public sphere in a democratic pluralist society through *theologia crucis*, reconciliation and proleptic openness.

Epilogue

This Epilogue is a critical reflection of the arguments I have proposed above. What distinguishes comparative theology in my argument is the social scientific experiment underlying a sociological (or more specifically, archaeological) analysis of elective affinity between religious ideas and material interests along with rationalization and power relations in a broader spectrum. The argument I have taken in each chapter, and the future direction it might take, can be summarised as follows:

1. A method of elective affinity is conceptualized in the sociological study of religious ideas and their practical ethical influence upon cultural, economic formation (the role of agent as ethical being in the cultural, economic field; purpose and value rationality). Archaeological enquiry of discourse (or episteme) is considered in its dissemination and discourse formation in terms of fitting (or technological) rationality between discourse, rationalization, institutional ratification, and power relations (objective side of discourse in power-knowledge interplay).

Given this, a method of elective affinity is elaborated in the subjective-ethical activity; here, agent praxis is explicated in reciprocity between status group and class in the economic realm (purpose rationality) as well as in the cultural semantic realm in dealing with sexuality and gender (value rationality). Value and meaningful action in the method of elective affinity are always involved in social facts of life and relevant to their reality under influence of life-world; they do not remain neutral in the ideal typical construction. They incorporate the historical critical principle (critical analysis, analogical imagination, correlation imbued with religious a priori) into a hermeneutical frame of reference for construction of models and meaning.

On the other hand, it is important to juxtapose a historical ontology with social system of episteme; a social scientific theory of elective affinity involves a social factual side of the division of labour, rationalization, specialization and power relations. The latter requires archaeological analysis of religious representations, the diverse field in social stratification, the domination system and its governmentality in terms of patriarchy, or androcentric principle, charismatic authority, legal-bureaucratic legitimacy, and bio-political strategy.

Archaeological enquiry in this regard is of hermeneutical character in reference to the life-world, while it explicates the history of effect and dialogical rationality in a symbolic, materialist manner by performing and rewriting effective history of those excluded and on the margins for the present. Language is translatable and communicable, but power-ridden and embedded with symbolic authority and violence. The cultural semantic realm is conceptualized with respect to genealogy of effective history concerned with epistemological rupture, transformation, and difference; it explicates the degree to which social influence upon language is embedded with its hierarchy, dominion and violence.

In the archaeological, semantic procedure, several steps are involved in the religious construction of reality: (1) Suspension is made concerning what is taken for granted (2) An appreciation or a critique is undertaken on religious ideas or texts as the source of the immanent critique (through critical exegesis), or as the reason of disgrace effect (through problematization); (3) A method of elective affinity is used in dealing with the regime of power in reference to its disgrace effect; (4) Anamnestic constitution of the innocent victim in society, culture and religion; (5) Immanent critique is exercised through adumbration, fusion of horizons, semantic retrieval, and its synthesis of truth, and meaning for contemporary relevance; (6) An ethical component and its practical intentionality are conceptualized at meta-ethical level and are committed to speech activity of *parrhesia* (discourse ethics); it reinvigorates the practical horizon of the sociological or archaeological hermeneutics in listening to the voice of those dominated on the margins, toward solidarity, change and emancipation.

This social scientific enquiry remains central in the study of comparative theology and religious construction of reality. Comparative theology provides an exegetical basis and semantic retrieval to render religious discourse and its effect more relevant to contemporary issues such as race, ethnicity, gender and sexuality.

2. The principle 'faith seeking understanding' is elaborated in terms of analogical enquiry in taking on the significance of religious experience of God *totaliter aliter* in terms of linguistic configuration of

similarity-in-difference; this stance does not discard the incommensurability of two compared entities; nor does it totalize or homogenize different thoughts, religious symbols, or cultural practices into the logic of sameness. The confessional epistemology 'faith seeking understanding' can be featured in exegetical language and renewed by looking at God's speech act, which can be heard in extra-ecclesiastical realms in an extraordinary, communicative manner; this perspective on intertextuality renews a limitation of one-dimensional fideism, or intratextual configuration of postliberal theology, deepening the horizon of faith in accordance with the symbol of reconciliation.

To engage the intertextuality between theology and comparative religions, it is helpful to refine cultural-semantic enquiry according to Geertz; it provides an insight into maintaining confessional particularity, while it acknowledges the other religious tradition in light of God's grace of reconciliation. Religious a priori or comparable commonality of religious experiences are not rejected but hermeneutically integrated and refined into comparative theological enquiry and construction.

3. Troeltsch's theocentric theology and his historical critical method for developing a constructive theology of comparative religions are important to consider. It is necessary, however, to reinterpret and critically revise his historical method and religious a priori through a lens of social scientific enquiry of life-world. The triadic principle (critique, analogy and correlation) is renewed and critically integrated in a linguistic, emancipatory fashion. Each life-world in each religious history can be comparatively explicated on its own terms, as advanced within the framework of a universal history of religion.

Furthermore, Barth's dialectical approach to the relation between revelation and religion is highlighted. Revelation is the sublimation of religion, in which Barth calls into question the domain of the problem (or disgrace effect of religion such as the holocaust, crusades and colonialism). Barth's understanding of God *totaliter aliter* is refined in a hermeneutical and sociological manner.

A particularity of revelation is not comprehended apart from God's inclusive grace of reconciliation, in which his theological insight has been brought into comparative theology and world religions. In the study of Pure Land Buddhism, Barth is convinced of the providential disposition within its teaching of faith and grace, despite difference regarding the name Jesus Christ. God may speak to the Church through the Pure Land teaching of compassion and solidarity, which is taken as an extraordinary way of communicating divine mystery. Barth's dogmatic theology enriches a constructive theology of comparative religions, critically complementing Troeltsch through God's speech act in a dialectical, analogical manner.

In appreciation of Barth and Troeltsch, Tillich's existential-phenomenological enquiry in the Buddhist-Christian context is discussed, while featuring his comparative theology in a sociological scientific frame. Tillich's existential eggshell can be broken and renewed, while it can be enriched in comparative theological reasoning in the procedure of dialogue, argument and learning in the exegetical work; it is also undertaken in sociological analysis of the elective affinity between religious discourse and its relevance with practical, material interests along with power relations.

4. In the comparative study of grace in Luther and Shin Buddhism, comparative theology is discussed in terms of identical pattern, differential, semantic retrieval, and synthesis, in which Luther and Shinran provide a resource of the immanent critique concerning economic development. For this constructive task, the historical study of Shin Buddhism, and Luther's teaching of justification, are dealt with at length. With the historical elucidation, a common pattern between them is outlined in terms of the tripartite model of grace of justification.

However, in scrutinizing the Buddhist idea of Emptiness and colonialism, there is a regime of problematization which concerns the source of ethical compassion. This is in contrast to what is falsified as an ideology for military invasion justifying colonialism. This refers to the conflict of interpretation with the tradition of Buddhism. This is also true of the symbolic meaning of the cross, whether it is elaborated as the theology of solidarity with suffering people or distorted as the theory of crucifix justifying colonial domination. This study shows the extent to which an ideal type would be blended with its irrational absurdity.

Comparative theology requires an analysis of religious discourse and material interests through a bio-political analysis of domination in subjugation of the human body in the colonial context. It shapes a spectrum of comparative theology in a postcolonial manner, in which 'Orientalism' is considered in a meticulous reading of the religious texts. This is done to transcend the colonized regime of the religious discourse. A critical exegesis comes to terms with suspending what is taken for granted, by exerting the immanent critique upon the problematic domain of the commentarial tradition. In sum, comparative theology remains confessional with a constructive endeavour, in which a semantic retrieval is sought from the source of religious discourse by engaging in the comparative reading of the other texts.

A religious construction of reality is applied to the comparative study of Islam. In undertaking a study of Islam, the Meccan model is retrieved as the source for human dignity, critical reasoning, and democratic potential. Islam has its own tradition in contributing to European civilization. Its own spirituality, rationality, religious humanism and ethics break through a Eurocentric mode of representation which reduces the uniqueness of Islam for its own interest of European representation. The comparative study of Islamic predestination and Calvinist election is featured to show how Islam's belief system would contribute to human responsibility and modernity.

5. A comparative theology in inter-religious relations facilitates an ethical project in a social scientific framework to promote prophetic religious morals and their value rationality in connection with their life-world and history of effect for responsible critique, solidarity and emancipation. Life-world enquiry locates the place of religion as the guiding principle penetrating the cultural realm, the practical style of life, and the erotic sphere of life. It investigates the degree to which religious discourse would be bound to hegemonic modes of signification or representation in dealing with sexuality, gender, race and ethnicity,

A phenomenology of the body appears to be diverse in social stratification, in which the category of sex, whether masculine or feminine, or differentials of sexuality, would be culturally produced and controlled through a bio-political type of dominion.

A religious construction of sexuality draws on the ultimate reality of *totaliter aliter* which transcends a metaphysic of gender substance, in which gendered discourse of heterosexual society is stratified and reified in society and culture. God is totally different, changing the system of inequality and violence in a gendered hierarchical society toward a new creation in expectation of a new heaven and new earth. God is infinite in safeguarding divine freedom against psychological reductionism or a gendered projection of the male God. God has come to life in Jesus Christ, who stands in deep solidarity and compassion for those who are silenced, marginalized and prostituted in the patriarchal world of religion and society. God's reconciliation in Christ continues to validate the subject matter of the gospel in recognition of the dignity and validity of people of other faiths.

Bibliography

Abe, Masao. *Zen and Western Thought*, ed. William R. LaFleur. Honolulu, HI: University of Hawaii Press, 1985.
Abrahamian, Ervand. *Radical Islam*. London: I.B. Tauris, 1989.
Amin, Samir. *Eurocentrism: Modernity, Religion, and Democracy*, trans. Russel Moore and James Membrez. New York, NY: Monthly Review Press, 2009.
____. 'The Implosion of Global Capitalism: The Challenge for the Radical Left,' http://andreasbieler.net/wp-content/workshop/Amin20-20implosion20 and20 audacity 20E 20 rev20final20(2).pdf
An-Naim, A.A. (1990), "Quran, Sharia and Human Rights: Foundations, Deficiencies and Prospects," *Concilium* 2, pp. 61–9.
Aquinas, Thomas. *Summa Theologica*, trans. The English Dominican Fathers. New York, NY: Benzinger, 1947.
Arrighi, Giovani. *The Long Twentieth Century: Money, Power, and the Origins of Our Times*. London: Verso, 1994.
Ayoub, Mahmoud M. *Islam: Faith and History*. Oxford: Oneworld, 2004.
Barth, Karl. *Ad Limina Apostolorum: An Appraisal of Vatican II*, trans. Keith R. Crim. Richmond, CA: John Knox, 1968.
____. *Anselm: Fides quarens intellectum*, trans. Ian W. Robertson. London: SCM, 1960.
____. *Briefe 1961–1968*, eds Jürgen Fangmeier and H. Stoevesandt. Zurich: TVZ, 1975.
____. *Christian Life, Church Dogmatics IV, Part 4, Lecture Fragments*, trans. Geoffrey W. Bromiley. Grand Rapids, MI: Wm. B. Eerdmans, 1981.
____. *Church Dogmatics* I/1/ I/2. IV/3.1, eds. G.W. Bromiley and T.F. Torrance. London and New York, NY: T. & T. Clark, 2004.
____. *Gespräche IV: 1964–1968*. ed. E. Busch. Zurich: TVZ, 1997.
Baudrillard, Jean. *Baudrillard: A Critical Reader*, ed. Douglas Kellner. Oxford and Cambridge: Blackwell, 1994.
Baum, Wilhelm and Dietmar W. Winkler. *The Church of the East: A Concise History*. London: Routledge, 2003.

Bellah, Robert N. *Religion in Human Evolution: From the Paleolithic to the Axial Age*. London, England and Cambridge, MA: The Belknap Press of Harvard University Press, 2011.

Bendix, Reinhard. *Max Weber: An Intellectual Portrait*. Berkeley, CA: University of California Press, 1977.

Benedict, Ruth. *Patterns of Culture*. New York, NY: Houghton Mifflin, 2005.

____. *Race: Science and Politics*. New York. NY: Modern Age Books, 1940.

Berger, Peter L. and Thomas Luckmann. *The Social Construction of Reality*. New York, NY: Anchor Books, 1966.

Bethge, Eberhard. *Dietrich Bonhoeffer: A Biography*. Minneapolis, MN: Fortress, 2000.

Bloom, Alfred. *Shinran's Gospel of Pure Grace*. Tucson, AZ: University of Arizona Press, 1965.

____. Com. and ed. *The Essential Shinran: A Buddhist Path of True Entrusting*. Bloomington, IN: World Wisdom, 2007.

Bloom, Jonathan and Sheila Blair. *Islam: A Thousand Years of Faith and Power*. New Haven, CT and London: Yale University Press, 2002.

Bonhoeffer, Dietrich. *Ethics*, trans. Neville H. Smith. New York, NY: Touchstone, 1995.

____. *Letters and Papers from Prison*, ed. Eberhard Bethge. New York, NY: Macmillan, 1971.

Bourdieu, Pierre. *Language and Symbolic Power*, trans. Gino Raymond and Matthew Adamson. Cambridge, MA: Harvard University Press, 1991.

____. *Masculine Domination*. New York, NY: Polity Press, 2001.

Bourdieu, Pierre. *Distinction: A Social Critique of the Judgment of Taste*. Cambridge, MA: Harvard University Press, 1984.

Bourdieu, Pierre and L.J.D. Wacquant, *An Invitation to Reflexive Sociology*. Chicago, IL and London: University of Chicago Press, 1992.

Braaten, Carl E. and Robert W. Jenson, eds. *Union with Christ: The New Finnish Interpretation of Luther*. Grand Rapids, MI and Cambridge: Wm. B. Eerdmans, 1998.

Busch, Eberhard. *Karl Barth: His Life from Letters and Autobiographical Texts*, trans. John Bowden. Grand Rapids, MI: Wm. B. Eerdmans, 1994.

Brassard, Francis. *The Concept of Bodhicitta in Śāntideva's Bodhicaryāvatāra*. Albany, NY: State University of New York Press, 2000.

Butler, Judith. *Gender Trouble: Feminism and the Subversion of Identity*. New York, NY: Routledge, 2007.

Calvin, John. *Commentaries on I and II Timothy*, trans. William Pringle. Rep. Grand Rapids, MI: Baker, 1993.

____. *Institutes of the Christian Religion* 2, ed. John T. McNeil, trans. Ford L. Battles. Philadelphia, PA: Westminster Press, 1960.

Ceperiano, Arjohn M. et al. "Girl, Bi, Bakla, Tomboy: The Intersectionality of Sexuality, Gender, and Class in Urban Poor Contexts," *Philippine Journal of Psychology*, 2016, 49 (2), pp. 5–34.

Chung, Paul S. *Comparative Theology among Multiple Modernities*. Cham: Palgrave Macmillan, 2017.

———. *Critical Theory and Political Theology: The Aftermath of the Enlightenment*. Cham: Palgrave Macmillan, 2019.

———. *Hermeneutical Theology and the Imperative of Public Ethics: Confessing Christ in Post-Colonial World Christianity*. Eugene, OR: Pickwick, 2013.

———. *Karl Barth: God's Word in Action*. Eugene, OR: Cascade, 2008.

———. *Martin Luther and Buddhism: Aesthetics of Suffering*, 2nd ed. Eugene, OR: Pickwick, 2008.

———. *The Spirit of God Transforming Life: The Reformation and Theology of The Holy Spirit*. New York: Palgrave, 2009.

Clooney, Francis X. *Hindu God, Christian God: How Reason Helps Break Down the Boundaries between Religions*. Oxford: Oxford University Press, 2001.

———. *Theology after Vedanta: An Experiment in Comparative Theology*. Albany, NY: SUNY, 1993.

———. *The Truth, the Way, the Life: Christian Commentary on the Three Holy Mantras of the Śrīvaiṣṇava Hindus*. Leuven: Peeters; Grand Rapids, MI, and Cambridge: Wm. B. Eerdmans, 2008.

Coates, Harper Havelock and Ryugaka Ishizuka. *Honen: The Buddhist Saint*. New York, NY: Garland Publishing, 1981.

Cobb, John B. *Beyond Dialogue: Toward a Mutual Transformation of Christianity and Buddhism*. Eugene, OR: Wipf and Stock, 1998.

Cohn-Sherbok, Dan. *Judaism: History, Belief and Practice*. London and New York, NY: Routledge, 2003.

Collins, Patricia H. *Black Feminist Thought: Knowledge, Consciousness, and the Politics of Empowerment*, 2nd ed. New York, NY: Routledge, 2009.

Cone, James H. *The Cross and the Lynching Tree*. Maryknoll, NY: Orbis, 2011.

Conze, Edward, trans. *Buddhist Wisdom: The Diamond Sutra and The Heart Sutra*. New York, NY: Vintage Books, 2001.

Davis, Brian. *The Thought of Thomas Aquinas*. Oxford: Clarendon, 1993.

Dawood, N.J., trans. *The Koran*. London and New York, NY: Penguin Books, 1999.

Dessi, Ugo. "The Pure Land as a Principle of Criticism," *Japanese Religions*. vol. 32 (1 and 2), pp. 75–90.

Diamond, Irene and Lee Quinby, eds. *Feminism and Foucault: Reflections on Resistance*. Boston, MA: Northwestern University Press, 1988.

Dilthey, W. 'The Rise of Hermeneutics (1900),' *Selected Works, IV: Hermeneutics and the Study of History*. Princeton, NJ: Princeton University Press, 1996.

Drescher, Hans-Georg. *Ernst Troeltsch: His Life and Work*. Minneapolis, MN: Fortress, 1993.

Duchrow, Ulrich. *Global Economy: A Confessional Issue for the Churches?*, trans. David Lewis. Geneva, Switzerland: WCC Publications, 1987.

Duchrow, Ulrich and Franz J. Hinkelammert. *Transcending Greedy Money: Interreligious Solidarity for Just Relations.* New York, NY: Palgrave Macmillan, 2012.

Dunne, John and Sara McClinton, eds. and trans. *The Precious Garland: An Epistle to a King.* Boston, MA: Wisdom Publications, 1997.

Durkheim, E. *The Elementary Forms of Religious Life,* trans. Karen E. Fields. New York, NY: The Free Press, 1995.

Ebeling, Gerhard. *Luther: An Introduction to His Thought,* trans. R.A. Wilson. Minneapolis, MN:

Fortress, 2007.

Ensminger, Sven. *Karl Barth's Theology as a Resource for a Christian Theology of Religions.* Bloomsbury: T. & T. Clark, 2014.

Ferrarello, Susi. *Husserl's Ethics and Practical Intentionality.* London and New York, NY: Bloomsbury, 2016.

Feuerbach, L. *The Essence of Christianity,* trans. George Eliot. New York, NY: Harper & Row, 1957.

Foucault, Michel. *The Archeology of Knowledge and the Discourse on Language,* trans. A.M. Sheridan Smith. New York, NY: Pantheon, 1972.

_____. *Discipline and Punish: The Birth of the Prison,* trans. Alan Sheridan. New York, NY: Vintage Books, 1977.

_____. *The History of Sexuality: An Introduction* 1, trans. Robert Hurley. New York, NY: Vintage Books, 1990.

_____. *The History of Sexuality: The Use of Pleasure* 2, trans. Robert Hurley. New York, NY: Vintage Books, 1990.

Gadamer, Hans G. *Truth and Method,* 2nd rev. ed., trans. Joel Weinscheimer and Donald G. Marshall. New York, NY: Continuum, 2004.

Gaonkar, Dilip P., ed. *Alternative Modernities.* Durham and London: Duke University Press, 2001.

Garcia, J. Neil C. *Philippine Gay Culture: Binabae to Bakla, Silahis to MSM.* Diliman, Quezon City. University of the Philippines Press, 1996.

Gayhart, Bryce A. *The Ethics of Ernst Troeltsch: a Commitment to Relevancy* Lewiston, NY: E. Mellen Press, 1990.

Geertz, Clifford. *The Interpretation of Cultures.* New York, NY: Basic Books, 1973.

Goddard, Hugh. *A History of Christian-Muslim Relations.* Chicago, IL: New Amsterdam Books, 2000.

Gomez, Luis O., trans. *Land of Bliss: The Paradise of the Buddha of Immeasurable Light.* Honolulu, HI: University of Hawaii Press, 1996.

Griffel, Frank. *Al-Ghazali's Philosophical Theology.* Oxford and New York, NY: Oxford University Press, 2009.

Habermas, Jürgen. *Between Naturalism and Religion: Philosophical Essays,* trans. Ciaran Cronin. Cambridge: Polity Press, 2008.

_____. *The Theory of Communicative Action: Lifeworld and System: A Critique of Functional Reason,* II, trans. Thomas McCarthy. Boston, MA: Beacon, 1987.

Harvey, Peter. *An Introduction to Buddhist Ethics*. Cambridge: Cambridge University Press, 2000.
Herdt, Gilbert. *Sambia Sexual Culture: Essays from the Field*. Chicago, IL: University of Chicago Press, 1999.
Hick, John. *God has Many Names*. Philadelphia, PA: Westminster Press, 1982.
_____. *An Interpretation of Religion: Human Responses to the Transcendent*, 2nd ed. New Haven, CT: Yale University Press, 2004.
_____. *Philosophy of Religion*. New York, NY: Prentice-Hall, 1963.
Hodgson, Marshall G. S. *The Classical Age of Islam*. Chicago, IL and London: University of Chicago Press, 1974.
_____. *The Venture of Islam: Conscience and History in a World Civilization, vol.1: The Classical Age of Islam*. Chicago and London: The University of Chicago Press, 1974.
Holmes, Mary. *What is Gender? Sociological Approaches*. London: Sage Publications, 2007.
Hubbard, Thomas K., ed. *Homosexuality in Greece and Rome: A Sourcebook of Basic Documents*. Berkeley, CA: University of California Press, 2003.
Huff, Toby E. and Wolfgang Schluchter, eds. *Max Weber and Islam*. London and New York, NY: Routledge, 1999.
Husserl, Edmund. *The Essential Husserl: Basic Writings in Transcendental Phenomenology*, ed. Donn Welton. Bloomington, IN and Indianapolis, IN: Indiana University Press, 1999.
Ives, Christopher, ed., *Divine Emptiness and Historical Fullness: A Buddhist-Jewish-Christian Conversation with Masao Abe*. Valley Forge, PA: Trinity Press International, 1995.
Jackson, Roger R. and John J. Makransky, eds. *Buddhist Theology: Critical Reflections by Contemporary Buddhist Scholars*. Richmond, Surrey: Curzon Press, 2000.
Jalbert, John E. "Husserl's Position between Dilthey and the Windelband-Rickert School of Neo-Kantianism," *Journal of the History of Philosophy* 26 (2) (1988), pp. 279–96.
Jones, Ken. *The New Social Face of Buddhism: A Call to Action*. Boston, MA: Wisdom Publications, 2003.
Jüngel, Eberhard. *Karl Barth: A Theological Legacy*, trans. Garrett E. Paul. Philadelphia, PA: Westminster Press, 1986.
Kant, Immanuel. *Critique of the Power of Judgment*, trans. Paul Guyer and Eric Matthews. Cambridge: Cambridge University Press, 2000.
Kaufmann, Gordon D. *In Face of Mystery: A Constructive Theology*. Cambridge, MA: Harvard University Press, 1993.
Keel, Hee-Sung. *Understanding Shinran: A Dialogical Approach*. Fremont, CA: Asian Humanities Press, 1995.
Kenneth K. Tanaka. *The Dawn of Chinese Pure Land Buddhist Doctrine: Ching-ying Hui-yuan's Commentary on the Visualization Sutra*. Albany, NY: SUNY, 1990.

Khorchide, Mouhanad and Ufuk Topkara. "A Contribution to Comparative Theology: Probing the Depth of Islamic Thought," *Religions* 2013, pp. 67–76 www.mdpi.com/journal/religions
King, Ursula, ed. *Religion and Gender*. Oxford and Cambridge: Blackwell, 2005.
Klappert, Bertold. *Versöhnung und Befreiung: Versuche, Karl Barth kontextuell zu verstehen*. Neukirchen-Vluyn: Neukirchener, 1994.
Knitter, Paul F. *Introducing Theologies of Religions*. Maryknoll, NY: Orbis Books, 2002.
_____. *No Other Name? A Critical Survey of Christian Attitudes toward the World Religions*. Maryknoll, NY: Orbis, 1985.
_____. *Without Buddha I Could not be a Christian*. Oxford: Oneworld, 2009.
Knitter, Paul F. and Chandra Muzaffar, eds. *Subverting Greed: Religious Perspectives on the Global Economy*. Maryknoll, NY: Orbis, 2002.
Kolb, Robert and Timothy J. Wengert, eds. *The Book of Concord: The Confessions of the Evangelical Lutheran Church*. Minneapolis, MN: Fortress, 2000.
Kraemer, Hendrik. *The Christian Message in a Non-Christian World*. London: Edinburgh House Press, 1938.
_____. *Why Christianity of All Religions?*, trans. Hubert Hoskins. London: Lutterworth, 1962.
Kulandran, S. *Grace in Christianity and Hinduism*. Cambridge: James Clarke, 2004.
Küng, Hans. *Christianity: Essence, History, and Future*. London and New York, NY: Continuum, 1995.
_____. *Islam: Past, Present and Future*, trans. John Bowden. Oxford: Oneworld, 2007.
Lindbeck, George. *The Nature of Doctrine: Religion and Theology in a Postliberal Age*. Philadelphia, PA: Westminster Press, 1984.
Luther, Martin. 'Admonition to the Clergy,' in Gunter Fabiunke, *Luther als Nationalokonom*. Berlin: Akademie, 1963. pp. 193–230
_____. 'Dear Christians, One and All, Rejoice,' in *Lutheran Book of Worship*, trans. Richard Massie. Minneapolis, MN: Augsburg Publishing House, 1978, no. 299.
_____. *Dr. Martin Luthers Vermischte Deutsche Schriften*, ed. Johann K. Irmischer. vol. 63. Erlangen: Heyder and Zimmer, 1854.
_____. *Lectures on Romans*, trans. and ed. Wilhelm Pauck. Philadelphia, PA: Westminster Press, 1961.
_____. *Luther's Basic Theological Writings*, 2nd ed., eds. Timothy Lull and William R. Russel. Minneapolis, MN: Fortress, 2005.
_____. *Luther's Works*, ed. Jaroslav Pelikan. St Louis, MO: Concordia, 1955–67.
Mahdavi, Mojtaba. 'Max Weber in Iran: Does Islamic Protestantism Matter?' pp. 9–10. https://www.cpsa-acsp.ca/ papers-2005/Mahdavi.pdf. pp. 1–21.
Malesevic, Sinisa. *The Sociology of Ethnicity*. London: Sage Publications, 2004.
Makransky, John J. *Buddhahood Embodied: Sources of Controversy in India and Tibet*. Albany, NY: State University of New York Press, 1997.

Marquardt, F.W. *Von Elend und Heimsuchung der Theologie: Prolegomena zur Dogmatik*. Munich: Chr. Kaiser, 1992.
Marx, Karl. *Capital, 1: A Critique of Political Economy*, trans. Ben Fowkes. London: Penguin, 1990.
McGrath, Alister E. *Iustitia Dei: A History of the Christian Doctrine of Justification*, 2nd ed. Cambridge: Cambridge University Press, 1998.
Marshall, David. *God, Muhammad and the Unbelievers: A Qur'anic Study*. Richmond, Surrey: Curzon, 1999.
Moore-Keish, Martha L. Christian T. Collins Winn, et al., eds. *Karl Bath and Comparative Theology*. New York, NY: Fordam University Press, 2009.
Nagao, Gadjin. *Madhiyamika and Yogācāra*. Albany, NY: State University of New York Press, 1991.
Nasr, Seyyed Hossein. *Islam: Religion, History and Civilization*. New York, NY: HarperOne, 2003.
Niebuhr, H. Richard. *Christ and Culture*. New York, NY: Harper & Row, 1951.
_____. *Radical Monotheism and Western Culture*. Louisville, KY: Westminster John Knox Press, 1970.
Nolan, Patrick and Gerhard Lenski, *Human Societies: An introduction to Macrosociology*. Boulder, CO and London: Paradigm Publishers, 2006.
Oberman, Heiko A. *The Harvest of Medieval Theology: Gabriel Biel and Late Medieval Nominalism*. Grand Rapids, MI: Baker Academic, 1963.
_____. *Luther: Man Between God and the Devil*, trans. E.W. Schwarzbart. New York, NY: Doubleday, 1992.
Otto, R. *The Idea of the Holy*. Oxford: Oxford University Press, 1958.
_____. *India's Religion of Grace and Christianity Compared and Contrasted*, trans. F.H. Foster. New York, NY: Macmillan, 1930.
Pangritz, Andreas and Paul S. Chung, eds. *Theological Audacities. Selected Essays: Friedrich-Wilhelm Marquardt*. Eugene, OR: Pickwick, 2010.
Pas, Julian. *Visions of Sukhavati: Shan-tao's Commentary on the Kuan Wu-Liang-Shou-Fo-Ching*. New York, NY: SUNY Press, 1995.
Peters, Ted. *God – The World's Future: Systematic Theology for a New Era*, 2nd ed. Minneapolis, MN: Fortress, 2000.
_____. *Sin Boldly!: Justifying Faith for Fragile and Broken Souls*. Minneapolis, MN: Fortress, 2015.
Radcliffe-Brown, Alfred. *Structure and Function in Primitive Society*. New York, NY: The Free Press, 1952.
Rahman, Fazlur. *Islam and Modernity: Transformation of an Intellectual Tradition*. Chicago: The University of Chicago, 1982.
Rahner, K. "Jesus Christ in the non-Christian Religions," in Karl Rahner, *Theological Investigations*. vol. 17. Baltimore, MY: Helicon Press, London: Darton, Longman & Todd, 1961–92, pp. 39–50.
Ramadan, Tariq. *Islam and the Arab Awakening*. Oxford: Oxford University Press, 2012.
_____. *Radical Reform: Islamic Ethics and Liberation*. New York, NY: Oxford University Press, 2009.

Repp, Martin. *Honens religiöses Denken: Eine Untersuchung zu Strukturen religiöser Erneuerung.* Wiesbaden: Harrassowitz Verlag, 2005.

Ricoeur, Paul. *Time and Narrative 1*, trans. K. McLaughlin and D. Pallauer. Chicago, IL: University of Chicago Press, 1984.

Russell Kirkland, "The Chinese Background of the Concept of MAPPÔ." http:// faculty. franklin.uga.edu/kirkland/sites/faculty.franklin.uga.edu .kirkland/files/MAPPO. pdf

Rendtorff, Trutz. *Theorie des Christentums.* Gütersloh: Gütersloher Verlaghaus Gerd Mohn, 1972.

Riley, Dylan. 'Bourdieu's Class Theory: The Academy as Revolutionary,' *Catalyst.* vol. 1. Nr. 2. (Summer 2017), pp. 117–36.

Ricoeur, Paul. *Hermeneutics and the Human Sciences*, ed. and trans. John B. Thomson. Cambridge: Cambridge University Press, 1981.

Rogan, Eugene. *The Arabs, a History.* New York, NY: Penguin, 2010.

Saeki, Yoshiro. *The Nestorian Monument in China*, rep. New York, NY: Macmillan, 1928.

Said, Edward W. *Orientalism.* London: Routledge, 1978.

Salvatore, Armando. "Tradition and Modernity within Islamic Civilisation and the West," in *Islam and Modernity, Key Issues and Debates*, eds. Muhammad Khalid Masud et al. Edinburgh: Edinburgh University Press, 2009, pp. 3–35.

Sansom, George B. *History of Japan to 1334.* Stanford, CA: Stanford University Press, 1958.

Shariati, Ali. *On the Sociology of Islam*, trans. Hamid Algar Berkeley, CA: Mizan Press, 1979.

Schellong, Dieter. *Bürgertum und christliche Religion: Anpassungsprobleme der Theologie seit Schleiermacher.* Munich: Chr. Kaiser, 1975.

Schmidt-Leukel, Perry. "Finding God in the *Bodhicaryāvatāra*: An Interim Report on a 'Christian Commentary to the *Bodhicaryāvatāra*,'" *Journal of Comparative Scripture*, no. 6 (July 2015), pp.9–34.

Schulze, Reinhard. *A Modern History of the Islamic World*, trans. Azizeh Azod. London and New York: I.B.Tauris Publishers, 2000.

Schütte, Joseph Franz. *Valignanos Missionsgrundsätze für Japan* 1. Rome: Edizioni Di Storia E Letteratura, 1951.

Seltzer, Robert M. *Jewish People, Jewish Thought: The Jewish Experience in History.* New York, NY: Macmillan, 1980.

Senghor, Leopold. *Negritude und Humanismus.* Dusseldorf/Koln: E. Diederich, 1967.

Sharf, Robert H. "The Zen of Japanese Nationalism," *History of Religions* 33 (August 1993), pp.1–43.

Shigaraki, Takamaro. "Shinjin and Social Action in Shinran's Teachings," trans. David Matsumoto. *The Pure Land.* n.s. (8–9) pp. 219–49.

Shinran. *The Tanni Sho: Notes Lamenting Differences.* Kyoto: Ryukoko University Translation Center, 1962.

_____. *A Translation of Shinran's Kyogyoshinsho* 4 Vols. Kyoto: Hongwanji International Center, 1983–1990.

Bibliography

———. *A Translation of Shinran's Songo shinzo meimon*. Kyoto: Hongwanji International Center, 1981.

Smith, Christian. *American Evangelicalism: Embattled and Thriving*. Chicago, IL: University of Chicago Press, 1998.

Smith, W.C. *Faith and Belief: The Difference between Them*. Oxford: Oneworld, 1979.

———. *The Meaning and End of Religion*. Minneapolis, MN: Fortress Press, 1991.

———. *Modern Islam in India*. London: Victor Gollancz Ltd., 1946.

Soh, C. Sarah. *The Comfort Woman: Sexual Violence and Postcolonial Memory in Korea and Japan*. Chicago, IL and London: University of Chicago Press, 2008.

Srinivasacbari, P.N. *The Philosophy of Visintidvaita*. Madras: Adyar, 1946.

Strong, John S. *The Experience of Buddhism: Sources and Interpretations*, 3rd ed. Boston, MA: Wadsworth, 2008.

Suzuki, D.T. *Collected Writings on Shin Buddhism*. Kyoto: Shinshu Otaniha, 1973.

———. *Essays in Zen Buddhism*. London: Rieder, 1950.

———. *An Introduction to Zen Buddhism*. New York, NY: Grove Press, 1964.

———. *Outlines of Mahayana Buddhism*. New Delhi: Munshiram Manoharlal Publishers, 2000; orig.: 1907.

———. *A Translation of Shinran's Yuishinsho-mon'I*. Kyoto: Hongwanji International Center, 1979.

Taha, M.M. *The Second Message of Islam*. New York, NY: Syracuse, 1987.

Tanner, Kathryn. *Theories of Culture: A New Agenda for Theology*. Minneapolis, MN: Augsburg, 1997.

Taylor, Charles. 'Two Theories of Modernity,' in *Alternative Modernities*, ed. Dillip P. Gaonkar. pp. 172–96. Durham, NC: Duke University Press, 2001.

Tenzin Gyatso, the Fourteenth Dalai Lama. *Essence of the Heart Sutra: The Dalai Lama's Heart of Wisdom Teachings*, trans. and ed. Geshe Thupten Jinpa. Boston, MA: Wisdom Publications, 2002.

———. *The Good Heart: A Buddhist Perspective on the Teaching of Jesus*, trans. Geshe Thupten

———. *Practicing Wisdom: The Perfection of Shantideva's Bodhisattva Way*, trans. and ed. Geshe Thupten Jinpa. Boston, MA: Wisdom Publications, 2005.

Jinpa, ed. Robert Kiely. Boston, MA: Wisdom Publications, 1996.

Thich Nhat Hanh. *The Heart of Understanding: Commentaries on the Prajñāpāramitā Heart Sutra*, ed. Peter Levitt. Berkeley, CA: Parallax, 1988.

Throop, C. Jason and Keith M. Murphy, 'Bourdieu and Phenomenology: A Critical Assessment,' Anthropological Theory Vol 2 (2), (2002), pp.185–207. http://cdn.preterhuman. net/texts/ science_ and_ technology /Throop20J.20and20Murphy20K.20-20Bourdieu 20and 20 Pheno menol ogy.pdf

Thurman, Robert A.F. 'Guidelines for Buddhist Social Activism Based on Nagarjuna's *Jewel Garland of Royal Counsels*,' in *Eastern Buddhist* 16 (Spring 1983). pp. 19–51.

Tillich, Paul. *Christianity and the Encounter of World Religions*. Minneapolis, MN: Fortress Press, 1994.

———. *Dynamics of Faith*. New York, NY: Harper & Row, 1957.

———. *On the Boundary*. New York, NY: Charles Scribner's Sons, 1966.

———. *Systematic Theology*, 1. III. Chicago, IL: University of Chicago Press, 1951, 1963.

Tracy, David. *Plurality and Ambiguity: Hermeneutics, Religion, Hope*. Chicago, IL: University of Chicago Press, 1987.

Troeltsch, Ernst. *The Absoluteness of Christianity and the History of Religion*, trans. David Reid. Louisville, KY: Westminster John Knox Press, 1971.

———. *The Christian Faith*, ed. Gertrud von le Fort, trans. Garrett E. Paul. Minneapolis, MN: Fortress.

———. 'The Place of Christianity among the World Religions,' in *Christian Thought: Its History and Application*, ed. Friedrich Hügel. Pp. 1–36. London: University of London Press, 1923.

———. *Religion in History: Ernst Troeltsch*, trans. James L. Adams and Walter F. Bense. Minneapolis, MN: Fortress, 1991.

———. *The Social Teaching of the Christian Churches*, I, II, trans. Olive Wyon. Louisville, KY: Westminster John Knox, 1992.

Troll, Christian W. *Dialogue and Difference: Clarity in Christian-Muslim Relations*, trans. David Marshall. Maryknoll, NY: Orbis, 2009.

Turner, Bryan S. 'Revisiting Weber and Islam,' *The British Journal of Sociology* 2010, pp.161–6. https://www.onlinelibrary.wiley.com/doi/pdf/10.1111/j.1468-4446.2009.01285.x

Ueda, Yoshifumi and Dennis Hirota. *Shinran: An Introduction to His Thought*. Kyoto: Hongwanji International Center, 1989.

Unno, Taitetsu. *River of Fire, River of Water: An Introduction to the Pure Land Tradition of Shin Buddhism*. New York, NY: Doubleday, 1998.

———. trans. *Tannisho: A Shin Buddhist Classic*. Honolulu, HI: Buddhist Study Center Press, 1984.

Wallerstein, Immanuel. *The Essential Wallerstein*. New York, NY: The New Press, 2000.

Weber, M. *From Max Weber: Essays in Sociology*, ed. and trans. H.H. Gerth and C. Wright Mills. New York, NY: Oxford University Press, 1946.

———. *The Protestant Ethic and the Spirit of Capitalism*, trans. Talcott Parsons. Mineola, NY: Dover, 2003.

———. *The Sociology of Religion*, trans. Ephraim Fischoff. Boston, MA: Beacon Press, 1964.

———. *Weber Selections in Translation*, ed. W.G. Runciman and trans. Erich Matthews. Cambridge: Cambridge University Press, 1978.

Wendel, F. *Calvin: Origins and Development of His Religious Thought*, trans. Philip Mairet. Durham, NC: Labyrinth, 1987.

West, Cornel. *Race Matters*. New York, NY: Vintage Books, 1994.
Williams, Paul. *Mahayana Buddhism: The Doctrinal Foundations*. London and New York, NY: Routledge, 1989,
_____. *The Unexpected Way: On Converting from Buddhism to Catholicism*. Edinburgh and New York: T. & T. Clark, 2002.
Yoshiaki, Yoshimi. *Comfort Woman: Sexual Slavery in the Japanese Military during World War II*, trans. Suzanne O'Brien. New York, NY: Columbia University Press, 2000.

Index

Abbasid caliphate, 125, 133, 138, 139, 140
Abe, Masao, 60-62
Abrahamic religion, x, xi
Absolute nothingness, 58, 60, 62, 64, 65, 195
Acosmism, 42, 45
Advaita Text, 50, 78, 111
Ahimsa, 66
al-Afghani, Jamal ad-Din,126
al-Banna, Hasan, 135, 136
al-Bukhari, 132
aletheia, 109
al-Ghazali, 141, 142, 152
al-Mahdi, 140
al-Mamun,140, 141
Ali, Muhammad, 126, 135,
Alternative modernities, 35, 119, 137
Amin, Samir, 121-127, 136
Analogans, 103, 106
Analogata, 103, 106
androcentric episteme, 179,
principle, 211
system, 176
Anfechtungen, 3, 8, 82
anonymous Christianity, 115
Anselm, 106
Anti-Semitism, 62
Aquinas, Thomas, 37, 74-76, 91, 142, 149
arcana Dei virtus,147
archeological hermeneutics,1, 211
enquiry, 210, 211
Aristotle, 18, 76, 139
Atman, 66, 110
Aufhebung, 3, 186

Augustine of Hippo, 75-77, 118, 160
Averroes, 138, 139, 141, 142
Avicenna, 139, 141, 142
Axial Age, xi, 66, 153, 154
Axial enquiry, 48, 67
religions, xi, 122, 153

Bakla, 174
Barth, Karl, 2, 3, 4, 98-120, 147, 162, 166, 186-189, 205-207, 212, 213
Bellah, Robert, 2, 66, 93, 94, 97,154, 204
Benedict, Ruth, 158, 159
Berger, Peter, 30, 98, 103, 104, 107, 119, 169
Beruf, 91
Bhagavad Gita, 66
Bhakti, 3, 6, 39, 45, 93, 98, 108, 111-113
biological dimorphism,183
Bio-politics, 51, 176
Bio-political enquiry, 63, 134
governmentality, 63
bisexuality, 178, 179
Boa, Franz, 159, 171
Bodhicaryāvatāra, 2, 47, 48, 53, 55, 56
Bodhicitta, 47, 53-58, 60
Bodisattva, 53-56, 59, 65, 67, 69, 83, 88, 95-97
Bonhoeffer, Dietrich, 103, 184, 208
Bourdieu, Pierre, 5, 7, 13, 29, 30, 168-170, 178, 179, 181
Brahman, 39, 45, 66, 110, 111
Brahmanism, 66
Brunner, Emil, 103
Buddhahood, 73, 74, 85
Buddha nature, 72, 73, 85

Buddhist axiality, 65-67
Buddhist theology, 74, 79, 81, 84, 85
Butler, J., 176

Calvin, John, 2, 3, 14, 122, 144, 147, 148, 159, 160
Caste system, 63, 66, 113, 199
certitudo salutis, 145
Clooney, Francis, 1, 47, 49-51, 64, 78, 98, 111, 112, 119, 204
Collage, 64, 65, 78
Collectio, 50, 204
Columbus, Christopher, 122
Comfort women, 48, 63
Commodity fetishism, 92
Cone, James, 174
Confucianism, xiii, 94, 95, 114
Correlation, 10, 14, 26, 30
Crusade, 114, 115, 212
Cultural-linguistic enquiry, 165, 166, 167
Cultural-narrative approach, 186
Cultural-semantic enquiry, 212

decretum horribile, 146
dependent origination, 47, 54, 56, 58, 66, 195
Deus absconditus, 81
Deus revelatus, 81
Dilthey, W, 2, 6, 16, 17, 25-28, 35, 36
disgrace effect, 49, 103, 202, 208, 212
Duchrow, U., xi, xiii, 92, 124, 130
dukkha, 62, 66
Durkheim, Emile, 130, 157, 160, 161, 166

economic traditionalism, 91
effective history, 211, 212
Eightfold Path, 55, 66, 73
elective affinity,1, 3, 11, 13, 51, 54, 92, 119, 120, 177, 186,195-196, 199, 201, 203, 206, 207, 210-213
Emptiness, 45, 47, 48, 52-56, 58-62, 65-67, 81, 85, 213
Enlightenment, 60, 65, 66, 73, 116, 119, 123, 124, 137, 142, 194
Epistemological relativism, 198
Epistemic rupture, 65, 71, 73, 201, 211, 212
Ethics of conviction, 150
Eurocentrism, 3, 17, 122-125, 127, 136, 137, 154

existential enquiry, 161, 162
extra muros ecclesiae, 109

Faith-epistemology, 31, 33
Feuerbach, L., 98, 103-106, 114
fides charitate formata, 77
fides Christo formata,77
fides efficax, 145
fiducia, 69, 85-87
Five Pillars of Islam, 129
Fiqh, 132,133
Foucault, Michel, 48-51, 63, 174-179, 199, 200-202
Four Noble Truths, 45, 66
French enlightenment model, 136
French Revolution, 123, 125, 126
Fusion of horizons, 51, 204

Gadamer, H.G., 28, 51, 202, 204, 205
Geertz, Clifford, 35, 165, 180, 202-205, 208, 212
Gratia create, 76

Habermas, J., 185, 202
Hadith, 131, 132, 141, 151
happy exchange, 77, 81
Heart of Wisdom, 58
Heart Sutra, 48, 58, 59, 61
Hegel, G.W.F., 16, 25, 30, 101, 105, 187
Henotheism, 161
Hermeneutic of narrative, 201
Hick, John, 26, 37-39, 161, 163
Hijrah, 128
historical critical method, 10, 15, 16, 17, 33, 34, 198, 212
Hodgson, Marshall, 125, 154
Holocaust, 61, 62, 115, 212
homo ethicus, 4, 51, 52
homo lector, 4, 47, 49, 50, 52, 113, 114
homo socius, 4, 51, 52
Honen, 68, 70, 71, 107, 112, 187, 188
House of Wisdom, 140
Husserl, Edmund, xiii, 25, 27-30, 53, 181, 197, 202

Ideal type, 8, 9, 10, 12, 198
idiographic inquiry, 27, 28
ijma, 151

Index   229

immanent critique, 3, 44, 48, 49, 50, 69, 79, 84, 92, 97, 99, 103, 114, 120, 121, 122, 127, 152, 190, 208, 211-213
Industrial Revolution, 123
inner-worldly asceticism, 95, 146
integralism,136
intertextuality, 88, 166, 180, 212
intratextuality,102, 212
iron cage, 42, 70,117, 119
Islamdom, 125
Islamic humanism, 154
Humanism, 150, 154
Predestination, 121, 122, 144
Protestantism, 122, 150, 151, 152, 155
Reformation, 151,
Traditionalism, 134
ijtihad, 151, 152

Jaspers, K., 153
jiri-rita, 95, 96

Kant, Immanuel, 15, 25-29, 36, 37, 104
Karma, 48, 57, 61-67, 85, 195
kathoey, 174
Kaufmann, Gordon, 31, 37, 38
Knitter, Paul, 23, 109, 110, 116, 119, 130
Kraemer, Hendrik, 101, 116
Küng, H., 76, 124, 126, 135, 136, 139, 140, 142, 148, 152

language games, 166, 204
Life-world, 4, 25, 27-31, 35, 52, 62, 78, 79, 120, 170, 181, 183, 184, 193, 195-198, 201-208, 210-214
enquiry, 3, 5, 40, 41, 150, 184, 214
approach, 150, 180, 202
clarification, 203
Lindbeck, George, 50, 156, 165, 166, 204
Luther, Martin, 1, 2, 68-97, 118, 126, 159, 188, 208, 213

Maimonides, Moses, 139
Malinowski, Bronislaw, 157
Mamluk model, 134, 135
Mappo, 69-70
Marx, Karl, 91, 168, 169
Meccan model, 3, 121,128-130, 132, 138, 153, 155, 214

Medina model, 3, 121, 128-130, 132, 134, 153
method of correlation, 162, 192, 198, 207
Moksa, 66, 112
Mozarabians, 138
Muhammad, 127-129, 130-132, 135-138, 141, 144, 146-149, 151-154
Multiple modernities, 1, 34, 35, 47, 51, 66, 92, 99, 108, 109, 115, 119
multivariate enquiry, 170
approach, 177
Muslim Brotherhood, 134-136

Nāgārjuna, 53, 54, 57, 59, 60, 61
Nahda, 121, 125-127, 142
Nanjing massacre, 61
National Socialism, 102-104, 112
Nenbutsu, 70, 71, 72, 85, 88, 188
Neo-Kantian school, 26, 36
Neoplatonism, 27, 139
Niebuhr, H.R., 6, 23, 156-161
Nirvana Sutra, 72
nomothetic enquiry, 28, 30
Nostra Aetate, 100, 115

On, 94, 95
Orientalism, 122, 128, 213
Otto, Rudolf, 82, 111, 112, 190, 192

Pact of Omar, 138
Pan-Arabism, 135
Pan-Islamism, 126
Parrhesia, 211
pederasty, 177, 178
Peters, Ted, 208
Politics of recognition, 155, 185
political Islam,135, 136
Post-Eurocentric orientation, 119
Postliberal theology, 50, 111, 165, 212
Practical syllogism, 147
Prapatti, 112, 113
privatio boni, 76
Protestant Islam, 3
Pure Land Buddhism, 2, 3, 45, 46, 68-98, 107, 189, 212

Qadar, 143

radical monotheism, 160, 161,
Rahner, Karl, 115
Ramadan, Tariq, 136, 137, 142, 152
Ramanuja, 39, 112
Reconquista, 122
Reformation, 124, 126, 151
religious a priori, 5, 15-17, 26, 27, 29-31, 33, 35, 36, 39, 41, 44, 100, 106, 108, 118, 196-198, 210-212
religious socialism,189
Renaissance, 122-5, 139, 140, 151
Rendtorff, Trutz, 116
Rennyo Shonin, 94, 95
Ricoeur, P., 180, 201, 205, 207

Said, Edward, 122, 123
Samsara, 66, 85
Śāntideva, 55-58, 60
Schleiermacher, F.D., 6, 17, 25, 35, 36, 100, 105, 106, 108, 159, 165, 197
Schmidt-Leukel, Perry, 55-58
Semantic circle, 30, 52-53, 57, 78
Sexual racism, 174
Shan-tao, 70, 71, 73,
Sharia, 132-134, 136, 153
Shariati, Ali, 150, 151, 153, 155
Shinjin, 69, 71, 85-87, 89, 188
Shinran, Shonin, 68-97, 107, 108, 112, 187, 188, 213
Shura, 151
sign-value, 175
signa posterior, 147
simul justus et peccator, 76, 188
Smith, Alfred C., 31, 32, 152, 181
Social Darwinism, 25, 34
Social humanism, 15
social stratification, 3, 7, 8, 12, 13, 51, 65, 68, 169, 170, 172, 179, 184, 201, 202, 207, 208, 211, 214
Sufis, 133
Sultanism, 133
Sunnah, 131, 151

Sunyata, 55, 60, 80, 195
Superimposition, 64, 65, 78
Suzuki, D.T., 59-61, 79-81
Symbolic violence, 65

Tat tvam asi, 183, 187
Taylor, Charles, 35, 119, 137
The Twelfth Imam, 131
The Umayyads, 131, 134, 138
Theonomy, 164, 190
Thick description, 165, 180, 203, 205
Tillich, Paul, 2, 4, 6, 37, 93, 156,161-166, 185-187, 189-195, 206, 213
Timotheos I, 140
Totalter aliter, xiii, 40, 99, 102, 105, 106, 108, 109, 118-120, 162, 181, 203, 211, 212, 214
Tributary world-system, 121, 122
Tripitaka, 99
Troeltsch, Ernst, 1, 2, 5-46, 99,100, 106, 108, 116- 119, 157, 185-187, 189, 192, 195-198, 201,206, 208, 211-213
Twelver Shiism,131

Ulama, 130, 132, 133, 141, 149
Umayyad Period, 131, 132, 135, 140, 143
ummah, 130, 148
Upanishads, 62, 66
Uttara Mimamsa Sutras, 111

Vedanta, 50, 57, 64, 78, 111

warrior religion, 132,133
Weber, Max, x, xi, 1, 3, 5 11, 13-15, 25, 36, 42, 69, 90-93, 97, 102, 116, 119, 121, 133, 134, 142, 144-152, 167-171, 177, 178, 185, 187, 198, 199, 200, 201
Wittgenstein, L., 166, 204

Yom Kippur, 128

zakat, 129
Zwingli, U., 115

Also by Paul S. Chung:

The Social Scientific Study of Religion

A Method for Comparative Theology

Foreword by Ulrich Duchrow

An overview of social scientific accounts of religion, providing a model for comparative theology.

In this study, Paul S. Chung charts the history of social scientific study of religion from the axial age to the present day, and thereby lays a foundation for a new model of constructive theology in the comparative study of religion, culture and society. Analysing the thought of Max Weber, Alfred Schutz, Pierre Bourdieu, Michel Foucault, Edmund Husserl, Max Horkheimer and others, Chung deals effectively with material interests, power relations and the history of race, gender and sexuality. The result is a synthesis that is at once innovative, critical, and applicable to current methodology in theology and the social sciences.

'Skillfully combining resources from a plethora of disciplines, Chung works out a comparative theological resource capable of tackling complex pluralities of the third millennium.'
– **Veli-Matti Kärkkäinen**, University of Helsinki

Published June 2022

Hardback ISBN 978 0 227 17766 2
Paperback ISBN 978 0 227 17765 5
ePub ISBN 978 0 227 17767 9
PDF ISBN 978 0 227 17768 6

Also by Paul S. Chung:

Postcolonial Public Theology:
Faith, Scientific Rationality, and Prophetic Dialogue

*An examination of Christian public
theology in a global context.*

Published 27 July 2017

Paperback ISBN: 978 0 227 17576 7
PDF ISBN: 978 0 227 90534 0

Church and Ethical Responsibility in the Midst of World Economy:
Greed, Dominion, and Justice

*An in-depth study and critique of global capitalism
and justice from a theological point of view.*

Published 26 June 2014

Paperback ISBN: 978 0 227 67999 9
ePub ISBN: 978 0 227 90156 4
PDF ISBN: 978 0 227 90155 5

The Hermeneutical Self and an Ethical Difference:
Intercivilizational Engagement

*A study drawing on diverse classical and
modern sources to for a postcolonial age.*

Published 26 July 2012

Paperback ISBN: 978 0 227 17381 7
ePub ISBN: 978 0 227 90102 1
PDF ISBN: 978 0 227 90101 4

Also by Paul S. Chung:

Asian Contextual Theology for the Third Millennium:
Theology of Minjung in Fourth-Eye Formation

A collection of essays exploring the development of the Asian theology of minjung, *and its role and influence in global Christian thinking. Edited by Paul S. Chung, Veli-Matti Kärkäinen and Kim Kyoung-Jae*

Published 29 April 2010

Paperback ISBN: 978 0 227 17331 2
PDF ISBN: 978 0 227 90299 8

Karl Barth:
God's Word in Action

An insightful analysis of the writings of the German theologian Karl Barth, emphasising the political and social relevance of his thought.

Published 27 November 2008

Paperback ISBN: 978 0 227 17266 7
PDF ISBN: 978 0 227 90323 0

Martin Luther and Buddhism:
Aesthetics of Suffering

A fruitful examination of the Lutheran theology of suffering in the context of the spiritual traditions of Asia.

Published 25 September 2008

Paperback ISBN: 978 0 227 17294 0
PDF ISBN: 978 0 227 90329 2